THE
LAST 100
DAYS

THE LAST 100 DAYS

THE AUSTRALIAN ROAD TO VICTORY IN THE FIRST WORLD WAR

WILL DAVIES

VINTAGE

A Vintage Australia book
Published by Penguin Random House Australia Pty Ltd
Level 3, 100 Pacific Highway, North Sydney NSW 2060
penguin.com.au

Penguin
Random House
Australia

First published by Vintage Australia in 2018

Addresses for the Penguin Random House group of companies can be found at
global.penguinrandomhouse.com/offices.

A catalogue record for this
book is available from the
NATIONAL
LIBRARY National Library of Australia
OF AUSTRALIA

ISBN 978 0 14378 496 8

Cover image: Unidentified officers and NCOs of the 13th Machine Gun
Company studying a map in a billet at Sailly-le-Sec,
Australian War Memorial E01942
Cover design by Ella Egidy © Penguin Random House Australia Pty Ltd
Typeset in Adobe Garamond Pro by Midland Typesetters, Australia
Maps by Alicia Freile, Tango Media Pty Ltd
Printed in Australia by Griffin Press, an accredited ISO AS/NZS 14001:2004
Environmental Management System printer

MIX
Paper from
responsible sources
FSC
www.fsc.org FSC® C009448

*To Major General Gordon Maitland, AO, OBE, RFD, ED (Retd),
and Mrs Dorothy Maitland.
Wonderful Australians.*

Contents

The Western Front

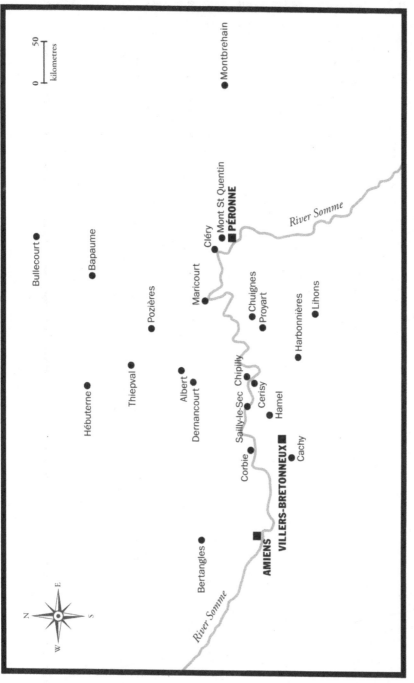

The Somme southern sector

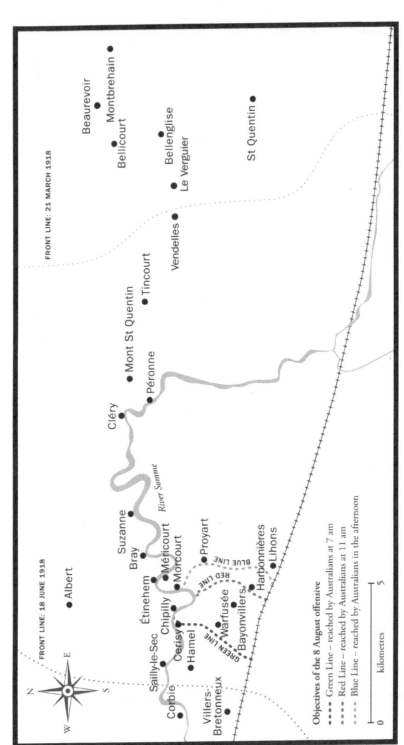

The Somme Valley

FRONT LINE: 18 JUNE 1918

FRONT LINE: 21 MARCH 1918

- Beaurevoir
- Montbrehain
- Bellicourt
- Bellenglise
- Le Verguier
- St Quentin
- Vendelles
- Tincourt
- Mont St Quentin
- Péronne
- Cléry

River Somme

- Albert
- Suzanne
- Bray
- Étinehem
- Méricourt
- Chipilly
- Morcourt
- Proyart
- Sailly-le-Sec
- Cerisy
- Hamel
- Warfusée
- Bayonvillers
- Harbonnières
- Lihons
- Corbie
- Villers-Bretonneux

GREEN LINE
RED LINE
BLUE LINE

Objectives of the 8 August offensive
- ▪▪▪ Green Line – reached by Australians at 7 am
- ▪▪▪ Red Line – reached by Australians at 11 am
- ▪▪▪ Blue Line – reached by Australians in the afternoon

0   5   kilometres

Introduction

In 1994, with an inquisitive mind and a heavy heart, I wandered the battlefields of the Great War, particularly the Australian operational areas along the Somme, and the Ypres Salient to the north, for the first time. I had been motivated to go after I had felt deeply affected by the interment of the body of an unknown Australian, taken from Adelaide Cemetery at Villers-Bretonneux and placed in the Hall of Memory at the Australian War Memorial, in November of the previous year.

Since that first trip in 1994, I have continued to go back to the battlefields of the Western Front to better understand Australia's sacrifice and contribution to the war effort. After 2004 I returned regularly to walk the battlefields and research a series of books on the Great War, starting with the edit of the now classic story *Somme Mud*.

The battlefields still draw me back. Even now, 100 years on from the destruction and death of the Great War, the battlefields of France and Belgium continue to reveal so much about the men who fought and died there. While the tortured earth, the vast fields of mud and shell holes, upturned wagons and remnants of dead horses and men have long gone, the landscape still tells a vivid story.

A few years ago the Australian public's attention turned from the Gallipoli campaign to the Western Front. The Great War centenary celebrations, starting with Fromelles and Pozières in

2016, increased this public interest in the area's history and saw a rise in the number of visitors to the Australian operational areas of the Western Front.

Yet there remains little understanding of the very last battles, indeed the last 100 days, that saw the Australian Imperial Force at its fighting best – Australians at last controlling and planning their own battles and their own destiny with an Australian, General John Monash, in command. In the lead-up to victory, the men of the AIF were more enthusiastic, energised and confident than they had been for years. The AIF, they knew, was a formidable fighting machine, feared by the enemy, respected by the British High Command, and celebrated by the people of their new nation.

Recently I visited the areas from Corbie to Montbrehain, tracing the Australians' advance in those last 100 days: first with the attack in early July at Hamel, up the Somme valley, across the river to Mont St Quentin and Péronne, and then east following the advance towards the Hindenburg Outpost Line and finally the Hindenburg Line itself. This is an area rarely visited by Australians, particularly the area around the lonely 4th Division Memorial above the St Quentin Canal near Bellicourt. While I had previously been east of Péronne, this was the first time I had studied the area and the Australian actions in any detail.

In the same way these important battlefields, stretching from Villers-Bretonneux to Montbrehain, had lacked visitors, it seemed very little had been written about them, or about the last 100 days of the war.

These battles of 1918 raged across beautiful country, particularly the Somme villages, and then out into the rolling green hills to the east. Even in August and September 1918 this area was not the shattered, desolate mud-fields of the Somme, but working farmland with fields of wheat, rapeseed and sugar beet, the terrain free of fence lines.

It is from these battlefield wanderings, and due to the absence of popular writing on this period of history, that my desire to tell this story began. I have always believed that to understand history, truly understand it, you must visit the areas where it took place. Though this won't always be possible, I hope this book will help to bring those places to life to tell the soldiers' stories.

In writing this history, I have relied on two main sources: the daily war diary entries from the fifteen AIF brigades and sixty battalions; and the battalion histories written after the war, including more recent work, particularly of the prolific researcher and writer Neville Browning. In this regard, I hope to capture the 'voice' of the time. I have aimed to tell these soldiers' stories not as a simple rewriting of details and events, but as an echo from the time; of these soldiers' matter-of-fact recounts of life on the ground, of their attitude to the enemy, and their varied responses to death and loss even as they marched to victory.

Will Davies
February 2018

ONE

Back on the Somme

At the beginning of 1918, the war had been fought for nearly three and a half years. By this point, few of the men who had left Australia for Gallipoli in late 1914 were still alive and, if so, were unwounded and sound of mind. The Australian Imperial Force's introduction to the Western Front was at the butchers' picnics at Fromelles and Pozières in 1916. Within the first two months on the Western Front, the AIF had seen nearly fifty per cent of its ranks decimated. Then the frightful battles of Bullecourt, Messines and Passchendaele in 1917 had dramatically thinned their ranks even further, leaving the AIF desperately short of men. In 1917 alone, the AIF sustained nearly 77,000 casualties, twice the casualties of the 1916 battles and three times the casualties of the Gallipoli campaign. To compound these losses, recruitment numbers were low in Australia, and two referenda had failed to indicate the public's support for conscription. Further, unlike their British allies or their German enemy, the men could not return home, see their family and loved ones, or breathe in the gum-scented air or the salty sea breeze. Australia was a distant memory. The Australians were exhausted, and death seemed inevitable.

The new year of 1918 opened with freezing weather. Blizzards raged across northern France, not unlike those of the frightful winter of 1916–17. Even though the Allies had learnt the lessons of hypothermia and trench foot, and the effect these had on the health and morale of men in exposed frontline trenches, men still suffered. But while the fighting slowed, men continued to train, recuperate and reorganise, and the generals and headquarter staff continued to plan and dream.

There was much to think about.

In November 1917, the Bolsheviks had seized power in Russia, and they had signed an armistice with Germany in December, bringing the fighting on the Eastern Front to an end. The Germans could now move a large number of men, guns and the vast accoutrements of war to the Western Front. For the British, this was a massive shift in the strategic balance of power. Faced with not only the loss of the Russian army, who, while ineffective, had tied up a large proportion of German land forces to that point in the war, now, suddenly, over sixty German divisions began moving from the Eastern to the Western Front.

While America's declaration of war in April 1917 had been welcome, its recent war with Mexico had shown the inadequacies of the US military. There were only 300,000 National Guardsmen, little matériel or war supplies, poor training and organisation, and no supply structure. As a result, initially only a few ill-equipped American troops arrived on the Continent. America's declaration of war was, in reality, a hollow promise. By June 1917, only 14,000 troops had landed and, by March 1918, only 300,000 men were in France, with few seeing any active service.

One positive result of the Americans' entry was that supplies from the US now flowed into Britain, which had been blockaded by German submarines since the beginning of the war. It was also becoming apparent, certainly to Germany but also to the Allies, that the chances of Germany now being able to win the war were becoming slimmer. Britain, unlike Germany, was highly geared to continue the war. The Second Industrial Revolution had seen mass production increase, with 200 new factories producing munitions and war matériel. One million women joined the industrial workforce, and thousands of others moved into farming for food production. The British army was the best fed and equipped on the Western Front, and its Dominion forces shared the bounty.

In Australia, the war dominated daily life across the nation, particularly the issue of conscription. The AIF, first raised in 1914, was purely a volunteer army and, initially, recruitment officers were overwhelmed with volunteers. As the war continued, with the volunteers suffering high casualties, the AIF faced a serious shortage of men. After the defeat of the second conscription referendum in December 1917 – the first had taken place in October 1916 – Prime Minister Billy Hughes resigned. However, due to the absence of a suitable alternative candidate, he was immediately sworn in again. Men still enlisted in the army, particularly after the lowering of age and health standards and height restrictions, but recruitment numbers continued to fall. In the country, rural production saw good profits for farmers from wool and wheat, particularly wool, which was requisitioned for the production of uniforms and blankets, reducing the incentive for men from these areas to enlist.

Within the AIF, there was great concern about low enlistments and the difficulty of rebuilding fighting battalions. The only possible replacements for injured men were men from specialist training courses and those on leave, the wounded men from hospitals in Britain and a trickle of new men from training camps on the Salisbury Plain in England. In Australia, by the end of 1917, recruitment was down to just 5000 men a month but 7000 were needed to retain battalion strengths, and even more should the

Germans launch further offensives. The coming of winter and possible spikes in sickness rates added to these concerns.

1917 had been difficult for the AIF. Although the Germans had withdrawn to the Hindenburg Line in March, the terrible fighting for the outpost villages north-east of Bapaume and the twin disasters at Bullecourt in April and May had deeply affected the men. Not only had the First Battle of Bullecourt resulted in 3000 casualties in twenty-four hours and the Second Battle a further 7000, but the Australians also by now carried a new, deeper contempt for the British High Command, and most men had little faith in the cumbersome and unreliable tanks they insisted on using. The success of the Battle of Messines in June was tempered by Australian casualties of 6000, and the involvement in the Third Battle of Ypres (more commonly referred to as the Battle of Passchendaele), from the Menin Road through Glencorse Wood, Polygon Wood, Zonnebeke and Broodseinde, had decimated the AIF's five divisions. Just like 1916, for the men of the AIF 1917 had been a year of suffering – from the Germans, the weather and the conditions, and the demands of the British High Command.

On 1 November 1917, the AIF serving on the Western Front in France and Belgium became a new entity with the forming of the Australian Corps. Billy Hughes had made representation to London 'that it was the wish of the Australian government that the Anzac troops "should be regarded as an army and that General Birdwood should command it" . . . strong feeling exists in Australia that Australian units should be self-contained. Conditions of service and personal character of Australian troops different from British troops.'[1] This push for an Australian army was taken up by prominent Australian journalist Keith Murdoch and a group of influential Australians in London. Murdoch had the ear of the British Prime Minister David Lloyd George and acted as an intermediary between him and Billy Hughes, particularly during Australia's two conscription debates. These took place at a time when Lloyd George and Field Marshal Douglas Haig, Commander of the British Army, had seriously different attitudes about the conduct of the war. Haig's response to the Australian request was that the timing was unsuitable and would hamper the overall campaign: 'It would affect the general conduct of operations so adversely that I regard it as both unwise and impracticable.'[2]

Haig's attitude was not good enough for Billy Hughes, given he had sent nearly 300,000 Australian troops to Britain and had 110,000 in the line. Another stern and direct telegram was sent to London reaffirming Australia's wish to have its own corps. This time the Army Council responded by directing Haig to begin the process of forming the Australian Corps under British General William Birdwood. The AIF had been under Birdwood's command since May 1915, from its very infancy, and Birdwood had seen it through Gallipoli, had defended it and supported it before the British High Command, and appreciated the distinct nature and fighting ability of the Australians.

With battalion numbers low, Birdwood suggested disbanding the 4th Division and creating a 'depot' division based in Boulogne, from which men could be reallocated to other AIF divisions. Under this plan, the 1st, 2nd, 3rd and 5th Divisions and their associated support groups, like artillery, medical, siege batteries, and the No. 3 Squadron of the Australian Flying Corps, were to comprise the new Australian Corps. While some divisions were delighted with the proposed change, others, particularly the 4th Division which would be relegated to the rear and facing disintegration, were not happy. The Australians, proud of their new formation and in a spirit of *esprit de corps,* clipped up the brims of their felt hats to clearly distinguish themselves from other Allied units. The level of resistance to Birdwood's plan meant that the 4th Division was never broken up, and instead men were brought in from a fledgling 6th Division to reinforce the other divisions.

While the Australian Corps remained under the overall command of Birdwood, there was a new emphasis on replacing senior English staff with Australians, particularly at a brigade and battalion level. Some of the British officers, however, had served in pre-war militia units in Australia, had joined the AIF in 1914, had been to Gallipoli and then to the Western Front, and had a close association with their units. As Australia's official war historian Charles Bean notes, 'they were also highly regarded by the diggers when, after their initial disregard, they accepted the colonials not on their behaviour and parade ground conduct, but on their fighting abilities and resilience.'[3] The contribution of these British officers over this time had been significant and, for many, it was a pity and a loss for the AIF to see them go.

By December 1917, the fighting on the Western Front had slowed and the men were looking to rest and survive the cold as well as the Germans. The British Expeditionary Force (BEF) occupied the line from the Passchendaele ridge south to the Somme. In places their front line was thinly manned – the French army was slowly being revived after their widespread mutinies – and their defences were poorly constructed. The lessons of the winter of 1916–17 had ensured better accommodation, particularly after the building of massive camps of the newly introduced

Nissen huts close behind the line. These huts were invented by a major in the Royal Engineers, Peter Nissen, and went into production in August 1916. They came in three sizes, were cheap to produce and could be erected very fast. Apart from troop accommodation, they provided orderly rooms, mess halls, classrooms and hospitals and, by the end of the war, over 100,000 of them had been constructed.

In November 1917, most of the Australian troops had been in Belgium in the area south of Ypres, particularly around Messines, Wytschaete and Ploegsteert. They were central to the recent fighting at Passchendaele, which had seen the Allies take the village and the area around Ypres, but at huge cost. The AIF had as a result become virtually unoperational and needed to be rebuilt and rested. As the Australians took over a large section of the Messines front, they found much work to do, particularly the completion of strongpoints along the main line of resistance. The defensive front line needed strengthening by moving forward posts closer to support, extending barbed wire and improving the accommodation of men in the line.

While major attacks were not carried out, active patrolling of no-man's-land and artillery duels with the Germans kept the men active. On 2 December, the 8th Brigade line came under artillery fire from the direction of Comines, with a number of direct hits on the cookhouse pillbox where a number of men were sheltering. The following day, a German corporal wandered into the 32nd Battalion lines and was captured, an event not uncommon given the maze of trenches and the low mist in the shallow valleys to the south-east of Messines.

A major focus for the AIF at this time was training, particularly in the rear areas and villages near Boulogne where Australian units were rotated for rest. Here they enjoyed hot baths and those with skin infections, particularly scabies, were treated with sulphur ointments. By December, the weather was closing in with snow and sleet, roads were icy and dangerous, and conditions were unfavourable for outdoor training. Also, few training facilities, materials and suitable fields were available. Heavy snow on the night of 22 December ended training until later in the month.

Christmas, even given the weather and the nearby Germans, was celebrated and enjoyed. No working parties were sent out; instead, Christmas carols were sung and men attended voluntary church services. The 11th Brigade diary notes, 'Snow falling – enemy heard last night singing and "cooeeing" and generally making noise in Christmas celebration',[4] it perhaps being a surprise that the enemy too celebrated this Christian occasion. Every effort was made by the senior commanders to celebrate Christmas as best they could, providing, along with a hot meal, wine, beer and other beverages for the men's pleasure. Christmas billies were also provided containing soap, tobacco, writing paper and various small luxuries for the men. Some senior officers, including divisional commanders, visited the men during their Christmas dinner, taking the opportunity to thank them for their fine efforts and sacrifice. All remembered the terrible winter on the Somme the previous year, and were grateful for the milder conditions and the thawing snow.

As the new year dawned, the AIF remained on the salient in the familiar areas south of Ypres. Apart from their active patrolling in no-man's-land and strengthening of the defences, life was relatively quiet, alternating between long periods in camps and frontline duties.

For the men of the 14th Brigade the entire month saw them training around the French village of Frencq, just north of Étaples and south of Boulogne. Throughout winter the weather remained mild, which was fortunate as the 'billeting was decidedly poor, but the distance from the forward positions of the Army area, the freshness of the country, the spells of fine weather, the opportunities for sport and competition, all combined to make a holiday of what might have been a very cold and muddy spell of training drudgery'.[5] When the men of the 14th returned to the line in the last days of January, they were fit, keen and in high spirits.

All five AIF divisions remained in Flanders, with two divisions holding a front of seven miles (twelve kilometres), a third in the support line, a fourth in reserve and one training on the French coast. Good work continued to strengthen the defences and salvage material.

Each night, patrols went out to capture prisoners for identification. One report stated, 'captured one Hun. Patrols met in no-mans-land. Shots were exchanged, but no casualties. German stated his unit – seemed intelligent and fairly willing to talk.'[6]

Despite the Australians' successes, and their bravery and sacrifice on the battlefield, their discipline was a continuing problem, as were the increasing rates of desertion. While the British had 677 cases of desertion across sixty-two divisions, the AIF had 171 across just five divisions, which had prompted Haig in mid-1916 to appeal to the Australian Government for the introduction of the death penalty. Haig's concern was that the lack of discipline within the AIF would lead to increased discipline problems across the entire army. Unless the Australians could be put under the Army Act, which had been enacted in the late nineteenth century to modernise military codes, the 'fighting efficiency would deteriorate "to an extent which may gravely affect the success of our arms".'[7] If the Australian Government agreed with the death penalty, argued Haig, it would be 'very sparingly' imposed. Even the New Zealand Government accepted the death penalty and, during the course of the war, five New Zealanders were shot, though at least one of them was actually an Australian.

Aside from desertion, a list circulated in March 1918 showed that nearly nine Australians per 1000 men were in field punishment, compared to one per 1000 for the British and less than two in other Empire forces.[8] Field punishment could be administered quickly, without the requirement that a convicted soldier be sent to prison. There were two types of punishment at the time: strapping or chaining a man to a gun wheel, fence or post for two hours a day for up to twenty-one days; and shackling a man for that period without him being fixed to anything.

Underlying these serious disciplinary problems was the Australians' rather loose approach to respect and discipline itself, which had long been an issue for the British High Command. This apparent lack of respect manifested itself in the men's attitude to saluting, showing respect to officers, obeying orders or accepting requirements placed upon them. Many Australian leaders argued that the issue of discipline in the AIF needed to be seen in a different way to that of the British army, as many of the men genuinely respected an officer for their leadership, bravery or concern for their soldiers. Many officers had risen through the ranks due to their service and leadership and were good mates with their men, which affected how the men behaved towards them. Also, from the time they enlisted, many of the Australians regarded themselves as part-time soldiers and, if asked, would probably have said they were a railway porter or a drover rather than a soldier. While home, and their previous callings, were a long way away and often years in the past, men remembered who they were. Peter Stanley makes this point with a cartoon by Cecil Hart in which a toffy English officer, backed up by a frowning, dismissive woman, states:

Officer: 'Don't you know what to do when you pass an officer? – You're a soldier aren't you?'
'No,' replies Private Anzac, 'I'm a farmer.'[9]

In another cartoon, where an officer confronts a young digger leaning, legs crossed, against a post, the conversation goes:

Officer: 'Why do you not salute?'
Anzac: 'Well, to tell you the truth, digger, We've cut it right out.'[10]

While discipline remained an ongoing issue for the Australians, the main focus for the Allies at the beginning of 1918 was an anticipated German offensive. As the diggers shivered in trench lines around Ploegsteert, Warneton and Messines, consolidating their line and bringing up supplies, or as they trained in the hutted camps in back areas, they knew the offensive was simply a matter of time – most likely when the spring thaw came.

Two

The German March
Offensive: All or Nothing

For the German High Command, 1918 was going to be a crucial year. Two elements were uppermost in the commanders' thinking and planning: the arrival of sixty German divisions from the Eastern Front, approximately 900,000 men, to bolster their troop numbers on the Western Front; and the fear of a million American troops entering the battle and dramatically shifting the balance of power. The response to both issues needed planning and careful thought, but what dominated their discussion was the desire for a decisive victory, with one last offensive to take Paris and drive the British into the sea.

At home, however, the German people were pessimistic and becoming increasingly hungry as the British naval blockade, which had been in place since the beginning of the war, started to bite. The Germans had pinned their strategic hopes on their own blockade of Britain to bring their enemy to its knees but it hadn't yet done so. The German hunger was a state of affairs that stretched back to the bleak winter of 1916–17, the 'turnip winter', when the German people substituted their potatoes and meat with turnips, which were usually fed to livestock. Soup kitchens were a common solution, yet many people died of malnutrition and sickness. At the same time, food was kept on farms and often not shared with those in the cities or in the German army, who found their rations reduced. To counter the resentment of the German people, the government introduced a programme, 'sharing scarcity', which went some way in restoring morale.

In a November 1917 speech to German military commanders, General Erich Ludendorff stated that the German army needed to launch an offensive by the end of February or early March the following year, before the deployment of American forces in large numbers would likely turn the tide of the war in the Allies' favour.

Planning began on what the Germans called the *Kaiserschlacht* – the Kaiser's Battle. The German command decided on an offensive that would push through the Allied front at strategic points and capture the key city of Amiens before striking quickly for Paris. The British army would then be in tatters, and any support it might receive from the French would be compromised by different languages, command structures and weapons. Then, after a cease-fire and armistice, the war would be won.

With the exception of the German army's initial invasion of France and Belgium, and the Verdun offensive, the Germans had so far fought a defensive war. Launching an offensive such as this required a major rethink. Since 1915, the Germans had developed and improved a new trench assault tactic that involved the cooperation and coordination of artillery with attack troops, the *Stosstruppen* or stormtroopers – mobile units armed with new Bergmann light machine guns. These elite troops could quickly bypass points of resistance, like machine-gun positions, and stream deep behind the front line to cause confusion and fear. They were followed by units who mopped up and dealt with prisoners while the attack surged forward. However, the success of this tactic would lie in dash and an offensive spirit, something the German army had not practised. As a result, over fifty divisions were withdrawn from the line for the training and attack man-oeuvres necessary for the planned offensive.

The crucial question was where would be best to strike: where along the French and British front, and against which Allied general, and which army? Thought was initially given to driving the British from the Ypres Salient, which had been fought over relentlessly since late 1914, but the weather and the muddy ground would pose problems. For the Belgians, it was the last small sector of their country in Allied hands, while for the British it was a lasting symbol of resolve, defensive spirit and sacrifice.

Believing the French would defend Paris while the British would focus on defending their supply ports on the Channel, the Germans opted to split the two armies by attacking at their junction. Ludendorff suggested Picardy in France, which was the boundary between the French and British armies, and also a line thinly held by British General Sir Hubert Gough's Fifth Army. The Fifth Army consisted of many composite units, which included new and inexperienced troops.

In the end, the Germans drew up a number of possible plans, including an initial offensive south of Ypres (Operation George), the Verdun offensive (Castor and Pollux), an attack around Arras (Max) and the Picardy offensive (Michael). Ludendorff toured the northern sector of the front in late December 1917, reporting on findings and further discussing options at a meeting with German commanders at Bad Kreuznach on 27 December. Ludendorff finally selected the focus as the fifty-mile (eighty-kilometre) front between Arras in the north and Mont St Quentin in the south. This offensive became known as Operation Michael.

★

The British and the French knew an offensive was coming, as they were aware of the Germans' troop trains arriving from the east, their strategic deployment of fighting divisions, concentration of artillery and seemingly endless build-up of ammunition stores. However, the Allies were confused as to where the offensive would be launched, and the Germans' delay into early 1918 increased their sense of paranoia and confusion. The British and French discussed the idea of placing thirty divisions in reserve, but the British had enough problems manning their own front as available men were so limited, and Haig had already reduced the size of a division from twelve to nine battalions. Also, the reorganisation that would be required, as well as the disruption to morale and the need to train officers, made a large reserve unrealistic. Instead, the British and French agreed to provide mutual support should any threat materialise.

The British had adopted the German idea of defence in depth, with up to twelve miles (twenty kilometres) of defence in three separate zones: the forward zone, a lightly held zone where only scattered posts might delay and break up an attack; a second line where the real battle would be fought, and the attacker exhausted and mopped up; and a third zone in the rear to despatch troops to precise areas under attack and to provide a final line of defence.

Since November 1917, German troops had poured into France until there was an estimated total of 150 divisions available for an offensive. This rose to 180 by February and, by late March, to nearly 200. Facing the British from Arras to La Fère and the River Oise were a total of sixty-five divisions, with over 6000 guns and nine tanks. To counter this, the British could muster only twenty-six divisions: twelve under General Sir Hubert Gough and fourteen under General Julian Byng. Ludendorff had enough artillery to attack along a thirty-one-mile (fifty-kilometre) front with guns spaced at twelve yards apart. This was less than the six yards per gun that the British had at the Battle of Passchendaele, but the German guns were far more intensive, especially with the *minenwerfers* (short-range mortars) of various calibres. Eventually, new planning saw the front extend to forty-four miles (seventy kilometres), into which the Germans committed between forty and fifty divisions with guns, including 1000 weapons from the Eastern Front, outnumbering the British by five to two.

Germany's Crown Prince Rupprecht, Commander of the German Sixth Army, expressed misgivings about the vagueness of the planning, the absence of a firm objective and the potential outcome should the offensive fail. While it had been agreed that an offensive of some sort must be launched, the fear was that the initiative would be lost and the effectiveness compromised by attacking at different points along the front. Nonetheless, while some modifications were made, the final orders for the battle were issued on 10 March, nominating 21 March as the start date.

Further plans were drawn up for an attack south of the River Oise (Operation Archangel) and north of Arras (Mars), which were to be the 'hinges' for the main attack. Further attacks were also in preparation north of Armentières at Messines and Kemmel (George II) for early April, as well as attacks further south near Rheims (Roland).

At 4.40 am on 21 March 1918, the German offensive began, falling principally on the weak defence line of Gough's Fifth Army at Picardy and the stronger defence line of General Byng's Third Army further north. The Germans had carefully selected targets, concentrating on British artillery, rear support areas and frontline defences. Their initial artillery barrage, in the first five hours of the attack, fired from 6500 guns over 1.2 million shells and mortars, which were mostly gas mixed with high explosive.

British gunners, now under heavy fire and gas, were forced to operate in gasmasks and, with the fog and smoke, found observation and target recognition difficult. Consequently, the SOS flares fired by their frontline infantry mostly went unseen. At the same time, the German stormtroopers moved through the ill-prepared and incomplete British defensive lines, avoiding machine guns and other strongpoints. They very quickly overcame the British defences and forced back the British troops, who were retreating in a disorderly rabble. Not only were the Germans using well-rehearsed infiltration tactics, but they also by this time had been re-equipped with lighter weapons, special padded uniforms and large bags for grenades.

The German advance surged on, completely shattering Gough's Fifth Army. By 9.30 am, the British had suffered an estimated 8000 casualties and, by the end of the day, had suffered over 38,000 casualties including 21,000 captured. The Germans, however, suffered more; nearly 40,000 casualties, of whom nearly 11,000 had been killed. The first day of the German offensive was more costly in combined casualties than the deadly first day of the Battle of the Somme.

On this opening day of the German offensive, the AIF troops were still in Flanders, where they had been since the close of the Battle of Passchendaele in November 1917. The war diary of the 1st Brigade shows them near the infamous Hill 60, south of Ypres, while the 2nd Brigade was in camp near Vierstraat, north-west of Messines. Other AIF brigades were at Zillebeke and Spoil Bank, Neuve Église, around Ploegsteert Wood, Wytschaete,

Locre and Meteren, and as far west as Lumbres near St Omer. While many were in training camps, like Vauxhall and Bulford, others were holding frontline positions, conducting raids and being raided. Near Hill 60, Allied artillery batteries were continually active, keeping German positions under constant bombardment, particularly at night.

On the morning of 21 March, news arrived at AIF unit head-quarters of the opening of the German offensive. Many units had received intense shelling at exactly the same time as the Germans attacked south of Arras, around thirty-four miles (fifty-five kilo-metres) away. The 3rd Brigade near Zillebeke reported, 'Enemy artillery increased in intensity to a regular bombardment at 4.30am. HE [high explosive] and all kinds of gas used.'[1] Nearby, the 8th Brigade reported 'At 4.40am enemy opened heavy bom-bardment all along our line and Messines Ridge. This continued until 6.40am when it fell on our front posts and enemy seen coming towards post no 2.'[2]

For the 14th Brigade, positioned near Wytschaete, heavy shelling fell along their front at 4.45 am, five minutes after the opening barrage to the south. Their war diary records, '7.25am, enemy raid on 55th Bn post. Dummy raids on posts. Apparently they are in conjunction with some larger operation.'[3] At this time, the brigade was hoping for a rest in the Merris area, 'but if the battle down south continues our rest will be very much curtailed in all probability'.[4] Concern spread as the men realised the situation was serious, and something they would quickly be involved in.

The 14th Brigade soon reported that, 'We have received news of the general attack on the 3rd and 5th Army fronts and on the French front in the Rheims sector. We had little news except that the bombardment started at 4.23am. Later information timed

1pm from GHQ to the effect that the enemy have attacked on a large scale and have entered forward system about Lagnicourt, Louverval and Bullecourt on the 3rd Army front and on the Fifth Army about La Fere.'[5] The fact that these places, which marked significant 1917 battlefields, had been taken by the Germans caused great consternation for the Australians, who had suffered so badly there.

With this ominous news came orders for the AIF units to be prepared to move south. Within hours of the offensive opening, the 9th Brigade received orders to move to Watou, west of Poperinge, and from there to Doullens and finally Heilly on the Somme. That day, Brigadier General Harold 'Pompey' Elliott attended a conference at divisional headquarters, and similar conferences were held by other AIF divisions. Elliott's 15th Brigade was at Ramillies Camp, near Mount Kemmel, when they received the order to move at short notice and hurry preparations. They were to move first to Meteren and on through countless small villages, finally ending 'in a reserve area guarding bridges crossing the Somme, from Aubigny to Vaux-sur-Somme'.[6]

On 23 March, the 14th Brigade reported that, 'Our war news today shows that the situation down south has developed very seriously. At 11.45 pm last night reports were to the effect that he [the Germans] had begun attacks again on practically the whole front and he appears to have gained a considerable amount of ground, especially on the Fifth Army front. Our news comes about 12 hours late and we wait anxiously for tomorrow's budget.'[7]

By 25 March, the AIF was on the move south. Unlike the British, they were rested and keen, and the 8th Brigade war diary noted, 'the spirit of all ranks is of the highest order and when we do come to close grips with the Boche, the traditions the force has made for itself will be supplemented by still greater deeds on the part of our men.'[8] Further, the war diary noted, 'all ranks in good spirits and very fit.'[9] It was time to defend, to fire on rows of German assault troops and settle old scores. The Germans were the ones running at the guns and providing the targets now, not the Australians, as had so often been the case in the past.

As the orders came in, each brigade and battalion began their move south. Many orders were confusing and contradictory, and changes were made while units were on the road as commanders tried to predict where they would be best positioned to stop the surging German advance.

The 4th Brigade, for example, began their move south starting from Neuve Église. Their journey took them to the point where they occupied a defensive line north of the Somme, from Souastre to Bienvillers-au-Bois. A similar course was taken by other brigades, with the focus on getting Australians into the line in front of Amiens to stem the German advance there.

Arriving on the Somme, the Australians faced the disheartening reality of seeing the Germans quickly overrun all the battlefields they had fought so hard for and won at such high cost earlier in the war. Gone was Bullecourt and the outpost villages, Bapaume, Gueudecourt, Pozières; even Albert and the leaning statue of the Virgin atop its cathedral. The history of the 22nd Battalion reads:

> The fluctuating fortunes of war had now enabled the Hun to
> overrun the old battlefields, capture Albert and bring his forces
> to the very gates of Amiens. The city was under fire, its splendid
> cathedral in danger, its streets littered with debris and tangled wire.
> The morale of the Twenty-Second was magnificent, and every

man was, at least temporarily, exalted by the emergency, and his knowledge of the seriousness of the time.[10]

The exaltation didn't last. The men were not happy to be back in the Somme, where the billets were considered 'poor and generally dirty'.[11] Places like the village of Dernancourt were famous for being filthy, lousy and uncomfortable. Private Lynch in *Somme Mud* states, 'How we hate the hole! Dirty dilapidated dwellings, remains of sheds and damp, foul-smelling cellars house our battalion. We're as mud-stained, wet and weary as the place itself.'[12] The 14th Brigade war diary mentions that, 'We rather expected something worse, and before very long we shall probably be spending our nights in the cold and wet without cover at all.'[13]

As the AIF streamed south, the Germans pushed further towards Amiens, a major Allied supply centre. Its railway terminus, station and marshalling yards were the target of two long-range German guns: the eleven-inch (twenty-eight-centimetre) Amiens gun on a railway siding near Harbonnières, and a fifteen-inch (thirty-eight-centimetre) naval gun in the woods near Chuignolles. With the Germans already through Albert, the Australians were spread in a line from the River Somme in the south through to villages as far north as Hébuterne and Saulty.

Adding to the confusion and the traffic were French civilians fleeing the fighting. In Barly, the French were packing up to leave as the Australians came into the village. A note in the 13th Battalion's history states:

Towards Bapaume could be seen the smoke of a burning village which caused them to hasten their loading. And then spontaneously it seemed, the inhabitants learnt that we were Australians. 'Les Australiens, Les Australiens' they were heard calling out to one another. The unloading commenced and later saw the furniture being carried back into the homes from which it had just been removed. 'Pas necessaire maintenant. Vous les tiendrez' an old man told one of our transports as he drove his empty wagon back into its shed. 'Not necessary now. You will hold them.'

'We'll have to see the old bloke is not disappointed,' said the Digger when the remark was translated to him.[14]

The first major action for the AIF was at Hébuterne on 26 March, when the 4th Brigade – made up of the 13th, 14th, 15th and 16th Battalions – just beat the Germans to the village, which was largely unoccupied, albeit with limited German patrols that had not by this time consolidated and secured it. As the brigade moved to take up its defensive position, British soldiers streamed westwards, warning that 'Jerry's got tanks galore'[15] and telling the Australians they were heading the wrong way. The 4th Brigade commander, General Charles Brand, had ridden his chestnut horse into Hébuterne, much to the amazement of the men, whereupon he rallied his officers and addressed them, 'Colonels, colonels, get your men assembled here just as they are.' As the men gathered around him, he said, 'I've just ridden into the place we are to attack.' One digger turned to his mate and said, 'Silly old blankard. You'll be getting shot,' to which his mate replied, 'You're a Dinkum Steve.'[16] There was indeed great respect for General Brand, who had taken the initiative to gain intelligence on the German situation in the village by himself.

Meanwhile, remnants of the British 19th Division were found outside the village exhausted, frightened and without food or water. When they learnt of the Australian relief, some broke down and openly wept.

As they entered the village, the Australians forced out German patrols and established a defensive line on the eastern side using overgrown trenches from the fighting in 1916. To cover the line, the 13th Battalion spread across the front of the cemetery, with the 15th to the north and the 16th to the south. The 14th remained in reserve. Realising they would be there for some time, the Australians made themselves comfortable, purloining live-stock and raiding the cellars for wine. Bean wrote of this time: 'Such conditions of warfare have never been known in the AIF and the campaign took on the complexion of a picnic, or of a children's escapade, a world removed from the experience of previous years. The conditions of the previous month in Flanders faded in memory like an evil dream.'[17]

Meanwhile, the Germans renewed their attack. Heavy shelling, often with captured guns and seemingly limitless ammuni-tion, now fell upon the Australian line. German frontal assaults were swept away with heavy casualties for the attackers. A 13th Battalion report on 3 April stated that one company of the bat-talion had noted 200 German casualties, with one Lewis gunner accounting for eighty, while the war diary stated: 'Enemy casual-ties were extremely heavy. 300 to 400 of the enemy were seen running away . . . and made excellent targets for our machine guns.'[18] Yet the men were soon exhausted from the endless work of digging, carrying supplies and patrolling. At night the cold kept them awake and the fighting meant daytime sleep was impossible.

The fight to hold Hébuterne was to see the 4th Brigade remain in position for over two weeks without relief. To their north, British divisions were rotated in and out of the line, but the Australians remained. A note to Colonel Douglas Marks, the Commanding Officer of the 13th Battalion, from General Brand simply stated, 'Dear Marks. The Corps Commander is afraid to let the defence of Hebuterne out of our hands.'[19] So the Australians stayed and took the fight to the confident Germans by continuing their patrolling and 'peaceful penetration', a quaint euphemism for trench raiding, which was a tactic the Australians specialised in.

Charles Bean summed up the men's attitude:

> in the present crisis, they [the Australian troops] could see how every blow counted towards the winning of the war. At last the Australians were being used where their fighting spirit told. They had stopped the enemy easily; they could see the Germans were disconcerted, prone to become bewildered and faint-hearted; in the maze of grass-covered trenches the German posts and patrols should be easily outplayed. The Australians therefore merely waited for better weather conditions and then continued to nibble at the German front, seizing a sap here, a length of sunken road there, battalions or companies acting on their own initiative.[20]

Further south, the Australians were facing the German advance on the Somme and Ancre rivers. The Germans were now just over twelve miles (twenty kilometres) from Amiens, and the situation was grim. If the Germans were able to get across the rolling farmland to the city, they could virtually take the train to Paris, and to victory.

French General Ferdinand Foch, a national hero after his 1914 defence of Paris at the First Battle of the Marne, declared, 'We must fight in front of Amiens. We must fight where we are now,'[21] while Field Marshal Haig uttered his famous 'backs to the wall'[22] remark to steady his troops. British General

Walter Congreve, VC, understood the danger along the Somme of a German breakthrough and said to General John Monash, Commander of the AIF's 3rd Division, 'Thank Heavens – the Australians at last,'[23] adding, 'At four o'clock today my Corps was holding the line from Albert to Bray when the line gave way. The enemy is now pushing westward and if not stopped tomorrow, will certainly secure all the heights overlooking Amiens. What you must try to do is get your divisions deployed across his path.'[24]

The Australians, well understanding their responsibility and role, had marched into the line determined to hold their position and win a place in military history for bold, audacious fighting and defence.

With the German capture of Albert, villages to the west towards Amiens had now came under direct attack and shelling. German troops advanced towards Dernancourt, where the AIF's 47th and 48th Battalions of the 12th Brigade had established a thin defensive line along the Albert–Amiens railway. The Germans quickly attacked and, on 28 March, made nine determined assaults on the railway embankment beside the village. The 12th Brigade's war diary notes, 'All attacks by the enemy were repulsed with heavy losses and machine guns, Lewis guns and riflemen were busy all day operating against wonderful targets.'[25] Australian snipers were also active, accounting for an officer and twenty other ranks killed and, on the following day, a further twenty-five Germans.

To support the extended front line, the brigade's 45th Battalion dug a strong support line on the hillside north of the village. Reports came in that a woman or women in the village were waving and pointing to where Germans were located in one of the houses, an incident reported by Charles Bean: 'She pointed behind her as though Germans were in the house. We waved to her to come over, but she shook her head. She also appeared to be using very unladylike language, probably using insulting words.'[26]

A number of sentry posts were established to cover the expanding front line. One of these, under Tasmanian Sergeant Stan McDougall, kept watch on a level crossing on the northern side of Dernancourt. As dawn broke on 28 March, a thick mist covered the valley, but the alert sergeant heard the slap of bayonet scabbards on the thighs of advancing Germans. He quickly warned his men, and they had just enough time to prepare as the Germans advanced out of the mist. Immediately, German stick grenades landed among his men, taking out a Lewis-gun team who had just begun firing into the advancing line. McDougall picked up the Lewis gun, firing and killing two German machine-gun crews.

As he advanced along the railway embankment, McDougall saw a party of Germans below him and immediately fired into the group, hosing them with bullets and leaving most dead. He then fired on another party of Germans advancing across the embankment, but by now his left hand was badly burnt on the casing of the Lewis barrel. His mate, Sergeant Lawrence, a Cloncurry station overseer, came to his aid, holding the gun so that McDougall could continue firing with his unburnt hand. For this action, McDougall was awarded the Victoria Cross. He went back to Tasmania after the war, married and had a career in the Tasmanian Forestry Department before his death at seventy-six in 1968.

Over the next week, attacks continued on the Australian line at Dernancourt as the Germans sought weak points in preparation for a larger assault. This came on 5 April, with some of the heaviest attacks ever experienced on an Australian line. The

Germans initially attacked the reverse side of the railway embankment and were driven off, but determined German attacks finally drove the Australians off the top of the railway embankment and back up the hill towards the 45th Battalion support line. Charles Bean described this attack as 'the strongest ever met by Australian troops . . . and one of the most difficult to resist'.[27]

That afternoon, the 45th Battalion counterattacked, charging down the slope and into the Germans. As they advanced they suffered severely, but once among the enemy their savage hand-to-hand fighting saw the Germans retreat in disorder, leaving the ground covered with their dead.

North and south of the Albert–Amiens road, the Australians were spread out to block the German advance. Brigadier General John Gellibrand's 12th Brigade was soon rushed to the valley between Millencourt and Hénencourt, villages familiar to the men from the fighting of previous years. To the south, another line from Morlancourt down to Sailly-Laurette on the Somme was also established by General Monash's 3rd Division. His 44th Battalion was ambushed on the night of 28 March with heavy casualties, but over the following two days the brigade launched a determined counterattack, resulting in significant German losses. The presence of four of the five Australian divisions in the region – the 1st Division was still further north – provided great reassurance to both the French and British High Command. Each day the Australian battalions improved their defences, carried up supplies of food and ammunition along a shortened supply line and even began peaceful penetration on the German lines. Amiens was safe for now, but given the number of Germans facing them, their challenge was to hold the line.

THREE

Saving Amiens

The AIF was now spread across the Somme and was blocking the German advance to the strategic railhead at Amiens in order to create a crucial defensive line. Meanwhile, the British army fell back and told the Australians that the Germans were coming in swarms, and were impossible to stop. The Australians relished the possibility of a good fight, with the Germans running at their guns and not the other way around, as had long been the case. The encounter with the Germans had yet more attraction for the diggers. An officer of the 56th Battalion noted, 'I overhead one of my platoon remark to his pal, "Struth Bill, we'll get some souvenirs now."'[1] The officer continues, 'They knew that probably within a few days they would be thrown into battle . . . against a mighty army flushed with success. Their manner would almost have led one to believe that they were about to participate in a sports meeting.'[2]

While Dernancourt was being held, thanks to the Australians along the line of the Albert–Amiens railway, battalions of the 9th Brigade were moving south of Villers-Bretonneux near Lancer and Hangard woods to plug a gap in the front line and join up with the French army.

At 10.30 am on 30 March, the 33rd Battalion marched towards the retreating British line as the rain came down. With them went the battalion cookers, and the men were served a hot meal, 'thus keeping the men warm and in good spirits'.[3] On the way, they were joined by four squadrons of the British 12th Lancers. The 33rd's Commanding Officer, Colonel Leslie Morshead, noted it was 'a proud privilege to be allowed to work with such a fine regiment [and be] judge of the splendid work they were doing for the Army at the present time . . . they cannot be too highly praised.'[4]

The proud British cavalry lifted the Australians' spirits while, about them, British stragglers and wounded passed in the other direction. Colonel Morshead noted in his report, 'During the whole time we were forward, men were constantly leaving the [British] line. There seemed to be no effort to check this straggling.'[5]

Gradually the cavalry moved ahead of the 33rd Battalion men and were soon heard to be engaging the enemy. They had quickly dismounted and advanced, taking the retreating, reluctant British soldiers with them. The cavalry attacked the enemy line, advancing against heavy rifle and machine-gun fire, and drove back the advancing Germans to re-establish the line. Morshead wrote, 'The lancers deployed at once and moved forward without flinching. All ranks displayed the greatest determination and eagerness to get to the Bosch with the bayonet.'[6]

Charles Bean relates the story of a young British cavalry officer keen to have a go at the Germans, who asked Colonel Morshead's permission:

'Oh, let's have a go at them Sir,' he pleaded. 'We'd dish them straight away.'

'Not I,' replied Morshead. 'What would your Colonel say!'

'Don't ask him,' urged the youngster, 'He's under your command, and if you order him he'll have to do it.'[7]

The 33rd Battalion continued onwards, pushing through Hangard Wood. Heavy German artillery fire on Lancer Wood, however, devastated sections of the wood and slowed their advance. Along with the 34th Battalion, the 33rd rested and waited for the order to continue forward, which came at 5 pm. Three companies began the advance towards Lancer Wood, a name given to the area by the 33rd and adopted by the British army. There the 12th Lancers had held their forward position, their machine guns covering the flanks.

The Australians emerged from the cover of the wood and into the open, keen to get at the Germans now lining the ridge and firing into their ranks. Immediately the Australians took casualties, particularly on the right where the attack was stopped.

Colonel Morshead, meanwhile, needed to consolidate his position and consequently attacked the German ridgeline at 8 pm, driving the enemy back and establishing a new line in the old German trenches. That night, the 33rd were relieved and, wet and cold, returned to Cachy, where the men were billeted in the aerodrome, full of stories of the spirited attack by the cavalry and proud of their brief action with them. However, their casualties were considerable, with five officers and twenty-eight other ranks killed, five officers and 157 other ranks wounded and eleven men missing.[8]

At 10 pm on 30 March, orders arrived for the 35th Battalion, who had moved up from Corbie on the Somme to Cachy, to be ready to move into the line. At 2 am they advanced. Leaving a reserve company in nearby Villers-Bretonneux, they took up a line east of the village, closer to Warfusée on the Péronne road and stretching south to Marcelcave.

The war diary of the 35th Battalion tells a story typical of the front line at this time. The first day of April dawned bright and clear, but with it came the serious wounding of Captain Eade, shot by a sniper. That night, a German patrol lost its way and was captured; two Germans from a Prussian regiment were killed, and another was captured and interrogated. The following day was very quiet but, again, a German wandered into the battalion's line and was captured. On 3 April, the enemy shelled Villers-Bretonneux and the line intermittently; one shell hit a billet, killing five men and wounding fourteen others.

Things were about to get a lot more active.

By 4 April, the Germans had moved up troops, determined to take Villers-Bretonneux. Ludendorff could sense victory and, although his exhausted troops needed rest and the long, extended supply lines needed consolidating, his eyes were on the Amiens prize only twelve miles away through the dust and haze. Villers-Bretonneux was important because, apart from the fact that the line of the old Roman road, which divided the French and British armies, ran through the town, the crucial railhead of nearby Amiens would, like Verdun, draw in the French army, who would be determined to defend it.

The Germans prepared to attack along a front crossing the old Roman road to Péronne and stretching south to Marcelcave and the northern trenches of the French army, less than a mile south. With the Australian 35th Battalion, which was manning the front line with three companies and one in reserve, were the British 6th Battalion London Regiment, the 8th Battalion Rifle Brigade and the 'Buffs': the Royal East Kent Regiment, one of the oldest regiments in the British army dating back to the sixteenth century. Behind them were the AIF's 33rd Battalion and the 9th Machine

Gun Company with eight guns, four in the line and four in reserve. In command was Lieutenant Colonel Henry Goddard, DSO, who was given the task of defending Villers-Bretonneux.

As the line stood-to, ready for a dawn assault, a heavy and concentrated barrage fell on Villers-Bretonneux at 5.30 am. Both high explosive and gas rained down, crashing among the 6th Londoners and inflicting heavy casualties, with over 100 men, including many senior officers, killed.

An hour later, the shelling shortened, falling along the front line. As it did, massed German troops were seen approaching along the Péronne road from the outskirts of Warfusée-Abancourt, three miles east of Villers-Bretonneux. They were in parties of about forty men each.

Immediately Allied machine guns, Lewis guns and rifles opened on them, ripping into their ranks and causing heavy casualties. The Germans fell back, but in the next hour they assaulted the line nine times. Each time they were driven back, the ground was strewn with their dead and wounded.

At 7 am, the Germans attempted a broad attack along the whole of the front, forming a wall of field grey uniforms, bayonets flashing, charging into the sustained British and Australian fire. The Allies fired an SOS flare and immediately an intense barrage fell upon the advancing Germans, tearing wide gaps in their lines. This barrage, and the heavy machine-gun and rifle fire, decimated the German attack.

Despite substantial losses, the Germans continued pressing the Allied line hard. When the Germans were 300 yards from the line, the British 8th Rifle Brigade on the left of the 33rd Battalion fell back in disorder, leaving the Australians' left flank dangerously exposed, a yawning gap in the defensive line. The Germans quickly exploited this, advancing along an abandoned trench and firing into the rear of the Australians. The machine guns withdrew and fell back, but not before one was overrun and captured and one taken out by German shelling. To counter these moves, the Buffs swung their left flank around and joined the 35th Battalion to stop the German advance, with the subsequent fire again decimating the German line.

Colonel Goddard ordered the 33rd Battalion, then in reserve in Villers-Bretonneux, into the line, taking up a position on the threatened left flank with eight more machine guns of the 9th Australian Machine Gun Company, making ten now in the line and four still in reserve. The Australians were supported on this flank north of the road by the 1st Dragoon Guards, who had ridden into the gap, quickly dismounted and joined the additional Australians, slowing the German advance.

At 11 am, as rain came down and the muddy ground impeded the German onslaught, the AIF's 34th and 36th Battalions came up from Bois l'Abbe to further strengthen the front line. Goddard now had the entire 9th Brigade engaged in the fight, with the enemy line 300 yards to the east.

The mud was also causing the Australians problems, as it was jamming weapons and rendering them inoperable. In response, remarkably, the Commanding Officer of the 6th Londoners offered clean Lewis guns to the 35th Battalion in exchange for their muddy ones.

Late in the afternoon, the British troops on the right of the Australians began to pull back in disorder, trickling through the battalion lines and reporting the Germans were advancing in thousands. A young subaltern, seeing the potential of his right flank becoming exposed, attempted to prevent their withdrawal, but the retreating troops had gone back too far, opening another gap in the line. The situation was critical.

To prepare for a counterattack, Colonel Goddard ordered forward the 35th Battalion, the 6th Londoners and the remaining four machine guns of the 9th Machine Gun Company, which had been held in reserve in Villers-Bretonneux.

Colonel Goddard moved to an exposed position swept by machine-gun fire and shells to better appraise his options. He then advanced the 36th Battalion, who moved forward 'in splendid order'[9] to counterattack south of the Villers-Bretonneux–Marcelcave railway line, thus protecting the right flank of the 35th Battalion. Their commander, Lieutenant Colonel John Milne, who had risen through the ranks of the old British Army, called to his men as they loaded magazines and prepared for the attack, 'Goodbye boys. It's neck or nothing.'[10] Then the companies moved off from the dead ground where they had shaken out. With them went 'a party of Queens'[11] – the Queen's Royal West Surrey Regiment – but a nearby unit of Buffs refused to join the attack.

The attack went in, assisted by the British cavalry, and the flank and forward line were restored. This counterattack was successful, with the enemy suffering considerable casualties and the Australians capturing four machine guns, which were turned on the Germans to great effect.

To further consolidate the gains, it was decided to advance the line forward again. The 9th Brigade moved out at 1 am on 5 April and, while German fire was heavy, few casualties were sustained. Men advanced and fired their Lewis guns from the hip, sweeping the German forward defences and overwhelming them. Rifle fire also took a toll on the German defenders and many surrendered, with thirty prisoners, including one officer, taken in the attack. Yet, despite these successes, the Allied line remained fragile.

At 8 pm, the 18th Battalion AIF relieved the exhausted men of the 35th, who had been fighting since the night of 30 March, had endured rain, cold and difficult conditions and, at times, had been the only battalion in the line. During that week, two officers had been killed and a further six wounded, while there were 283 casualties of other ranks. After a relatively quiet day, the men of the 35th silently filed out of the line and moved back to a temporary rest area at Bois l'Abbe, before returning to the aerodrome at Cachy. However, even out of the line, they were not safe. On 6 March, two men were killed and three wounded from German shelling. The battalion moved back to cellars in the destroyed town of Villers-Bretonneux, where another man was killed and two more wounded. These fatalities continued for the next few days until they moved to Gentelles, further behind the line.

On 10 April, Major General R. L. Mullens, Officer Commanding 1st Cavalry Division, wrote to General Monash to thank him for the 9th Brigade's assistance:

> I was very much stirred by the courtesy of your officers and
> their desire to do everything in their power to help. As you
> know, we had a curious collection of units to deal with, and
> it was a very real relief to know that I had your stout-hearted
> fellows on my left flank and also later on my right flank and
> that all worry was therefore eliminated as to the safety of our
> flanks. Your order for the placing of your heavy guns and
> batteries so as to cover our front was of very real assistance,
> incidentally they killed a lot of Huns, and was much
> appreciated by us all.[12]

Colonel Benson of the 6th Londoners also wrote, 'The counter attack of the 36th Battalion was got away very rapidly and efficiently. The greatest credit is due to the OC (Milne) of the 36th who organised and launched the counter attack, and to his battalion for the spirited way in which it was carried out. This officer undoubtedly retrieved a very awkward situation.'[13] Sadly, while Milne had survived the attack, he was killed on 12 April, when a shell landed on his headquarters.

The successful defence of Villers-Bretonneux pushed two German divisions back in what became known as the First Battle of Villers-Bretonneux. While the German offensive had failed to take the town, it had pushed back the British Fourth Army and, to the south, the French, providing tantalising views to the Germans of Amiens and its Gothic cathedral shimmering in the distance.

Ludendorff now turned his attention to Flanders, launching Operation Georgette. Though the Australian 1st Division had just arrived on the Somme, they were quickly recalled back to Flanders to protect the vital railhead at Hazebrouck, the main supply centre for the British. The town was also the gateway to the Channel ports, and its loss would have had a devastating effect on resupply and morale.

When the Australians arrived at Hazebrouck on 12 April, they were deployed to a defensive line across the front of the Nieppe Forest. The 1st and 2nd Brigades were spread along a front of nearly six miles, an area usually defended by two divisions. The 2nd Brigade's 8th Battalion had a front of 3000 yards; 1000 yards per company, each comprising about 200 men at this time.[14]

When the Germans attacked on 14 April against the 3rd Battalion at Gutzer Farm, they came in waves and were mown down, so tightly packed were their ranks. The Germans took the farm, but the Australians retook it, only to then be driven out by heavy German machine-gun fire on two sides. Throughout the afternoon, the Germans pressed their attack on the Australian line, but were driven back. The strong defence by both Australian and British troops saved Hazebrouck, and by the end of April, Operation Georgette was over.

Sixty miles south, on the Somme, the Allied line of the Fourth Army was predominantly held by Australian units along a front of seventeen miles. This 'was due to the daily reoccurring fears of a German breakthrough to Amiens, and the necessity for buttressing the much-tried British infantry with reserves of first rate quality'.[15] General Henry Rawlinson, Commander of the British Fourth Army, which included the Australian Corps, summed up the situation in his diary: 'I feel happier about the general situation and I now have three brigades of Australians in reserve, so I think we will be able to keep the Boche out of Amiens.'[16]

While the situation had indeed stabilised, the Germans still retained the strategically important Hangard and Lancer woods south of Villers-Bretonneux, an area which became the focus of the next stage of the Allied defence.

The task of taking Hangard Wood was given to the AIF's 5th Brigade. Rather than launching a major attack, small units of troops were to advance through the two sections of the wood and form a defensive line along the road that ran along the wood's eastern edge and faced the open ground to Lancer Wood further east. The main attack would be undertaken by two companies – one from the 19th Battalion and one from the 20th Battalion – and on either side would be flanking platoons for protection.

41

Early on 7 April, the two attacking companies moved out, the 19th under the command of Captain Clarence Wallach, one of five Wallach brothers who had enlisted. When the anticipated artillery barrage did not come, Wallach led his men across the open ground towards Hangard Wood. German machine guns opened on the advancing line, killing two officers and taking out many of the men. Wallach was badly wounded, having been shot through both knees.

At this point, Lieutenant Percy Storkey took command. He and eleven men pushed through the low regrowth of the wood and, on hearing a German machine gun to their south, wheeled around and came upon the rear of a number of German machine-gun pits, where the enemy troops were firing towards the advancing Australians. Twenty yards from the Germans they were spotted. Storkey charged, yelling as he went. The Australians 'got in quickly with bombs, bayonet, and revolver'.[17] Storkey demanded the Germans' surrender, but three hesitated so he shot them with his revolver, at which point it jammed. His men slipped the pins from their grenades to threaten the Germans, who then quickly surrendered. Thirty Germans had been killed, and three officers and fifty men were captured and quickly escorted to the rear. Australian casualties were 151 officers and men.

With Operation Georgette in Flanders stalled by mid-April, Ludendorff again turned his attention to Amiens and Villers-Bretonneux. Over the next few weeks, the Germans brought down troops, guns and supplies.

Facing them were the British 8th Division, which had been savagely dealt with during the German March offensive, losing

250 officers and about 4500 men. To replace these losses, and as the British were desperate for reinforcements to fill the ranks, they had lowered the enlistment age, allowing 140,000 reinforcements to be sent to France to help stall the attack. However, these reinforcements were mere boys. An Australian noted in his diary, 'For two days companies of infantry have been passing us on the road – companies of children. English children, pink faced, round cheeked children, flushed under the weight of their unaccustomed packs, with their steel helmets on the back of their heads and the strap hanging loosely on their rounded baby chins.'[18] Some British units were made up of sixty per cent new, young recruits who, as Bean states, 'till a week before had never fired a shot'.[19] While General Rawlinson was concerned about using these untrained troops in so important a defensive task in the Somme, pressure from both Foch and Haig made it necessary to push these lads into the line.

A German prisoner captured by the French told the Allies that an attack would come on 16 April. While this didn't eventuate, the Australians brought up the 5th Division, and battalions from the 14th Brigade moved to the north of Villers-Bretonneux in readiness.

Early on the morning of 17 April, the Germans drenched the town with mustard gas, sometimes at a rate of one shell every two seconds. The shelling lasted from 4 am until 7 am, by which time the Australians had suffered nearly 700 casualties. The gas formed a coating and, if touched, blistered their skin. Men were especially affected in tender parts of their body, particularly their eyes, throat, under their arms and in the crotch. It was later found that the Germans had fired 12,000 gas shells made up of mustard gas, sneezing gas and phosgene gas into the town.

Again it was learnt from captured Germans that a further attack would come, this time on 24 April, which would be preceded by a heavy gas bombardment and would include fifteen German tanks, something not seen before in battle. Aerial photographs appeared to confirm this plan, as massed German troops could be seen lining trenches to the east of the town.

At 4.45 am on 24 April, all hell broke loose along a six-mile front from Villers-Bretonneux south into the French sector. The bombardment was intense and included a mix of gas, particularly mustard. Shrouded in fog and smoke, the Germans advanced on the British line to the east of the town, with visibility down to 100 yards. Soon reports came in confirming that the enemy were supported by tanks and that the British line was folding, with men streaming back.

Brigadier Harold 'Pompey' Elliott, Commander of the Australian 15th Brigade, was to the north-west of Villers-Bretonneux on high alert for such an attack. He sent forward two patrols, which established a line on the east side of the town and attempted to collect stragglers, many of whom were found without a rifle or equipment. Elliott also laid out his Lewis guns.

By now German units were in Villers-Bretonneux and were swarming across the open fields to the south-east, where the defensive line ran from Monument Wood. Elliott was chafing at the bit to initiate a counterattack, but the British had reassured his commander, General Talbot Hobbs of the 5th Australian Division, that their help was not required, something that rankled both men.

In the front line, things were not going well for the young British recruits. To the south-east, three German tanks appeared out of the mist, supported by infantry. They lumbered forward, each tank an iron pillbox bristling with machine guns. Attempts to stop them by Lewis-gun fire failed and the tanks rumbled forward, crossing the British front line. Men crouched low in the trenches as the tracked monsters crossed a yard above their heads. Many British troops were cut off or killed, but others were able to fall back into the town and along the railway cutting.

At Monument Wood, the British resisted and dealt high casualties on the advancing enemy as they crossed the open land towards Hangard Wood, but the British were overrun. Six German tanks advanced and four more broke through at Hangard Wood, pushing the British defenders back to the outskirts of Cachy, to the south-west of Villers-Bretonneux. As in other parts of the line, the appearance of the tanks out of the mist and smoke created panic, with men fleeing back towards Villers-Bretonneux itself.

It was at this time that the first tank-on-tank engagement in the war occurred, with three British Mark IV tanks taking on the lumbering German prototypes. While all tanks were damaged and the battle inconclusive, it was a watershed technological moment. Nonetheless, with the supporting infantry, the German tanks swept around the flanks, cutting off the retreat in many places and capturing 2400 British troops.[20] One German tank alone captured 175 British soldiers. As dawn broke the situation became very grim, with British troops withdrawing in disarray, many without weapons.

The looming threat to Amiens was not lost on General Rawlinson or General Foch. By 8 am on the 24th, German units held the north and south of Villers-Bretonneux and were advancing rapidly towards the western outskirts.

At noon, Foch ordered Rawlinson to recapture Villers-Bretonneux, but Rawlinson had already ordered the Australian

13th Brigade under Major General Thomas Glasgow to bring his men forward and take the town 'that night at the latest'.[21] At 9.40 am, Glasgow had received his orders and by 11.15 am, his men were marching to Bois l'Abbe on the western side of the town. He was fully aware of the importance of his mission and the nature of the task ahead, having conducted a personal recce at Cachy of the switch there, a long communication trench across the line of an enemy advance or a junction in a trench system. However, Glasgow remained concerned for his men, noting, 'Poor chaps, they're in for a tougher time than they realise.'[22]

Rawlinson also ordered Pompey Elliott's 15th Brigade to be ready to attack at 8 pm. (The 15th Brigade, who had suffered so badly at Fromelles in July 1916 and had matters to settle with the Germans, supported the move, coming up from the flats on the Somme and quickly taking a position close to where the Australian National Memorial at Villers-Bretonneux stands today.) Glasgow, however, reasoned that it would still be light at this time and his men of the 13th, without any preparatory barrage, would be exposed to German fire across the bare approach to the east of Hill 104. He noted, 'If God Almighty gave the order, we couldn't do it by daylight.'[23] He argued for a later attack, needing the time to prepare his men, get to the start line and have the cover of darkness. It was finally agreed to attack at 10 pm.

Glasgow and Elliott met briefly at the nearby village of Blangy-Tronville at 8 pm, where they sorted some differences and settled on the plan to encircle Villers-Bretonneux with the 15th Brigade to the north and the 13th Brigade to the south, cutting off the superior German forces within the town boundaries.

Elliott was pleased to have the 13th on his right, trusting his fellow Australians. He and Glasgow agreed the full moon would assist the attack, and requested there be no barrage to alert the

Germans. What was most important, given the failed counter-attacks attempted during the day, was to retake Villers-Bretonneux and re-establish the British line of the previous morning. Orders were passed down, with Captain Harburn of the 51st Battalion telling his men, 'The Monument [Wood] is your goal and nothing is to stop you getting there. Kill every bloody German you see, we don't want any prisoners and God bless you.'[24]

At 10 pm, against Glasgow's advice, a bombardment fell on Villers-Bretonneux, removing the element of surprise. His 13th Brigade moved from their start line and began their advance of two miles. The men of the 51st Battalion on the left took heavy machine-gun fire from Aquenne Wood, but Second Lieutenant Cliff Sadlier, with Sergeant Charlie Stokes and a bombing party, attacked through the woods, eliminating two machine guns and their crews. Wounded, and without his bombers, all of whom had become casualties, Sadlier attacked a third machine gun with his revolver, killing the gun crew and capturing the weapon. For this action he was awarded a Victoria Cross.

North of the village, Elliott's 15th Brigade did not get into position until two hours later, and began their attack at midnight. Their approach had been silent but once the order to charge was given, the cry went up, 'Into the bastards, boys.'[25] Heavy German machine-gun fire swept into the ranks and men fell, but the charge surged on. Quickly they overran machine-gun posts, shooting or bayonetting the German gun crews. Charles Bean noted, 'for the time being, the men had thrown off the restraints of civilised intercourse and were what the bayonet instructors of all armies aimed at producing by their tuition – primitive, savage men.'[26] The Australians reportedly said that 'they had not had such a feast with their bayonets before'.[27] While flares lit the sky, the Germans were silhouetted by the burning village behind them and 'old scores were wiped out two or three times over'.[28]

Elliott's 15th Brigade reached the north-eastern corner of Villers-Bretonneux, wheeled and dug in on an arcing front along the Hamel road, their backs to the town. At this time they had not linked up with Glasgow's boys south of the town, and neither brigade had succeeded in closing the gap and bottling up the Germans as planned.

Enemy troops were still coming and going into the town, oblivious to the Australian encirclement. Bean notes that, 'many Germans came along the road from the town "apparently quite unconcerned, smoking cigarettes" and from the other direction arrived a party of them pulling a hand cart with trench mortar shells. All were allowed to approach, and then abruptly challenged and made prisoners.'[29] In another incident, Major Kuring of the 59th Battalion saw a large party of men approaching, challenged them and, after a brief firefight, captured twenty Germans and four light machine guns.

In an attempt to link the two brigades, two patrols moved out before dawn on 25 April but were quickly engaged by German machine guns in scattered posts, and a number of Australians were killed and wounded. Lieutenant Simpson of the 60th Battalion had all his men hit, but was able to drag the wounded to cover, eliminate a German post and, for the remainder of the day, hold the post, sniping Germans as the opportunity arose. Meanwhile the second patrol was also finding stiff opposition, and no further efforts were made during daylight to link up the two brigades.

South of the town, Glasgow's 13th Brigade was holding a line between the town and Hangard Wood with the assistance of British units. At 9 am, two blindfolded Germans were paraded at

52nd Battalion headquarters bearing a message from their commander that requested the Australians to surrender. The German sergeant major informed the Australians they were surrounded on three sides by superior forces, and they should surrender to avoid serious loss of life. If not, he threatened to 'blow you to pieces by turning the heavy artillery onto your trenches'.[30] It was explained to the Germans that this had to be referred above, but, in the meantime, another German arrived with another demand for the Australians to surrender.

When Glasgow received the request by field telephone, his answer was clear and unambiguous: 'Tell them to go to Hell.'[31] The three Germans, meanwhile, were led away into captivity, much to their relief.

By early 26 April, the front line was joined and Villers-Bretonneux totally encircled. The 13th Brigade had 1009 casualties, including a total of 365 officers and men of the 51st Battalion. Elliott's 15th Brigade had 455 casualties but, given the success of the combined attack, these casualties were considered reasonable though regrettable. British casualties were about 7000 in the 8th and 58th Divisions, and German casualties were about the same.

The Australian recapture of Villers-Bretonneux was broadly celebrated and brought 'great fame to the Australian infantry',[32] with the Australian Corps recognised as a major factor in the slowing and then turning of the German offensive north and south of the Somme.

Field Marshal Haig had sent a message on 25 April stating his 'congratulations to the III Corps Commander and the troops engaged particularly the 13th and 15th Australian Brigades on the most successful and important operations carried out in the neighbourhood of Villers Bretonneux'.[33] Some months later, on 20 July, Haig wrote, 'A night operation of this character, undertaken at such short notice, was an enterprise of great daring. It was carried out in the most spirited and gallant manner by all ranks. The 13th Australian Brigade in particular, showed great skill and resolution in their attack, making their way through belts of wire running diagonally to the line of their advance, across very difficult country which they had no opportunity to reconnoitre beforehand.'[34] General Rawlinson was also impressed, and expressed 'his appreciation of the excellent arrangements . . . and the gallantry and determination exhibited by all troops'.[35]

The attack reaffirmed the effectiveness of the Australian troops, especially when allowed their own planning and timing. Even the British High Command was starting to recognise that the Australians needed to fight in their own unique, perhaps peculiar way. The officers understood the Australian attitude, their commitment and their perseverance and, most importantly, the trust that existed between Australian units which meant that they would not let down their mates, nor fall back or vacate the line.

It should be kept in mind, however, that the success at Villers-Bretonneux, and the halting of the Germans across the Somme and in front of Amiens, was not singularly an Australian victory. The Australian part in the action, while significant, was not undertaken without help.

Bean was careful not to exaggerate the Australian achievement of March to April 1918. He wrote:

It has frequently been claimed that the Australian infantry divisions stopped the advancing Germans in their previously victorious progress towards Amiens and also towards Hazebrouck . . . if this claim means that the Germans continued to advance until they came up against Australian troops hurriedly brought to the rescue, and that these were the troops that first held up the enemy on the line on which the offensive ended, it is not literally true of any important sector of the Somme front . . .[36]

A footnote in Bean perhaps best describes the Allied opinion of the Villers-Bretonneux attack:

Brigadier General Grogan of the 23rd British Brigade, who was in an even better position to know the nature of the achievement, has generously described it as 'perhaps the greatest individual feat of the war – the successful counter-attack by night across unknown and difficult ground, at a few hours' notice, by the Australian soldier'.[37]

In Villers-Bretonneux the front line now ran to the east of the village, facing the Germans at the eastern end. This was a dangerous place, where the land was flat, windblown and devoid of any cover. The new front line comprised a series of gun pits and hastily dug trenches, which made communications, resupply and movement both difficult and dangerous. As it was devoid also of trees or any landmarks, the area was confusing and men on both sides of the line became lost or wandered into each other's trenches. To provide cover and a degree of safety, a communication trench protected by wire was dug, allowing hot food to be brought forward and for the relief troops to enter the line and move on to the scattered posts with a greater degree of safety.

Just south, the Germans now held Hangard and Monument woods, where attacks by French Moroccan units had failed. The French had been keen to force the Germans back from the town. For this task they brought in Moroccan troops and elements of the Foreign Legion, but had made little headway against stubborn German resistance. Their attack had been observed by the Australians, who initially watched with admiration before witnessing the colonial troops suffer heavy losses.

On 28 April, the AIF's 4th Division took over. The 4th Brigade, recently moved from the defence of Hébuterne in the north, occupied the trench line that crossed the old Roman road to Péronne. Nightly they sent patrols into no-man's-land, raiding German trenches and creating panic. A German record notes 'that the days were quiet, but by night our opponents, Australians, were very active'.[38] These were the days of 'peaceful penetration', or trench raiding.

Another initiative undertaken by AIF battalions along the line was 'nibbling'. As Colonel Douglas Marks, the commander of the 13th Battalion, described it:

> The policy of nibbling forward was one at which the 13th
> Battalion excelled, no night passing without our advancing a
> Lewis gun or a few snipers to form a post which later became a
> J.O.T. [jumping off trench] for another nibble, which irritated
> Fritz so much that he became extremely jumpy and nervy
> sending up all night continuous streams of flares and bursting
> out spasmodically into fits of hurricane strafe.[39]

However, the Germans had taken control of the old British aircraft hangars opposite the corner of the Hamel road, which allowed them to mass troops undetected, sometimes just fifty yards from the Australian line, for assaults on the Australian trenches. The Germans also had well-sited and well-protected machine guns among these hangars. The recapture of Villers-Bretonneux had been a victory for the Allies, but the situation remained grim.

FOUR

Hamel: A Test of New Tactics

On 1 June 1918, Major General John Monash was promoted to lieutenant general and given command of the newly formed Australian Corps. Combining the five Australian divisions into one corps under the command of an Australian had long been a wish of the Australian Government, even given the high regard the Australian troops had for General William Birdwood. Monash was seen as the right choice. He was proud of his troops and wished to see them undertake an attack of his making, one he could assert was an Australian initiative in planning and execution. As a result, Monash put to General Rawlinson the idea of an attack against Hamel, a small village just three miles to the northeast of Villers-Bretonneux. This would drive the Germans from the heights on the south side of the Somme, push back the threat to Amiens and further disrupt the Germans' plans to resume their offensive. It would also bring the Allied line on the south bank of the Somme up to the defensive line that the Allies had established on the north bank, which now lay some way ahead.

John Monash was a Melbourne University graduate in engineering and law, and had initially joined the Garrison Artillery, where he was appointed a lieutenant in April 1887. He held various part-time ranks before being appointed commander of the 4th Brigade in late 1914. Monash had started the war as a lieutenant colonel and had served at Gallipoli before being transferred in 1916 to the Western Front, where he was promoted to major general. In June 1916, he took command of the newly raised 3rd Division. Two years later, taking up his new role as commander of the Australian Corps, in the surroundings of the beautiful château at Bertangles, five miles north of Amiens, he began planning for an attack on Hamel.

In particular, Monash sought a means to harness his men's aggressive fighting ability in a new and determined way. His engineering mind realised the potential of carefully coordinating the elements he had at hand: infantry, artillery, air support and, in particular, tanks. While Monash was initially keen to make this 'primarily a tank operation',[1] like the rest of the AIF he vividly remembered the disastrous involvement of tanks at Bullecourt in 1917, where the tanks supporting the troops had either been destroyed or had broken down, and the Australians had suffered enormous losses. However, the new British Mark V tanks were far more reliable and the crews better trained. If Monash was to involve tanks, it would take some convincing of both his officers and men, along with the provision of suitable numbers of tanks to support his planned attack.

By mid-June, the Australian line had pushed forward, particularly to the north of Villers-Bretonneux closer to Hamel. From the ridgeline, the Australians could look across the rolling ground to Vaire and Hamel woods. Visible too was the shattered village of Hamel and, beyond, the low flats stretching north to the treeline and the ponds that bordered the Somme. Further north again was the rising ground on the north side of the river, with Sailly-le-Sec visible among the trees, the scene of ferocious fighting by the 3rd Australian Division in late March and early April.

From this vantage point, the Australians continued their active patrolling, nibbling and peaceful penetration. They could watch the Germans threading their way through Vaire Wood along Hun's Walk, a communication trench through the wood, bringing up supplies and conducting their reliefs. They could also watch the effect of their artillery, crashing along the opposite ridge, in particular onto the German position, the Wolfsberg, situated on the top of the hill above Hamel. The Germans also kept up a continual strafe of the Australian lines, not only along the front, but well back into Villers-Bretonneux and the communication lines past Bois l'Abbe on the road from Amiens.

At Bertangles, Monash was hard at work planning his attack. He envisaged an infantry force made up of brigades from the 2nd, 3rd and 4th Divisions to ensure a spread of casualties. Along with his chief of staff, Brigadier General Thomas Blamey, Monash visited the assembly area of the new Mark V tanks and was greatly impressed, for here was 'an instrument to lighten the task and the losses of the infantry and render possible the Hamel operation'.[2] The Australian command, and certainly the fighting battalions, had not been familiar with the success of the tanks at Cambrai in November 1917, nor with the improvements both in tactics and fighting capability.

After Monash had seen the tanks in operation and spoken to the commander of the 5th Tank Brigade, Brigadier General Anthony Courage, he drew up a plan of attack primarily based around tanks. Monash initially planned for one battalion of tanks, a total of thirty-six, but revised this to sixty, which he estimated would be enough to cover his front of about three miles with one tank every 250 yards. He also adopted the idea of three waves of tanks: an advanced section of fifteen tanks, followed by the main body of twenty-one tanks and a support line of nine tanks to mop up, plus four carrier tanks and a further company of tanks.

However, on 25 June, at a conference at divisional head-quarters, the British tank commanders argued for there to be no artillery barrage. The Australians, well remembering the failure of the tanks at Bullecourt, quickly quashed this idea. The operation went back to being an infantry attack supported by tanks rather than a 'tank operation'.

For Monash, the task was now one of rethinking the coordination of tanks in a new offensive way, particularly with infantry and the other elements at his disposal. With tanks, he needed to accept a number of problems: speed and capability, the noise of their engines and the reluctance of tank crews to follow the barrage. Monash needed to cover this loud engine noise and revving, and to carefully time the arrival of the tanks so they could move forward with the infantry. Too early and they would find themselves moving into the falling barrage; too late and the infantry would be left to fight without their assistance.

Artillery became another important element of Monash's plan. Guns were to be brought up at night as close to the front as possible, dug in and carefully camouflaged. It was crucial the Germans be unaware of the presence of these guns, which meant they were not to fire until the attack began. They were then to move forward and provide covering fire along the new line. Monash used his heavier artillery to fire in a desultory and random fashion at all hours of the day or night leading up to the attack, onto the open areas across which his troops would advance. These shell holes were carefully placed and then mapped to provide cover, a clever tactic that was typical of Monash's planning, and his desire to reduce casualties. He also used smoke shells, drenching the front-line trenches to cover the advance of the infantry and to deceive the Germans about the actual point of attack.

The Australians manning the front line from the Roman road to the Somme naturally had no idea of the planning underway. They were continuing with active patrolling, gathering intelligence and nibbling forward. At times these tactics led to mishaps, as was the case of a 13th Battalion patrol on 20 June when two officers, Captain Irvine and Lieutenant Lilley, out gathering intelligence on German positions, were fired on by Australians in the front line, killing Irvine and wounding Lilley.

Battalions were rotated into and out of the line continually, with the men returning to areas west along the Somme or to villages further to the west past Amiens. Training continued in these villages as did sojourns in the *estaminets*, cafes selling alcoholic drinks, in Amiens.

It was not until 25 June, after the briefing to divisional commanders, that battalion commanders were notified and briefed on the proposed attack. At this meeting, Monash went over his idea of coordinating various offensive elements, and the role of the tanks, aircraft and artillery. Monash also detailed the plan for a creeping barrage, the use of smoke but no gas, and the resupply of troops through the use of carrier tanks and airdrops. The attack was to take ninety minutes from the advanced start line to be laid down, across the rolling slope, through Vaire Wood and the village of Hamel, ending at Wolfsberg, above and to the east of the village.

Another element in the attack was the inclusion of the recently arrived American army. While America had declared war on Germany on 6 April 1917 and landed troops in Europe that year, they had had little involvement in the war so far. From May 1918, American troops were slowly entering the areas far behind the front line and an agreement was reached between Field Marshal Haig and the US Supreme Commander, General John J. Pershing, to attach American units to Allied units for training purposes.

When American troops were moved to Allonville just outside Amiens, and into the Australian back area, Rawlinson saw the Americans' position as an ideal training opportunity for them, and thought that 2000 American troops would boost the Australian Hamel operation. After seeking Haig's approval, Rawlinson spoke to General Read, the Commander of the US Second Army, who agreed to provide up to a battalion of men. In turn, it was suggested to Monash that he include a battalion of American troops in the attack, something he immediately agreed to. On 22 or 23 June, the Americans became part of the operation, with initially four companies, and later a further six, included in Monash's planning. Monash even decided to stage the attack on 4 July in their honour.

From the beginning, American and Australian troops got on well. The Americans were aware of the reputation of the Australians and when one digger asked, 'Are you going to win the war for us?' the quick reply came, 'I hope we'll fight like the Australians.'[3]

There were, however, immediate problems with the inclusion of the Americans. General Pershing had to consider orders from President Woodrow Wilson that included certain conditions for the inclusion and deployment of American troops. While Pershing was happy for the American troops to train with Allied forces, Wilson demanded that they always operate under American command, an impossible requirement if they were to be included in Monash's plans. As a result, Pershing withdrew ten companies of his troops from the Hamel operation. Monash had factored in these American companies, interspersing them with the Australian units. Removing them would totally disrupt his plans. Annoyed by Pershing's decision, Monash informed Rawlinson that if the American troops were withdrawn he would call off the operation. Pershing's order also infuriated the American troops, who were keen to see action. Some, it was said, replaced their uniforms with Australian uniforms and simply ignored the order to withdraw. In the end, about 1000 Americans were included in the attack.

With the build-up of essential supplies of food, water stores and ammunition dumps, and recces by officers and senior NCOs near Hamel and Vaire Wood, it soon became obvious to the Australian troops that a 'stunt' was underway.

The serious work of offensive engineering began with the digging of communication trenches and the laying of buried cables. Assault ladders were brought forward while other men disassembled the barbed wire defences, rolling them up or cutting lanes out into no-man's-land.

From the start, Monash imposed a high level of security on the operation. Along the front, all movement of men and guns occurred at night and was well camouflaged before dawn. Troops were to remain out of sight with as little obvious activity as possible, yet active and aggressive patrolling continued at night. Even the pontoon bridges laid across the Somme to bring the guns were disassembled and hidden before dawn, and the tracks made by marching men and wagon wheels covered and removed.

At Monash's headquarters at Bertangles, few notes were made at meetings and few maps marked with the lines of advance and details of the attack. Everything was then collected and locked away at night, all as part of Monash's thorough planning.

Apart from the tanks allocated to the attack, Monash had a substantial allocation of artillery: 326 guns or howitzers, plus 313 pieces of heavy artillery. In the weeks before the attack, he began a daily strafe of the German lines and back areas at 3 am with a mix of high explosive, gas and smoke. While this tactic was normal before an attack, it would not only cover the approach of the tanks and the noise of their engines, but it would also affect the German defenders. The enemy, he believed, would associate gas with smoke, forcing them to don their gasmasks and, in so doing, reducing their fighting effectiveness. On the morning of the attack, he would eliminate gas from the mix, but hopefully the Germans would still be wearing gasmasks when the attack began.

Following Monash's detailed briefings in late June, the battalion commanders understood and accepted his thoroughness, and appreciated his extensive preparations for the attack, and his concern with the safety of the men and with reducing casualties. Monash explained the increased allocation of the artillery, tanks and air support, and the inclusion of the Americans across the Australian front. A key factor determining the effectiveness of tank movements was the allocation of Australian scouts to guide them to their targets and to direct their fire.

The troops, too, were getting ready. They knew from the preparations, the movements at night and the build-up of supplies that the day of the attack was near. Many of the battalions were camped along the Somme, particularly around the pretty town of Corbie, with its ancient cathedral and winding streets. Men enjoyed the river, swimming and blowing up fish with grenades, an activity which continually brought disciplinary action from above and annoyed the locals, but this and raiding the orchards became regular occurrences during these warm, clear days in high summer. The men also prepared themselves by repairing equipment and uniforms, cleaning rifles, sharpening bayonets and submitting their will to the orderly room.

On 2 July, Prime Minister Billy Hughes visited the front and spoke to the troops, expressing the nation's pride in their achievements:

> Your deeds, the history of this war, are the basis upon which the future nation of Australians will be brought up. You have fought to keep alive the ideal of freedom and to save Australia from the domination to which, if Germany won, we would certainly be subjected. While you are doing that abroad, we pledge ourselves to look after your interests at home.[4]

Even given Hughes' support for the two conscription referenda, he was well received by the men.

On the same day, Australian battalions began filtering into the line, and by dawn the following day they were ready for the attack. Forward posts were now established, and the start tapes were laid out under cover of darkness on the night of 3 July to ensure they were not discovered by German patrols. Down on the flats around Hamelet, the tanks were assembling for the attack as the artillery stood ready. For the troops along the front line, a distance of three miles, all that remained was to remove the last of the barbed wire and assemble along their start tapes.

While the battalion commanders had carefully briefed their men, had provided aerial photographs and a 'message map' to send back reports of their position, even they did not know 'zero hour', the time the attack would commence, such was the level of Monash's secrecy. At 6 pm on 3 July, orders went out via telegram to the battalion commanders that zero hour was to be 3.10 am the following morning. The battalion commanders briefed their company commanders, who in turn briefed their platoon commanders, who briefed the men. The AIF command knew that it was crucial all the men clearly understood the task, the objective and the timings of the attack. It was a lesson they had learnt earlier at Messines in 1917, where nearly everyone of rank was taken out, but the diggers had needed to continue the attack and carry out the orders.

The night of 3–4 July was very quiet. A mile behind the line, the tanks assembled, their engines throttled down and covered by the low-flying aircraft. Just after midnight, the attacking battalions filed out of their trenches and silently took up their positions along their start tapes, in some areas in waist-high wheat. As they settled down, the men contemplated their responsibility. This was the first operation wholly planned and undertaken by Australians and the reputations of the AIF, their commander General Monash and the Australian nation rested on their success or otherwise.

The Germans, meanwhile, slept in their dugouts deep in the chalk or in their billets in Hamel, totally oblivious to the storm of fire about to descend upon their front.

Back behind the Allied line, on the flats near the Somme, there was one heart-stopping moment. As the line of lumbering tanks made their way forward, a German flare spiralled into the air and hung there for two minutes, 'showing up an area below as if vignetted in half-daylight,' Charles Bean wrote.[5] The tension was intense, not the least because surprise had seemed assured.

At precisely 3.10 am, the guns opened all along the front, crashing as they did every morning around that time. But now the hidden guns opened up; a total of 362 field guns and 302 heavies, as well as 111 Vickers guns,[6] swept the three miles of the enemy front. While the barrage fell heavily along the front, raising the dust 200 yards ahead of the Australian start line, Vickers guns fired at a sharp angle in the air, laying down a curtain of machine-gun bullets like hail. These fell in thick bands, catching any Germans in the open. Others fell short on the assembled Australian and American troops, and 'several shells dropped short and exploded . . . annihilating them'.[7] One shell in ten was a smoke shell, and thick white smoke swirled around the front. But this time there was no gas, not that the Germans knew as they struggled into their gasmasks, accepting this was the same barrage that had been falling on them each night for the past week. Many curled up in their warm beds and went back to sleep.

With rifles slung, the Australians advanced towards the line of falling shells, ready to hug the barrage once it made its first lift after four minutes. Meanwhile, 'the American troops, intermingled with the Australians, were impressed with the casual attitude of the veteran Diggers.'[8] As they moved forward through the gaps in the wire, and as German flares lit the sky, shells crashed from the flats on the Somme south to the Roman road, hiding the advancing Australians in a barrage 'almost as deep as at Messines'.[9] Knowing the German artillery response would be swift, the men moved quickly to follow the barrage, out into no-man's-land and away from the falling German shells along the support and reserve lines.

Within five minutes of zero hour, the tanks began to arrive. They shuffled forward slowly, waiting for the barrage to lift another 100 yards before they advanced with the infantry into the wall of dust and smoke. By now, the Australians were overrunning the front line of German posts and, within a few minutes, German prisoners were streaming back, bleary eyed and bewildered, their hands high above their heads. Many were found to be mere boys. The Germans, like the Allies, were running out of men.

Men of the 43rd Battalion rushed the German line, completely surprising the German garrison and taking four Maxim guns with their covers still on. They raced on, with Germans fleeing their wild advance. In other places surrendering Germans were captured with their gasmasks on.

Ahead, the line of shells crashed down upon the known German positions, advancing at a rate of 100 yards every three minutes. Apart from the front and support lines, the shells also fell among the German artillery batteries in the rear with devastating accuracy, such was the range-finding technology of artillery by this time. On the right of the attack, the 13th Battalion headed across the Villers-Bretonneux–Hamel road and into a quarry. Their young commanding officer, Douglas Marks, received a message from his advancing men 'by means of a most efficient German field telephone captured in a previous fight'.[10] Bean noted that 'everything seemed to be going well'.[11]

The Australian advance was rapid, the eager troops unencumbered by mud or a determined German response, and keen to hug the barrage. To the left, the Queenslanders of the 15th Battalion passed relentlessly through the wire and overran an area known as Pear Trench before their three allocated tanks even had time to arrive. The Queenslanders, whose losses had been heavy in the advance, 'killed right and left in both the trench and the sunken road that ran through the redoubt'.[12] So quick was the Australian advance on Pear Trench that the machine guns were found to still have their covers on, and surrendering Germans were still wearing gasmasks.

In the fighting for Pear Trench, one German gun continued firing, taking many men out of the advancing line. A Lewis gunner, Private Henry Dalziel, clamped another magazine on his gun and, drawing his revolver, charged the enemy, shooting two gunners and capturing their position. For this action, he was awarded the Victoria Cross. Similar acts of bravery took place all around. There was Private Berry who, after losing his team to a machine gun, organised more ammunition and attacked and destroyed the gun himself. In the fighting at nearby Kidney Trench, Thomas Axford took a German position and was awarded the Victoria Cross.

The bravery of the signallers was also noteworthy. Many telephone lines ran across the open countryside to the rear, but they were cut by shots and shells, and the tanks that crisscrossed the front. Signallers were continually repairing broken wires, always exposed to snipers and machine guns working in open areas. A 13th Battalion signaller, John Harris, whose mate had already been wounded, ran out over 500 yards of cable, keeping his line in repair all day and adding a bar to his Military Cross.

To allow the attacking battalions to reform and reorganise, and for battalions like the 44th to leapfrog through, a halt was called to the artillery barrage after an advance of 1000 yards. The 44th advanced through Hamel village with little resistance, clearing buildings and cellars and capturing a large number of prisoners. They also erected a French tricolour flag, something which quickly brought down German artillery fire.

After Pear Trench, the next expected obstacle was Vaire Wood on the far right of the attack. The wood was attacked by the 4th Brigade, who wheeled around the southern edge to line up with the other advancing companies behind the stationary barrage. Bean wrote: 'The men of the extending companies had been told to take their tactic from rugby football, looking upon Vaire Wood as the scrum, their task being to double round it like the scrum halfback and make for the corner yards to the north.'[13] This was 'a risky movement and can only be entrusted to first-class troops'.[14] The attack had begun on a frontage of 400 yards, but this manoeuvre around Vaire Wood would broaden it to 1250 yards, the length of the final objective at the top of the ridge behind the wood.

Initially strong opposition was encountered on the edge of the wood, but this was overcome with the aid of six tanks that, working in pairs, quickly destroyed any opposition. German troops were pulling out and moving back along the Hun's Walk communication trench towards Accroche Wood, where they were joining the German defence at Wolfsberg above the village.

By 4 am, as the light was beginning to spread across the battle-field, the Australians were close to taking all their objectives. At 4.18 am, the 13th Battalion's 'A' Company reported they had captured 200 unwounded prisoners and fourteen machine guns, and were now on their objective and in contact with the 15th Battalion on their left.

To ascertain the position of the advance, low-flying Allied aircraft sounded klaxon horns at 4.40 am as a signal for the Australians to light small flares in their positions, which were then marked on maps that were quickly flown back to head-quarters. Observers on the heights on the northern side of the Somme reported, 'Tanks everywhere beyond Hamel, beyond Vaire Wood,'[15] no doubt welcome news to Monash.

In his book *Jacka's Mob*, Lieutenant Edgar Rule of the 14th Battalion describes mopping up Vaire Wood behind the initial advance. Seeing a line of German heads in a trench, he called on them to surrender, which they did, but as he approached, he was fired upon. Rule called up a tank, whereupon the trench again surrendered and he was surprised to see 'a crowd of young boys. We could not kill children . . . [so] with a boot to help them along, they ran with their hands above their heads back to our lines.'[16]

Back at the 13th Battalion position above Vaire Wood, its young colonel, Douglas Marks, was surprised to see a pile of stores already in position. 'Why, what's this?' he asked one man, who replied, 'It's from our tank, sir.'[17]

Monash's plan included the use of four carrier tanks (modified fighting tanks) for resupply, a major advance in battlefield logistics at the time and the 'outstanding lesson of the battle'.[17] From just one of the four carrier tanks came 134 coils of barbed wire, 180 long and 270 short screw pickets, forty sheets of corrugated iron, fifty petrol tins of water, 150 trench mortar bombs, 10,000 rounds of ammunition, four boxes of No. 36 grenades and sixteen boxes of No. 23 grenades.[18] Throughout the course of that day, the four tanks carried supplies that would normally have required the work of 1200 men.

Another innovation was the idea of an Australian pilot, Wing Commander Lawrence Wackett, who would later go on to become the father of the Australian aviation industry. Troops were instructed to lay out large white cloth panels on the ground in a 'V' shape (for Vickers), and aircraft then parachuted small-arms ammunition onto the markers. During the course of the battle, ninety-three boxes of ammunition – nearly 112,000 rounds – were delivered by this method.

Meanwhile, the new tanks were making an impact. As daylight arrived, the tanks became even more effective, operating more closely with the infantry. German machine-gun positions could be engaged with grapeshot or simply 'rubbed out' as the tanks drove backwards and forwards over enemy positions. Bean recounts, 'At various parts of the battlefield, tanks levelled out by their weight whole lines of shelters and rifle pits along the edges of banks and sunken roads.'[19] The diggers were concerned about the wounded being run over by tanks, particularly in the wheat, but a system was established of marking the wounded with a rifle planted vertically in the ground by the bayonet. Returning tanks also became effective in collecting the wounded and returning them to aid posts.

With tank support, the Australians advanced through Hamel, taking 300 Germans captive, most of them found in cellars and dugouts in the town. One observant digger, Lance Corporal Boyce Vincent Schulz, identified the line of a buried German cable ending at a house in the village. Taking a German-speaking American, they knocked on the door and, speaking German, were invited in. They promptly captured a battalion commander and his staff, effectively blocking communications to the rear. In fact, the overall attack had been so swift that in many German positions no reports were despatched nor warnings given before they were overrun.

During the build-up around Hamel before the attack, Monash had staged diversionary attacks on the north side of the Somme around Morlancourt, and as far north as Albert. These attacks continued when the main attack on Hamel was launched.

One of these attacks, on the river flats, had not gone well. The Victorians of the 15th Brigade had attacked across marshy land bordering the river, where it was impossible to dig trenches and boggy areas needed to be avoided. The dummy attacks, while diverting attention from the advances further north, drew heavy German fire.

The Australians consolidated their positions, dug in and ran out wire. Here they found that German trenches were scattered, poorly dug and badly camouflaged, with some trenches used as open latrines. But they also found German snipers active, forcing the wiring and digging parties to ground. Australian snipers were brought up, claiming twenty-one hits and, aided by the use of Stokes mortars, they were able to eliminate the German snipers, but not before they had inflicted a number of casualties on the Australians. Little was achieved by these feints, and they resulted in disproportionate casualties. In one case, a raiding party of 200 men of the 55th Battalion were caught in the open, with a third becoming casualties.

The final objective of the Australians at Hamel was the high ground above the village at Wolfsberg. It was captured with slight losses and the taking of many prisoners, but by mid-afternoon the Germans had reorganised and were putting in strong counter-attacks. German artillery was also ranged across the ridgeline after dark, and a party of 200 Germans attacked up the communication trench that ran to the east, supported by shelling with mustard and phosgene gas, briefly dislodging the Australians and causing Monash some concern.

The 43rd and 44th Battalions counterattacked, driving the Germans back. Bean writes, 'The enemy fled helter-skelter over the open with the Western Australians after them, bombing, snap-shooting, and firing Lewis guns from the hip.'[20] By the time the counterattack had ended, the Australians had captured six officers and fifty other ranks, along with ten machine guns, and had released eleven Australians who had earlier been captured.

For the Australians it had been a good day and, for General Monash, a brilliant victory. Given ninety minutes to take the objective, they took it in ninety-three minutes. The casualties, however, totalled 1400, including 176 Americans. German casualties were estimated at 2000, including 1500 prisoners, 177 machine guns, thirty-two *minenwerfers*, as well as a secret new German 0.53-calibre anti-tank rifle.

The Germans had been at a disadvantage from the start. Fresh troops had just entered the line; as many of the Australian soldiers had noticed, most were young, and some were mere boys of sixteen with no battle experience. German defences were in places badly sited, their trenches were shallow and only thin belts of wire protected their front. Prior to the attack, the Germans had been continually harassed by peaceful penetration. One German, quoted by Charles Bean, said, 'You bloody Australians. When you are in the line you keep us on pins and needles; we never know when you are coming over.'[21]

Yet Monash, and the success at Hamel, deserved recognition and celebration. The action established a new line and pushed the Germans further away from Amiens. The attack also saw an offensive action against the run of play, unexpected and potent, that demonstrated Allied resistance and determination.

Of most importance for the Allies was the success of the new tactics introduced by Monash, tactics that would alter the course of the war. Hamel provided the Allies with a new appreciation of close coordination and planning, which gave them an edge at a crucial time. Monash had advanced what was current practice by improving the timing, and by using aggressive, reliable troops.

News of the Australian success spread quickly and lifted the morale of the Allied armies. At his headquarters in Bertangles Château, Monash was not only proud of his success and that of the Australian Corps, but also overwhelmed with praise and congratulatory telegrams and letters from Allied prime ministers, politicians, and even General Pershing. Field Marshal Haig had written to Billy Hughes, asking him to 'please convey to Lieutenant General John Monash and all ranks . . . my warm congratulations on the success which attended the operation carried out this morning, and the skill and gallantry with which it was conducted.'[22]

Haig and Rawlinson were delighted with the success at Hamel, particularly to counter the condemnation the High Command had received after the disastrous and costly German March offensive and the absence of good news since. Indeed, Haig had great faith in Monash; he wrote, 'Monash is a most thorough and capable commander, who thinks out every detail of any operation and leaves nothing to chance.'[23] Haig was relieved to see pressure taken off Amiens through strong offensive action.

The Supreme War Council sitting at Versailles welcomed the news of the first Allied victory since Ludendorff's March offensive had begun with much jubilation. The French Prime Minister Georges Clemenceau visited the Australian 4th Division at Bussy-les-Daours, near Amiens, and spoke to the men in English. In part, he said:

When you Australians came to France, the French people expected a great deal of you . . . We knew that you would fight a real fight, but we did not know from the very beginning you would astonish the whole continent . . . I shall go back tomorrow and say to my countrymen, 'I have seen the Australians. I have looked in their faces. I know that these men . . . will fight alongside us till the freedom for which we are all fighting is guaranteed for us and for our children.'[24]

The battle, though small by Western Front standards, was to change the Allies' future offensive tactics.

FIVE

Nibbling East

The attack at Hamel confirmed the widely held belief that neither side could claim a decisive victory, nor even a strategic advantage. Like two punch-drunk boxers bashing each other about the ring, bloody and bruised, one always rose for another blow, another attack. But it remained to be seen which of the two could sustain this pummelling, the pain and the blood, and maintain their resolve and morale.

The various German attacks from the March offensive were now petering out, and the Allied generals Foch and Haig had discussed the idea of a Somme initiative. Their aim was to protect Amiens not by a strengthening of the defensive line, but by counteroffensive. Their planning had before this point been long-term, with consideration given to a war stretching until 1920. However, Operation Georgette, the German offensive of mid-1918 in Flanders, postponed this idea. Now, with the Australian successes in Villers-Bretonneux and Hamel, and the end of the Germans' Operation Michael, new Allied offensive plans, which included the French, Americans and the British along a broad front, began to be considered.

Ludendorff's offensive plans had not yet fully played out, however. On 27 May, he had launched Operation Blücher-Yorck, with the Germans attacking on the Aisne, in particular the strategic Chemin des Dames Ridge to the south of the French sector. The offensive started with 4000 artillery pieces firing high explosive and gas, followed by the assault of seventeen stormtrooper divisions. By nightfall they had opened a twenty-five-mile (forty-kilometre) gap in the Allied line, gaining ten miles (sixteen kilometres) of territory and, within a few days, they had taken 50,000 Allied prisoners and captured 800 guns. They were now only thirty-six miles (fifty-six kilometres) from Paris. Though this attack finally stalled on the Marne through German exhaustion, high casualties and supply problems, the Allied High Command realised there was still fight in the German army and cancelled offensive action on the Somme.

The German advances of Operation Gneisenau in June and Friedenstrum in July, while initially successful, finally ended Ludendorff's offensives. One further planned offensive, Operation Hagen, was also cancelled by 7 August. By the end of July, when the last attack flickered and died, Germany had lost 227,000 killed or missing, 765,000 were wounded and a further 1,960,000 – one fifth of the German army – were sick, many from the influenza pandemic. As well as these losses, the effect of the offensives' failure on German morale was enormous.

The initiative now passed to the Allies. General Foch, the supreme commander of all Allied forces, wanted to counterattack; the question was where it would take place. Like Ludendorff, Foch needed to consider his long front line. He saw advantages in the Somme region, not the least being the apparent neglect of the Germans to strengthen their defences, relying instead on re-occupying the old French Amiens outer defence line. Perhaps they saw the Allies as beaten and unable to mount an offensive, underestimating their recuperative powers, the industrial output of Britain and the supply line from America. Foch also needed to relieve the pressure on Amiens and Paris, where further threats were feared given recent German attacks on the Marne.

Encouraged by Haig, General Rawlinson submitted an attack plan in mid-July which was approved by both Haig and Foch. From the start, the plan was based on two crucial elements: surprise and secrecy. The Australians, under Rawlinson's British Fourth Army, as well as the Canadians under General Arthur Currie, were to be used for the advance in the British sector. Haig had offered the Canadians to Rawlinson, who welcomed these seasoned and successful troops for inclusion in his planning. The Canadian troops and the five divisions of the new Australian Corps would form the vanguard for the attack, which would incorporate the lessons learnt at Hamel and include the new tanks and equipment now available. There was much to do beforehand – the current line to consolidate, planning, training, the vast logistics of troop movement and supply, intelligence gathering – all under the cloak of tight secrecy.

New techniques and weapons, such as the successful use of tanks at Cambrai in 1917, artillery that was more comprehensive and had improved accuracy, sound detection and more Lewis guns (light machine guns) had significantly improved AIF performance by 1918. Better, faster and more reliable communications were also an integral part of the Hamel success, particularly the effective use of reconnaissance planes to track and report the attack. Pilots marked on maps the movements of German and Australian troops, and the maps were then dropped to motorbike riders who quickly despatched them to the relevant headquarters. Consequently, Monash and battalion commanders had current information on the progress of the battle within minutes, compared with the slow, tedious communication systems of the past.

Through July and into early August, planning continued at a feverish pace. Once the line for the attack was determined, detailed planning started. It was decided to attack along a front of

25,000 yards (14.2 miles or 22.7 kilometres) from Morlancourt south to Moreuil. The British in the north would have a front of 5000 yards; the Australians, south of the Somme, 7500 yards; the Canadians, on the Australians' right flank, 7500 yards; and the French, at the southern end of the line, 5000 yards.[1] The front line was across well-drained farmland, free of craters and extensive wire, and north of the Roman road, generally flat and ideal for tanks. The area had been well photographed, and detailed typographical maps were produced in colour for broad distribution.

As at Hamel, the offensive elements of the attack – the infantry, tanks, artillery and aircraft – needed close coordination. Attention needed to be given to medical organisation, meteorology, communications, engineering works, training and preparation, rail and road movements and resupply, along with intelligence on German disposition and strength. This involved detailed planning for the logistics and movement of trains, motor lorries and guns, the build-up of supply dumps and engineering work. Secrecy needed to be maintained and the offensive kept from the men, even while the massive build-up stated the obvious.

Rawlinson's plan, the details of which were drawn up by Monash, involved fourteen infantry divisions (one British, five Australian, four Canadian and four French), three cavalry divisions, 3000 guns and 650 tanks. The broad attack would have an average objective of 10,500 yards (six miles or ten kilometres) and would be initially undertaken with three objectives: the 'Green Line', the 'Red Line' and finally the 'Blue Line'. Once an objective line was reached, the following division, brigade or battalion would then leapfrog the first unit and continue the advance. This broke down to a setpiece advance for 3000 yards under a protective barrage, a further advance of 4500 yards in open warfare relying on tanks instead of artillery, and a further exploitation zone of 1500 yards if this could be achieved. To minimise fatigue, the leapfrogging divisions would be brought up close to the start line and rested, with the initial attacking divisions passing through them before crossing the start line.

Artillery was to be quietly moved into the line at night and carefully camouflaged before dawn. This was to be checked by aircraft from the Australian Flying Corps No. 3 Squadron every day and carefully watched. Guns were not to fire before the opening of the offensive so their locations would remain concealed, and there would be no ranging shots on targets, the guns' accuracy having been checked at a specially prepared artillery range behind the lines.

Once the attack started, the lighter artillery needed to be quickly hitched up and moved forward with the advance, particularly the rapid-firing eighteen-pound guns. Detailed barrage maps were drawn up, providing precise timings and distances for guns to keep up the barrage just ahead of the advancing troops. In all, there would be eighteen brigades of field artillery with six guns per battery – 432 guns in all – plus mortars and medium and heavy artillery, for a total of 680 guns for the Australian advance.

As with Hamel, coordinating the infantry with the artillery barrage needed careful planning. It was proposed that from zero hour, the line of the barrage should be straight along the whole front, falling 200 yards in front of the infantry start line. It was hoped that the artillery could not only eliminate all known German artillery, but could lay down an accurate barrage line for the infantry to follow and reduce inaccurate firing or 'drop-shorts' – shells falling among the advancing lines of infantry.

Tanks, too, were crucial. At Hamel, the Australians had learnt the value of tanks and would never again fear their presence, while the British tank crews had been impressed with the morale and fighting qualities of the Australians. Yet the operation of tanks required training, and it needed to be demonstrated that tanks were a suitable, and indeed necessary, alternative to artillery. On 9 July, the 7th Battalion practised with tanks near Rivery on the outskirts of Amiens to rehearse cooperation, in particular signalling. Similarly, on 29 July, the 27th Battalion was taken to a tank park north of Amiens where 'they practiced the latest methods in tank and infantry co-operation'.² This training continued so that most units spent time during July and early August practising signalling and learning how to work with, and protect, tanks.

Aircraft were also a major element in the offensive. It was found that the noisy, slow-flying Handley Page bombers would cover the noise of tank engines. These bombers were to fly up and down the line, night and day, particularly in the days immediately before the attack. Reconnaissance aircraft were also important for aerial photographs and intelligence gathering, and fighters worked to protect both the bombers and the reconnaissance aircraft.

The No. 3 Squadron was also preparing for the big day. Throughout July, it had continued its work bombarding German artillery and photographing German positions. This was particularly important when the Australian line was extended south to Cachy and Hangard, where up-to-date reconnaissance photos of the German lines were urgently required. On 17 July, four RE8 aircraft that were directing artillery fire onto a German position by radio were caught in a severe hailstorm with lightning and high winds. Unable to reach their aerodrome, they were driven down and landed behind the Allied lines with no injury or damage. Other squadron aircraft became involved in aerial dogfights, in one case shooting down a German albatross fighter who had just destroyed four British balloons in quick succession.

Though inclement weather often grounded reconnaissance flights, the Australian Flying Corps kept a close watch on the movement of German batteries. The Germans were at the time replacing real guns with dummies, a diversionary tactic, and these were logged and noted so that Allied artillery could fire on these German positions to continue the deception and cover their own plans for the upcoming offensive.

On the day of the offensive, the squadron would have three different tasks. 'A' flight was to carry out artillery patrols, calling down counter-battery fire on enemy artillery batteries. 'B' flight was to conduct counterattack patrols, seeking out concentrations of enemy infantry whose position they would radio to the artillery and then, flying directly over the concentration, drop a red flare to indicate the position to the Australian infantry. 'C' flight contact patrols were to work with the attacking infantry, identifying individual units by simple field signals and signs, and relaying these positions back to headquarters either by radio or by dropping marked maps at division or corps headquarters, or army report centres.[3] Both 'A' and 'B' flights also had the task of dropping phosphorus bombs along the Morlancourt ridge to obscure German observations from this area.

With the speed of the anticipated advance, a forward radio station was established in Aubigny to continually test the radios carried in aircraft, and to be ready to warn artillery of any unexpected breakthroughs so that artillery would not fire on lines of advancing infantry. As Bean notes, 'The perusal of the battle-orders for the aeroplanes and every other arm engaged in the attack affords a fascinating insight into both the machinery of modern battle and its scientific employment.'[4]

Throughout July, while the Allies built up their troops and supplies for the planned offensive, the infantry war continued. In particular, the Australian tactic of peaceful penetration was a regular pastime, supported and encouraged by Monash and his divisional commanders. Major General Rosenthal, commander of the 2nd Division, had watched with interest as this tactic was developed informally within battalions. He encouraged his brigade commanders to undertake raiding where possible, particularly against the weak defensive German line where the troops were demoralised by the failed offensives and reinforced by young, inexperienced soldiers.

German defences at this time were generally scattered and often in poorly constructed trenches. Many of the German trenches were in the old French defensive trench line east of Amiens, and lacked barbed wire and obstacles. Australian units continued to nibble away at the German line, pushing outposts into no-man's-land and linking these with a continuous trench line.

On the night of 16–17 July, a raiding party from the 19th Battalion, made up of two officers and fifty-six other ranks, raided two German positions near Villers-Bretonneux. The attackers quickly overran the German posts, with the enemy bolting as the Australians fired into their backs, killing seventeen and wounding twenty, and coming away with three prisoners. While two Australians were killed and a further eight wounded, this aggressive action spread fear among the Germans. Unknown to the Australians at the time, this raid also disrupted a planned German attack on the Australian line, allowing the battalion to push their front forward. While this was perhaps the slow way to Berlin, it kept the initiative with the Australians and enhanced morale, self-confidence and determination.

Around this time, there was an incident with a man from the 25th Battalion. The private had been ordered to locate the flanking

Australian battalion and make contact, then return and report in. He made contact but, walking back to his unit, he became lost and wandered into a German post. The Germans quickly disarmed him and were marching him to the rear when they were fired upon, and his guard was wounded. The Australian ran into a wheat crop and hid, waiting for the darkness. However, as he was so close to the German line, he did not find an opportunity to escape overnight and had to spend the following day also in hiding. He finally made his way back into the Australian lines the following day, having had nothing to eat or drink for two days.

In a raid by the 25th and 26th Battalions, also on 16–17 July, the Australians attacked what was known as the 'mound', a low rise or hummock of high ground south of the railway line and east of Villers-Bretonneux that dominated the Australian line and needed to be eliminated. An attempt had been made on the night of the 15th to secure no-man's-land by capturing two enemy outposts, but the attack had failed. When this new attack went in, there was heavy fighting, with the Germans leaving their trench line with fixed bayonets to take on the advancing Australians. This was an unusual move, as the Germans normally fell back when attacked, or surrendered.

During the attack, 'C' Company, on the right, reached a spot called Jaffa Trench, but mistakenly thought this was the objective and propped. The mistake was fortunate, as the fork off the trench contained around 200 Germans and the small remaining band of Australians – two officers and about twenty men – would have been easily wiped out. In the end, both the outposts and the mound were secured, with the 25th Battalion capturing twenty-eight and killing an estimated sixty enemy troops, plus capturing two heavy and two light machine guns. The battalion had one officer and twenty-three men killed, and a further sixty-eight wounded.

Later that day, sentries spotted 250 Germans moving up Jaffa Trench and through a grain crop towards the mound. After an Australian SOS flare went up, the artillery landed high explosive among the advancing Germans, and when Lewis guns and rifles joined in, the results were devastating. When the firing stopped after fifteen minutes, over 100 Germans lay in front of the Australian line.

Two hours later the Germans again deployed, moving forward until they were only fifty to 100 yards from the Australians, ready to counterattack. Again the artillery opened on the advancing lines and accurate Lewis-gun fire, directed by Lieutenant Cecil Auchterlonie, scythed into the Germans. They were mowed down and a further 150 fell. For his decisive action, Lieutenant Auchterlonie was awarded a bar to his Military Cross, which he had received only two weeks before at Hamel. After this, the 25th Battalion was withdrawn, but their short time in the line had seen fifty-four men killed and a further 158 wounded, leaving a battalion of only 473 men at less than half their effective strength.

Apart from raiding and nibbling, Australian troops were also tasked with identifying German units for intelligence reports. This required a small fighting patrol of an officer and a few men raiding a German trench, grabbing prisoners and bringing them in for interrogation. A typical note in the 40th Battalion history notes:

That day enemy identification was asked for and a lieutenant, R. S. McKenzie, took out a patrol of seven ORs to procure it. They moved from our line at 10pm and went about 800 yards down to the Hamel–Warfusée road where they located an enemy post. Lieutenant McKenzie left his party about 30 yards from the post and crawled forward with Sergeant A. H. Richards towards it. They got within 10 yards of it, threw bombs in and rushed. They found two men in the post and Lieutenant McKenzie shot one and secured the other as a prisoner. Bombs were at once thrown at them from another post in the rear and Lieutenant McKenzie was wounded. He sent the sergeant off with the prisoner while he made his way back more slowly to join up with his patrol. Just as he reached his patrol they were attacked by an enemy patrol, who threw bombs among them, fired a few shots and ran, severely wounding Sergeant Richards and one of the men. Rifle grenades were by this time bursting on the road where a patrol was and our party moved off with the prisoner, carrying two of the wounded, both of whom later died. Lieutenant McKenzie was able to walk back slowly without assistance.[5]

The Germans, on the other hand, showed a marked decrease in aggression and in their fighting morale. Aside from being understrength, many units were, like British units, filled with poorly trained younger men, many of them boys. As the 40th Battalion history notes, 'During this period [July] in the line, there was a marked decrease in enemy artillery and an increase in our own which gave us a fairly quiet time in the trenches.'[6] The 22nd Battalion reported, 'During the concluding days of July, the German offensive spirit definitely collapsed,'[7] while the 24th Battalion reported, 'Fritz was plainly nervous, displaying many signs of unease.'[8] Later, the 24th reported that Germans around Monument Wood south of Villers-Bretonneux, including the elite 2nd Grenadier Regiment, 'were rather passive and showed no desire to fight'.[9] A 19th Battalion intelligence report dated 17 July, under the title 'ENEMY ATTITUDE', simply reads, 'Alert'.[10]

The old Roman road between Villers-Bretonneux and Péronne was the boundary between the British and French armies, which was the reason Ludendorff had expended so much energy and men along it. For the Australians in early to mid-1918, their deployment just over this line and south of Villers-Bretonneux brought them in contact with the French army for the first time. In *Somme Mud*, Private Edward Lynch of the 45th Battalion writes about coming into contact with the French army:

> A noise on our immediate right. A man is running towards us. He jumps down amongst us. Two arms wave, two hands flicker in our faces. Two anxious, excited eyes jump at us. A little black goatee beard is bobbing up and down under our noses. A hole opens in the beard and 'Aux Armes! Aux armes! L'ennemi!' the man excitedly gasps, and his imploring eyes burn into each face of the post as he asks if we understand him. I answer in my best French that I understand him. He jumps at me and calls me 'comrade' half a dozen times, and I tell him we are on guard already. Then he dives at me and get a mouthful of bristly beard, and before I know what's what, the excited beggar is kissing me for all he's worth. I jump back, getting rid of that mouthful of beard and hear the boys roaring and rocking in mirth.[11]

The 24th Battalion, on the very right end of the Allied line, connected with the most northern French units, in this case the

Algerian troops, and reported, 'On our right were the Third Zouaves Regiment who were enthusiastic in their praise of the Australians. They posted the following notice: "*Vivent les Australians, qui nous donnent des cigarettes*" which translates to "Hurray for the Australians who offer us cigarettes".'[12]

On the night of 30 July, an advance party from the 13th Battalion completed their relief of French colonial troops in Aquenne Wood, west of Villers-Bretonneux. Here the Australians found the French to be 'methodical and thorough in their handing over and the defensive scheme of the area was carefully explained and also the role of the Battalion in case of penetration of the defences by the enemy. The condition of the trenches was excellent and communication with the rear could easily be maintained in daylight by means of numerous communication trenches.'[13] Colonel Douglas Marks was also impressed, recording in his diary, 'French are very methodical in their trench organisation. Best relief we have had. Sanitation their weak point.'[14]

Also coming into the line now in greater numbers were the American troops, organised under three different formations. There were eight regular Army divisions, seventeen National Guard divisions and eighteen National Army divisions formed by men drafted for National Service. While they were late in arriving, the impact of this new injection of men and matériel was soon felt, relieving both the French and British sections of the front.

After Hamel, the Americans continued to be involved with the Australians, especially in training behind the lines. For example, the 7th Battalion had five American officers and eighty men attached for experience, while the 40th Battalion sent two officers and four NCOs to Querrieu, where a training trench was built so untried soldiers could carry out routine duties as they would in the front line and learn 'Australian methods of scouting and patrolling'.[15]

After their experiences together at Hamel, the Australians had a genuine respect for these newcomers, although the US troops still had a lot to learn. American Command ignored Allied experience and offers of advice, and took the 'American way' of doing things. It showed. While Australia had 60,000 dead in the Great War from the Gallipoli landings in April 1915 until early 1919, the Americans lost nearly the same amount of men in just the last five months of the war.

Also new for the Australians was the arrival of the Canadians on this sector of the front. The Australians greatly admired their colonial cousins, particularly their aggressive fighting qualities and their great successes, like the taking of Vimy Ridge in April 1917. The Germans also respected the Canadians, believing that wherever the Canadians appeared in the line, an attack was imminent. Their deployment therefore required great secrecy and the careful invention of suitable 'excuses' to cover their movement.[16] One widely spread story was that the Canadians were to be moved south to counter an expected renewed German offensive on the Somme and so, without arousing German suspicions, four Canadian divisions were quietly spirited into the support lines.

Meanwhile, along the front, routine patrolling, nibbling and peaceful penetration continued. Men were keen to undertake aggressive patrolling, and battalion commanders were never short of volunteers.

On 6 July, a party from the 20th Battalion had just moved into the line from Morlancourt and were occupying newly captured trenches above Hamel at Accroche Wood. Soon their position was taking sniper fire. Corporal Wally Brown, a Tasmanian, crept out with two grenades, having located where the fire was coming from. Racing across the open, he was soon under fire from another post and forced to ground. He rose and raced on, hurling a Mills bomb, which fell short. He leapt into the post, quickly knocked a German down with his fist and threatened the other in the post with his remaining grenade. One officer and twelve men emerged from a dugout and surrendered, whereupon Brown guided them back to the Australian lines under heavy German fire. Major General Rosenthal, a supporter of peaceful penetration tactics, recommended to Monash that the Victoria Cross be awarded to Wally Brown for his audacious attack, but also to encourage others to undertake raids of their own.

While British units shunned small-scale offensives, preferring to rest and rebuild their battalions and their armies, the Australians continued with these tactics. At night, active patrolling was carried out, right up to the enemy wire, which in many places was sparse and easily crossed. It was later heard that the continual activity of Australian patrols had prevented the German wiring parties from going out in fear of being killed or captured. 'Cutting out' sections of German trench made German patrols reluctant to extend into no-man's-land. Australian frontline units 'owned the night', and it is now known that the aggressive tactics of the Australians 'shook the German troops facing the Australian Corps'.[17]

As an indication of this aggressive work and the success of 'bush tactics', as a German general described this activity, the AIF captured eighty-five officers and 3700 men, thirty-eight trench mortars and 400 machine guns. The 22nd Battalion history notes, 'A letter captured from a Hun in one of our raids . . . mentions a dread of the Australians "who creep up to our posts at night like cats, killing and carrying off".'[18]

Secrecy remained key, however. There was a moment of concern in the 24th Battalion headquarters when, after establishing their headquarters in a chalk pit, they later found a German buzzer installation that looked very suspicious. A buzzer was a simple telephonic contrivance to allow Morse code to be transmitted on poor lines or over long distances. This particular installation 'was designed to record all conversations in the vicinity and transmit them to the Hun'.[19] While there was much speculation as to whether it was still able to transmit, it was a concerning time for the commanding officer. Naturally the device was quickly dismantled, but its discovery and capability remained a mystery.

Up and down the line, the diggers were getting ready for the next action. In camps behind the line, equipment was replaced and repaired, and clothes washed. Men showered and exchanged their underclothes and torn tunics, cleaned their rifles and sharpened their bayonets on the large stones set up for the purpose. Some received local leave to Amiens or the nearby villages to enjoy chips, meat and fried egg plus beer and *vin rouge*. A solid training programme continued, along with sports meetings and inter-battalion competitions. Swimming parties were organised in the afternoons, weather permitting, but the incessant thunder of artillery meant the war was never far away.

To be prepared for the opening of the Allied offensive's first stage, the Australian Corps was assembled on the Somme. The 1st Division, which had been holding the line to the north, were at the time marching south from their deployment areas in Flanders around Hazebrouck, Strazeele and Merris, where they had held the German advance in March and April, and had been retained there to secure the line. They, like the Canadians who were secretly moving from Arras, were to join the rest of the Australian Corps, taking up positions behind the 4th Division.

Monash needed to bring to bear not only new tactics and the application of a range of weapons on the offensive, but also his strong, impressive intellect, his engineering experience and skills, his supportive staff and also, through his confidence and respect, his beloved AIF. Most of all, he wanted to put his men in the forefront of the offensive, at the very vanguard of the assault, for it was here he believed success and victory would come.

SIX

The Days Before the Allied Offensive

By the end of July 1918, a series of conferences between Generals Foch, Haig and Rawlinson completed the overall planning for the Allied offensive. Rawlinson then held eight conferences with the Canadian General Arthur Currie; the British III Corps Commander, General Sir Richard Butler; Lieutenant General Charles Kavanagh of the Cavalry Corps; and Australian Corps' General John Monash.

On 21 July, when the date of the offensive was still only provisional, Monash met with Rawlinson, but he departed on the 23rd for London and returned to Bertangles on the 30th. The next day, Haig arrived. Monash was able to report to him, 'I have all the threads of the operations in my hands.'[1] Monash called a conference of his divisional commanders, where he asked for their individual plans. Any queries or questions raised at this meeting were addressed in a memorandum sent out the following day. The wheels were in motion for the great counterattack.

Haig had a range of ideas. First, he wanted an 'unlimited offensive', while Monash stressed that there 'is no intention of carrying the exploitation of the success eastwards of the Blue Line (the third objective)'.[2] Second, Haig favoured Canadian units over Australian ones as he felt the Australians came with a number of problems. Apart from the perceived ill-discipline of the troops – and the fact that the death penalty was not an option with them – the Australian battalions were understrength. Their brigades had been reduced from four battalions to three, in line with the new British formations, and the idea of bringing light horsemen from Palestine had been rejected. The Canadians had four divisions at full strength, with reinforcements on hand to make up any losses. Haig was also aware that the deployment of Australian troops into offensives where there was a chance of high casualties needed Prime Minister Billy Hughes' approval. Nonetheless, Haig accepted that the best option was for the Canadians and the Australians to form the vanguard, using all their divisions in the offensive. Third, Haig was keen to see the use of cavalry in the offensive, and told Rawlinson to make 1st Cavalry and a company of Whippet tanks available to Monash. These would be deployed on the Australian right flank in the hope of breaking through and creating chaos after the taking of the Red Line.

Along with these provisions, both the Canadians and the Australians would be given a brigade of tanks, each comprising four battalions of fighting tanks – 144 in number – and a company of twenty-four carrier tanks. The British III Corps would have one battalion of Mark V tanks – thirty-six in number – and the Cavalry Corps two battalions of Whippets. The AIF was allotted forty-eight tanks (two tank companies, each of twenty-four tanks) to lead each division to the first objective, the Green Line. A further twenty-four tanks, along with any that had survived the initial advance, were allotted for the second stage of the attack, to the Red Line. For the third stage, the 'exploitation' phase, thirty-six Mark V tanks, one tank to 250 yards of front line, were allocated to get them to the Blue Line.

It was proposed that the French, situated south of the Canadian divisions, would attack simultaneously with five divisions on the first day, adding more divisions as the advance progressed, with as many as thirty divisions involved within a few days as the Third French Army joined the offensive. Like Haig, Foch kept details of the attack from his senior officers until the last possible moment, with divisional commanders only receiving details a week before the offensive was to be launched.

To divert attention from their plans for the Somme, the Allies made diversionary attacks in expected places and kept up the shelling, successfully playing into the Germans' expectations while secretly moving troops to the south at night.

By late July, the Germans were beginning to appreciate the shift in the balance of power. Though still on an offensive footing, they were reluctantly conscious that the Allied armies were not defeated and were, in fact, being bolstered by American troops and British troops transferred from Palestine. If there was to be a threat of Allied counterattack, it was believed it would come from British attempts to recover lost ground in the north around Mount Kemmel and Ypres or along the Lys, and north around Arras. They believed the French would attack east of Rheims.

On 23 July, the Allies began to move into position. The side-slipping of the British Fourth Army's boundary south, the relief of the Australian 5th Division by the British III Corps north of the Somme, and the takeover by the 4th Division of the northern part of the French line were considered by all, including the Germans, as just routine readjustments and redeployments – nothing to raise alarm or concern. Most importantly, the Germans seemed to remain unaware that Canadians were coming into the line.

The great fear among the Allied commanders, however, was that captured Allied troops might divulge news of the coming offensive while under interrogation, or even hint at the build-up of men and stores. This was first tested with the capture of Sergeant Samuel Acton and five men of the 51st Battalion by a German raiding party in the early hours of 4 August. High Command naturally feared the men might talk, not about details of the attack, which they knew nothing about, but about the extent of the build-up, the presence of the Canadians and the concentration of guns, stores and ammunition. As it happened the Germans found out nothing, and within twenty-four hours, after no further enemy raids, High Command was relieved. In German documents captured soon afterwards, it was found that the sergeant 'refused to make any military statement and could not be shaken in his resolve by any means employed'.[3]

More ominously, a large number of British prisoners were captured near Morlancourt on 5 August, just across the river and close to the 8 August start line. The AIF's 29th and 32nd Battalions had advanced the line there 1000 yards on 29 July, inflicting heavy casualties on the enemy. The night of their attack was cloudy and dull, and the recent rain had turned the communication trenches into wet, muddy channels, so the going was very heavy. The attack on a three-company front in two waves was made on a frontage of 2500 yards, with the objective being the enemy system of trenches. The 8th Brigade's war diary recounts:

> The artillery opened at zero and was very effective. At zero plus
> three the attacking troops moved forward, following the barrage
> closely. The first line of enemy trenches was reached and on
> the left the enemy fought our men with the bayonet. A bitter
> hand-to-hand fight ensued to which our men showed their

superiority with this weapon and practically the whole of the front line troops opposite the left assaulting battalion were killed. On the right, the enemy managed to get a machine gun into action, but it was speedily overcome and the crew killed together with the garrison of the post numbering in all 20.[4]

By 1 am, 'word was received that all objectives were captured and mopping up, consolidation and exploitation were in progress.'[5] With this swift action, the Australians were able to capture the German front line and the support companies, with the estimate of enemy dead at 200. The action secured the heights above Morlancourt and the high ground further south of the Bray–Corbie road. Three small German counterattacks were driven off, and one enemy party that attempted to gain access to the Australians' left flank was wiped out by two Lewis-gun crews. The Australian battalions lost two officers and sixteen other ranks were killed, while three officers and 141 other ranks were wounded, and three missing.

The determination of the men is exemplified by the courage of a 29th Battalion runner, Private Edwin Eric Baulch, a 24-year-old driver from Warrnambool in Victoria. He had been wounded early in the attack but carried on. Sent to deliver a message to his commanding officer, he was moving along a communication trench when a gas shell burst at his feet, blinding him. Unable to see, he began crawling, groping his way forward, determined to deliver his message 'which contained information urgently required'.[6] In this terrible condition, he was found by his CO. His first words, on recognising his CO's voice, were, 'I have a message for you sir.'[7] Baulch rejoined his battalion in early September and returned to Australia on the *Medic* at the end of May 1919.

The new line was taken over by the British 55th Brigade the following day but the Germans quickly counterattacked, pushing the British back 1000 yards to the vicinity of a quarry where matériel and ammunition for the coming offensive were stored. In the following days, British counterattacks, while relentless, were unable to recapture the lost ground, a serious concern for Monash as his left flank on the north side of the Somme was now exposed.

The British retreat, with the loss of ground that resulted, was also strongly felt by the Australian troops after their hard-won fight a few days before. Bean notes:

ever since the arrival on the Somme–Ancre peninsula they [the Australians] had been steadily gaining ground, and they had never felt the slightest doubt in their ability to hold it. Yet here, as at Villers Bretonneux, no sooner had the front line been handed over to the British troops than the enemy seized it.[8]

The Germans reported capturing eight officers and 274 men, creating enormous concern that details of the planned offensive would be fed to the Germans. As Bean writes, 'it was almost inconceivable that no hint of the coming offensive would leak out.'[9] As night fell on 7 August, however, there was no indication that the Germans had any knowledge of the offensive, which, concludes Bean, was 'very remarkable evidence of the staunch-ness of the average Englishman in such a predicament'.[10] This and other incidents where men stumbled into the German lines, or were captured in no-man's-land, also did not lead to the Germans acquiring valuable information about the offensive.

The reason for this, of course, was that none of the soldiers knew anything. Had this been 1916, the coming offensive would have been common knowledge in cafes and *estaminets*, in un-coded transmissions, lost maps and idle talk. But things were very different in 1918. Communications were far more secure, and coded messages had become standard for radio transmission. Security was tight at Monash's headquarters in Bertangles Château where maps, plans and documents were numbered, and their distribution limited. Details of the attack were known to only a few officers; for example, senior officers of the AIF's Pioneer Battalion had no definite information until thirty-six hours before the attack, even though their role involved long-term preparation.

The troops were not dumb, however. Those who had been transferred to the Somme from the north had a shrewd suspicion that they would not have been transferred there unless something major was in the planning. In the 46th Battalion, 'The rank and file had absolutely no idea what was happening, they knew that an attack was imminent, but when and where was an absolute mystery to them. Little did they know that they were about to be involved in one of the greatest allied offensives of the war.'[11]

Training schedules were also a giveaway, as they focused on musketry and Lewis-gun training, along with the familiarisation with German weapons and tactics. There had been toughening-up exercises, route marches, swimming in the Somme and sports meetings, and concerts at night – all for fitness and morale. And then there were the inspections and battalion parades: 'A few inspections from the heads and it's a case of "into the line" again. We know it only too well. It's not the first time we've seen the cooks inspecting the geese.'[12]

The men would also have been aware of the extensive preparation and organisation going on around them, with fourteen infantry divisions, three cavalry divisions, over 3000 field guns, 450 tanks and seventeen RAF squadrons all concentrated west of

Villers-Bretonneux along the Somme. As the men watched, huge dumps of stores were created, guns were brought up and camouflaged, roads repaired and bridges built and then disassembled before dawn, water points laid out, command and medical posts erected and equipped – all at night and all in secret. Between dusk and dawn, the roads were a seething mass of traffic, guns, limbers and marching men, all arriving without confusion and haste. And then, with the arrival of dawn, just the normal activities of an active front line.

The men of the AIF took confidence from their belief in their celebrated general, and trusted his planning, resupply and concern for their welfare. Knowing the importance of fresh troops, Monash ordered that the men be billeted as close as possible to the start line and that they be given complete rest for the day or two preceding the attack.[13] He also made it clear that, after thorough planning and deep consideration of the details of the offensive, there would be no last-minute changes, an important step to gain the confidence and trust of his officers, and ultimately his men: 'Thus every commander knew exactly where he stood, and the "order, counter-order, disorder" sequence that had marred so many military enterprises, was happily eliminated.'[14]

Monash was also concerned about the condition of the roads, especially the Roman road where the cavalry would form up on the night of 7 August, so he had engineers build a track there during the night. He also had two cables buried within 1000 to 1200 yards of the start line, 'and the provision included trench or loop-sets of wireless for each brigade'.[15] He located headquarters as close to the front as possible, ideally within line of sight of the advance, and carefully allocated separate roads for motor traffic, horse-drawn vehicles and tanks. He also cleared lanes for the return of the wounded.

There was also the unresolved issue of the projecting Chipilly ridge, high ground rising from the northern bank of the river. Chipilly was a key defensive position for the Germans and had been discussed in the earliest planning days of the offensive. In June, Monash had proposed that the heights north of the river be attacked, which was undertaken by two Australian battalions on 31 July. The British were left with two objectives: the first, Mallard and Célestins woods, and the second, the Chipilly Spur, including Gressaire Wood and part of the Bois de Tailles.

Another major concern for Monash was a possible gas attack in the vast forming-up areas stretching back two miles from the front, particularly in the forested areas like Bois l'Abbe, and Hangard and Lancer woods. Should this happen, the artillery were instructed to immediately commence counter-battery fire, forgetting the need to hide the guns, and quickly eliminate the threat of gas on the massed troop formations. Contingency plans were also crucial.

On the morning of 7 August, a letter from Monash was issued to the battalions as part of the final briefing. From this, Bean states, 'Monash applied to it his full power of minute forethought, immense care, and pellucid exposition, and even in this night march the men felt that whatever might lie in front, all was right behind them.'[16]

Battalions were assembled in the afternoon and commanding officers briefed their men on the upcoming attack, explaining the night advance to the start line, the deployment, the leapfrogging and the objectives. It was Monash's policy to ensure that the men knew as much about the battle ahead, their objectives and the supporting arms and preparations made. While these details could be shared with the enemy, the benefits were the impact on morale and the knowledge that the men went into the attack fully briefed on what was expected of them. With low recruitment levels in Australia and dwindling reinforcements, battalions had become more self-sufficient – even, some argued, elitist[17] – and totally reliant on their command structure, their quartermaster and an emphasis on welfare, health and training. At this time, the men heard Monash's letter to the troops, which said in part:

> For the first time in the history of this corps all five Australian
> Divisions will tomorrow engage in the largest and most important
> battle operation ever undertaken by the Corps. They will be
> supported by exceptionally powerful artillery and by tanks and
> aeroplanes on a scale never previously attempted. Because of the
> completeness of our plans and dispositions, of the magnitude of
> the operations, of the number of troops employed and the depth
> on which we intend to overrun the enemy's positions, this battle
> will be one of the most memorable of the war and . . . we shall
> inflict a blow upon the enemy which will make him stagger
> and will bring the end appreciably nearer. I entertain no sort of
> doubt that every Australian soldier will worthily rise to so great
> an occasion . . . for the sake of AUSTRALIA, the Empire and
> our cause.[18]

So secret were Monash's plans that zero hour was not finally fixed until twelve hours before the attack. The weather and fog, crucial factors in the attack, could not be predetermined. The actual time for zero hour was to be relayed to battalions by a simple code: if it was to be before 4 am, the minutes would be in issues of butter, and if after 4 am in issues of jam. When zero hour was fixed at 4.20 am, the order went out to send twenty rations of jam to headquarters at once. One officer, not privy to the code, actually believed this was a serious request and searched high and low among his men to part with their jam ration. Not long after a runner turned up at battalion headquarters and presented the adjutant with a small parcel of jam, saying, 'With Capt. Bisdee's compliment, sir, he can't get 20 rations, but here's enough for 12.'[19]

An hour before sunset on the evening of 7 August, a random German shell of small calibre fell among supply tanks lined up in an orchard on the northern outskirts of Villers-Bretonneux. One tank caught fire, igniting the others. As the flames spread, tanks began exploding due to the mortar ammunition, petrol and other flammable contents within them. All but three were destroyed, a serious setback to the 5th Division as these were the tanks for their resupply.

More importantly, as a result of this shelling there were questions about whether the Germans had learnt of the offensive, and if not, what they would make of this enormous conflagration so close to the front. Would they follow up with a more intense bombardment, or be ready when the attack was launched? It was a tense and worrying time for the 5th Division's commander, General Hobbs, whose tanks were destroyed, and for Monash and his staff waiting in the rear. Fortunately, the Germans didn't seem to realise that this conflagration was evidence of a massive build-up close to their line.

The moonlit night was bright and clear, though a chill in the air kept the men alert, particularly as they waited to move out. To make conditions more challenging, a ground fog arose. Closing their quarters and leaving their tent lines, the men moved out in single file, some coming up along the towpath by the river, where the faint smell of gas lingered in the air. Battalions moved along access roads on predetermined lines of advance, through Villers-Bretonneux and past Hamel. To assist the advance, petrol tins with battalion numbers punched into them, into which a lit candle was placed and set up on poles, marked the lines of advance to the tapes.

It was not only the infantry divisions that would mount the attack moving forward, but also the supporting divisions, specialist units, resupply, medical services and ammunition that would maintain the attack over the coming weeks. The 6th Machine Gun Company moved from their camp at 6 pm, led by mounted officers. As their captain was keen to avoid marching and unnecessarily tiring his men, they sat in GS (general service) wagons with limbers following them, carrying their sixteen machine guns, gear and ammunition. The battalion history notes, 'The sight of the loaded waggons brought forth many pleasantries from less fortunate individuals who wanted to know "where's the picnic?" Passing through Glisy and to the left of Blangy-Tronville, the cheery party moved on.'[20] With them, men, wagons, motor lorries, tanks and cavalry moved towards the line.

The night remained quiet, with random shelling and contacts up and down the line, but nothing to indicate the Germans were aware of the enormous build-up under way. At the southern end of the line, at 12.30 am, the 27th Battalion started to move along the edge of Villers-Bretonneux, arriving at their assembly point at 3.30 am. Almost immediately, the Germans began shelling the 7th Brigade front north of the railway, the shells falling mainly on the 26th and 27th Battalions as they formed up. Counter-battery fire quickly smothered the German batteries, but only after the 27th Battalion had sustained fifteen casualties.

Hour upon hour, battalions of eager, confident Allied troops marched along the approach roads, a seemingly endless procession stretching back ten miles. Everything and everyone was moving forward, the men conscious that every possible contingency had been considered, every opportunity noted, and that victory, even revenge, was within grasp.

The men were heavily laden for the task ahead. Each carried a rifle and 200 rounds, a bayonet, rations for two days, two water bottles, four Mills bombs, a pick or shovel and five sandbags. Others carried stretchers and flare pistols, while specialist units, like bombers, were issued smoke and rifle grenades.

Earlier in the night, the tapes had been carefully laid out by intelligence officers and engineers using hand signals; this was dangerous, silent work, yet work that was important to the forming-up of the attacking battalions. Occasionally a German flare would light the sky, forcing the men to remain in whatever position they were when the flare went up. Standing in the glow would have been a frightening experience, as they waited until the flare gradually floated to earth and went out. Also working away were the sappers, cutting holes in the barbed wire for the attacking troops to move forward. Private J. S. Finney of the 44th Battalion noted:

At times we would hear the muffled snip of the wire cutters . . . that seemed like the crack of a whip. We knew then that another stumbling block in the form of a wire was cut. It was now Fritz who took it into his head to gives us a good-night salvo and overcame his 'iron rations'. We get down full length in the nearest hole and patiently wait (as there is nothing we could do) until he's considered he's done enough. On this ceasing, he traversed a machine gun two or three times and then settled down for the night. After waiting a few minutes, we soon get going again and was not long in getting the job through.[21]

The men were excited about the possibilities of an offensive, and the opportunity for 'ratting' (stealing from) prisoners. Many were in high spirits, like those of the 39th Battalion who, a few hours before going forward, 'held a high carnival in Corbie. Fancy costumes had been found in one of the houses. They "dressed up" and sang appropriate songs until it was time to march to the assembly point. Shortly after 11pm the platoon marched out of Corbie.'[22]

Other men were not so happy, having been left behind to form the 'nucleus' of their battalion should there be high casualties in the attack. Many pleaded with their officers to be allowed to go, stating they had been in the battalion since the early days, but these were the very men who needed to be retained. Leaving a battalion nucleus out of a battle was a common practice, so that should the battalion be wiped out men would still remain as the foundation to rebuild it. Generally men were happy to be part of this nucleus, but not on this important occasion.

It was feared the dense fog would prevent British aircraft taking off but somehow they did, and their contributing noise was crucial to cover the advance of the tanks. With the continual roar and buzz, 'the tank engines, throttled down, were inaudible even to the waiting Australians except a few who were very close.'[23] With the tanks, long lines of troops moved silently forward, marching by company with sections advancing twenty yards apart, past the guns lined practically wheel on wheel, the camouflage thrown aside and their crews standing ready. Mixed in were men of the 13th Light Horse Regiment, distributed earlier among the four divisions, to undertake traffic control.

Not all men were advancing. The Regimental Medical Officer for the 44th Battalion, Captain S. L. Germon, noted, 'One of the men of the battalion was sleeping in a hole in the ground, somewhat like a grave. During the night a tank passed right over the hole, awakening and startling him considerably, but in no way damaging him.'[24]

The engineers, too, were busy. They erected prefabricated bridges at points along both the river and the canal at Fouilloy east of Corbie, and near the ferryman's house, 'Circular Quay', at Vaire-sous-Corbie. As the advance continued, they constructed bridges at Gailly and Bouzencourt. They also searched dugouts for traps and mines, tested and repaired wells, established horse watering points, did reconnaissance work and placed signposts. Anticipating the destruction of roads, Monash allocated each company a stretch of road to maintain, for example, 'C' Company the road from Hamel to the front line, and 'A' Company the road through Cerisy. For this, a store of stone and brick rubble was compiled and its transport made ready, with thirty-two tip trays provided, fully loaded and parked at Vaire for crucial road work.

By 3.45 am, the assembly was complete. Lying on the ground along their start line, 100,000 men were spread out in wheat fields and flat grasslands in the rolling hills south of Villers-Bretonneux, in woodland and among undergrowth or in the swampy lowland along the Somme waiting for zero hour. With them, nearly 350 Mark V tanks plus 120 supply tanks spread along a fourteen-mile front, all covered by 3000 guns. Ahead, the Green Line, 4000 yards out; then the Red Line, a further 5000 yards away; and finally the Blue Line, 1000 yards beyond that.

The men awaited the attack with keenness and confidence, eager to come to grips with the enemy. They checked their mates' equipment, ensuring nothing rattled and everything was in order.

Monash had instructed that a hot meal be served to the men before starting out and this had been done at midnight, with the cookers moving right up to the line to follow the advance. Nearby, asleep and unaware, were six divisions of German troops, oblivious to the grim, bloody day ahead.

SEVEN

Der Schwarze Tag:
The Black Day

By 4 am, the men lying in the wheat were getting cold as the fog thickened and closed about them. In the centre of the Australian line, the 17th Battalion made their last preparations. At 4.10 am, the company commanders' order to 'stand to' was carried down the line in a low whisper, while a silent runner reported the men all present. Word also passed down the line that it was ten minutes to zero hour.

The seconds ticked by as thousands of eyes watched the slow sweep of the illuminated second hand on their carefully synchronised watches: 4.19 am, one minute to go. The final minute ticked away and then 3000 guns lit the sky, turning night into day and sending a line of bursting shells deep into German-held territory. Mixed in was a machine-gun barrage fired by lines of Vickers guns, sending a rain of bullets into German positions.

Private J. S. Finney from the 44th Battalion described the scene:

The Trench mortars started and almost immediately afterwards came a peculiar whirring, pulsating sound tearing the air into a turmoil and then down came that wall of steel, smoke and flames as if a curtain had been suddenly dropped from the heavens.

It was a magnificent sight, as far as the eye could see. On the right and left it was raining that peculiar muddy red flame. Intermingled with this were Fritz Very lights in all colours, making a vain call for a counter barrage, but it was evident the call was unheard.[1]

At the southern end of the line, another Australian private noted in his diary the opening movements of the attack:

We hopped the twig at 4.20 am. Fritz heard us forming up before and dropped a barrage. They had to grin and bear it for an hour. The one big gun of ours went off a way back. Our barrage came down with a crash. There were thousands of 18lbs, 4', 6' 8' even up to 15' guns. Most of the heavies got onto his gun positions. All his gunners must have scuttled for their dugouts at once as the barrage stopped as quickly as ours opened. As soon as the barrage fell away we went in lines.[2]

Along the extended front, men cheered the barrage as it crashed ahead of them, bringing up dust and smoke to add to the dense fog. In the crashing tumult, shouts of command rang out, and the clamour was such that men had to yell to be heard. Lieutenant Binder of the 59th Battalion described the barrage like 'being behind a curtain of rushing noise'.[3]

The men rose like dark phantoms from the earth and, with rifles slung and cigarettes lit, they moved towards the wall of descending shells 200 yards ahead of them. The nerves of battle quickly passed as a wave of excitement and adrenalin flushed through the advancing men. The Australians were confident: they were fit and well trained and, most importantly, they trusted their officers and mates.

The fog had become so thick that, in places, visibility was reduced to a few yards. Officers advanced using prismatic compasses, but the crashing line of shells and the flashes ahead in the distant fog gave the men some sense of direction. However, contact with units to either side was impossible and men soon became mixed, while the advancing tanks just ahead of the men became less effective due to the poor visibility.

The advancing line was soon among the first German advance posts and dugouts. Rifle fire and the explosion of grenades indicated the men were now in contact with the enemy. As Private R. Fryer-Smith wrote, 'We come across a few enemy dugouts here and yelled at the Hun to come out and if he is not out in a few seconds, a Mills bomb is hurled into the opening and that is the end.'[4]

In the 27th Battalion, the men advanced 'with the confidence as great as the moment',[5] mopping up as they went. Within a short time, large numbers of the enemy were captured and sent back to the Australian rear. After his advance was held up by a German machine gun, the 27th's Sergeant Grant quickly outflanked the enemy in the smoke and fog, capturing the post of two officers and forty-seven men along with two machine guns. He was recommended for a Victoria Cross but was killed later, on 3 October, just hours before the notification of his Distinguished Conduct Medal was to reach battalion headquarters.

After three minutes, the first 'lift' occurred, the barrage moving forward a further 200 yards. Fearful of the German retaliation, the men were surprised that no enemy shells had fallen yet. They realised that the Allied batteries allocated to counter-battery fire had done their job, smothering German artillery positions and depriving the enemy of the much-feared reprisal barrage. Also, the enemy gunners had no definite targets, and the assault had already overrun their front line and was advancing steadily behind the creeping barrage on their very positions. It was later discovered that in the days before the attack, the enemy had been short of ammunition and had restricted their firing.

Advancing along the towpath on the north of the river, the 39th Battalion traversed the swamp and struck only desultory enemy machine-gun fire and the occasional shell dropping short from their own guns. Thick belts of barbed wire half-hidden in the grass and reeds, however, retarded their advance. The first enemy seen while a platoon was negotiating these entanglements were German machine gunners, hurriedly retreating through the fog, carrying their gun. The shots that were fired at them missed.

The 39th soon found themselves on the outskirts of Sailly-Laurette, having had only one man wounded in the advance. Pushing into the village, they came across abandoned German machine guns and, soon after, the crews hiding in a cellar. The Germans were challenged and threatened with Mills grenades until they came out, hands above their heads. Forty prisoners and eight machine guns were captured and sent back under escort.

The advance of the 42nd Battalion at the very north of the Australian line was slowed due to the swampy ground along the river and the broken country in the dense fog. A tank supporting the battalion also found visibility limited, and at one stage was heading for the river before two officers from the battalion climbed on top and, with great difficulty, warned the crew.[6]

The advance through Accroche Wood south of Hamel by the 43rd Battalion was achieved nearly without firing a shot. They were quickly followed up by the 34th, who mopped up. On the northern edge of the wood, the 35th Battalion, however, encountered stiff resistance. The Australians charged and eventually cleared the trenches, allowing the advance to continue towards the heavily defended Gailly ridge to the east of the wood. By this time, the tanks were moving ahead of the advance and crossing the wheat field, clearing it of enemy resistance.

As the fog began to lift, the full extent of the fighting was revealed. Across the vast expanse of the battlefield could be seen long lines of artillery and limbers, general service wagons, ambulances, pack animals and lines of troops all relentlessly moving forward. As the enemy defences were not strong, there was little damage to the roads and the ground, except along defence lines and machine-gun posts, and the wooded areas and villages were totally destroyed. The pioneer units and engineers were quickly at work repairing roads, filling in shell craters and checking for booby traps and mines.

This was the 3rd Pioneer Battalion's first experience of open warfare, free of trench lines and churned-up ground. As their history notes, 'the sight reminded one of a great field day in pre-war days. Here one saw every arm of the service concentrating, coming and going: wounded tanks returned to be inspected and temporarily patched up, gun teams waited for orders for the move to new positions, engineers and tunnellers opened and inspected wells, advanced dressing stations sprang up.'[7]

While most of the German artillery had been knocked out, German batteries north of the Somme began firing across the river on the long lines of concentrated targets. As the fog cleared, German artillery in Mallard Wood in front of Chipilly began enfilading fire upon the 42nd and 44th Battalions, inflicting a number of casualties. This attack, along with long-range machine-gun fire, indicated the British III Corps had not reached their objective. Again, the flanking British units were not keeping pace with the Australian advance. Most of these German guns were quickly silenced, but the slow advance of the British was to become a major, recurring problem.

By now, as the AIF battalions had become mixed, men needed to be rounded up and reorganised. They did their best to keep moving forward, following the line of falling shells as they closed on the Green Line, but platoon commanders had little control of their men. As the 44th Battalion reported, the officers 'simply became individuals, blind to everything except what he tumbled over and not knowing anything about the unit he was supposed to be in command of. The diggers, when they found themselves isolated or lost, simply pressed on always in the direction of the barrage. There was no sitting down waiting for orders.'[8]

Meanwhile, the tanks could be heard but not seen. Eventually the thinning mist allowed the tanks to move on points of resistance, but the tanks began hitting contact mines, causing their tracks to be stripped off. Other tanks had dropped out, having hit obstacles in the fog, or had been ditched, but few had been damaged by German fire.

Initially, the 13th Light Horse reported the advance due to the inability of the circling aircraft to see through the fog. As it cleared, low-flying aircraft with special markings flew along the line, sounding their klaxon and firing white flares, a signal for the men to light trench flares to indicate their position. The observer could then map the troops' position. The map was then quickly flown back to headquarters, where it was dropped in special despatch bags.

At the southern end of the line, the Australians were operating with the Canadians, the boundary between the two defined by the railway line that ran from Villers-Bretonneux southeast. This was the first time two Dominion corps had formed the nucleus of an attack, although the Australians and New

Zealanders had fought side by side on the slopes of Passchendaele the year before.

Soon after the attack started, German machine-gun fire slowed both the Australians and the Canadians until, after a duel between Lewis gunners and the Germans, the advance could move forward. The Germans, however, kept up a constant defensive fire and on approaching Marcelcave, the first occupied village, Lieutenant Mason, MC, of the 21st Battalion, crossed the railway and assisted the Canadians in the fortified Jean Rouxin Mill, and after 'a vigorous bomb fight, drove the Germans out'.[9]

As the 28th Battalion advanced with the Queenslanders of the 26th Battalion, they came under heavy fire and, upon reaching a strong belt of wire at Card Copse near the railway at the southern end of the advance, with no tank support the men were forced to ground. Needing to maintain the pressure of the advance, Lieutenant Alfred Gaby of the 28th Battalion found a break in the wire and charged the German trench line. Walking along the top of the parapet with his revolver, he fired down into the cowering Germans. Daunted by his audacious attack, fifty Germans with four machine guns surrendered, allowing the advance to progress. For his bravery, Gaby was awarded the Victoria Cross, but he never knew of his award, as he was killed by a sniper while encouraging his platoon in fighting near Framerville three days later.

In the middle of the line, the 17th Battalion was also lost in the fog. The 'B' Company commander, Captain Finlay, who had been originally commissioned in the field at Gallipoli, pushed his men forward and met little opposition. His first objective was the village of Warfusée which he passed to the south side, where, with the assistance of the tank 'Buffoon', was able to capture three 4.2-inch howitzers. The battalion history tells a typical story:

> During the advance, a fine example of boldness and enterprise was given by one of 'B' Company's young section leaders. Lance-corporal P. L. Anderson. The fog had begun to lift and revealed a party of about 50 Germans retiring hastily across the company's front, obliquely from the right flank. They had with them three machine guns. Anderson, who was a footballer and in first class condition, straight away led his section, which was on the left flank, so as to head off the enemy. Outstripping his men, he succeeded in holding up the Germans who surrendered immediately when they observed Anderson's section bearing down on them.[10]

Continuing the advance on Warfusée, four machine guns were captured by Captain Edward Harnett of the 17th Battalion. Soon after, a battery of four 4.2-inch howitzers were seen, their crews racing to hitch them up to escape. The Australians shot the German horses and quickly overran the guns, but the crews escaped. Then Harnett came upon a battery of 5.9-inch howitzers firing over open sights, point blank into the 7th Brigade. His men captured the guns along with one officer and forty-five gunners. German resistance evaporated, and Harnett and the 17th Battalion rushed on with the assistance of five tanks, which levelled buildings that lay in their path.

As the 17th and the 18th Battalions moved forward, Germans appeared, with their hands held high, out of the town's cellars, one of which was a German headquarters. The Germans were disarmed and formed up on the road, before being marched to the rear to the overflowing POW cage at Villers-Bretonneux.

By this time prisoners were flooding back through the Australian line. As reported in the 25th Battalion history:

> The Hun was on the run by then. Thousands of them coming
> through our lines with hands up. Our men pounced on them and
> lifted all their valuables. Watches, coins, postcards etc. galore.
> Then we saw a grand sight. The Cavalry. We had cleared his
> trenches. They had clear going and off they went.[11]

At the cage in Villers-Bretonneux, prisoners were lined up, awaiting their turn to be admitted. One group of sixty-six prisoners had been sent back under the charge of one Private Murray. When asked what happened with the prisoners he replied, 'Well sir, we started off well, but I could not catch-up with the bastards.'[12]

On reaching the first objective, the Green Line, the advance stopped. The barrage, however, continued, falling 400 yards ahead of the rapidly consolidating line, while the heavy guns fired on German back areas and predetermined targets, often to the limit of their range. The 27th Battalion history notes:

> It is doubtful whether less experienced troops could have reached
> the objective, so deep within the enemy lines, with practically
> only the controlling fire of our artillery to guide them and had the
> men sought cover from the point blank action of the enemy field
> guns, instead of rushing their positions, fearful casualties would
> have inevitably have resulted among the great mass of troops
> concentrated in the rear area.[13]

With the arrival of the advancing battalions at the Green Line around 7 am, the immediate priority was establishing a defensive line in anticipation of a swift German counterattack. Patrols started to move out into no-man's-land to probe the enemy defences, which were quickly found to be in disarray. With patches of fog remaining and visibility still limited, aggressive patrols cut out German posts, surrounding them and capturing their garrisons to further advance the line.

While the consolidation continued, some German shells still fell along the newly established front line. One shell hit a carrier tank of the 44th Battalion while it was being unloaded. Fortunately no one was inside, but the concussion of the blast started the tank engine: 'It went at full speed down the hill, and coming to a very steep bank, rolled over and over to the road at the foot, where it lay on its back out of action.'[14] Meanwhile, German matériel was salvaged, and valuable information and maps were discovered and quickly sent back to headquarters. Both German and Australian men and horses were buried, their graves carefully noted for later retrieval.

What quickly became clear was that casualties for the first four hours of fighting were exceptionally light. The 43rd Battalion reported three killed and five wounded, and the capture of 100 prisoners, twenty-five machine guns (including ten heavies), one section of field guns, one anti-tank rifle and a large amount of signals and other equipment. The 27th Battalion had five men killed, and one officer and forty-two other ranks wounded. In their advance, they captured 200 Germans, nine 77-millimetre guns, one wireless plant and twenty-five machine guns. Similarly, the 42nd Battalion on the river captured 300 prisoners, three 77-millimetre guns, twenty-five machine guns, seven trench mortars and a large quantity of ammunition and stores, all at a cost of a few casualties. This was in line with a 40th Battalion observation that as they followed up the first waves, 'In advancing over this recently captured ground the fact that struck us most was the very small number of our dead.'[15]

Private Edward Lynch, the author of *Somme Mud*, was a member of the 45th Battalion attacking that day as part of the 4th Division's advance on the northern end of the line, and refers to finding dead German soldiers:

We're at the old enemy front line trench now. It is an open sepulchre, blown and smashed to pieces. Dozens of dead everywhere and not a whole man amongst them. Limbless and headless they lie coated in chalk, torn and slashed by the shelling. Slashed in life and slashed again in death. Killed by our remorseless shelling. Killed that we may advance.

He found Australian dead also:

Ahead of us we see the broken embankment of a machine-gun emplacement. We move nearer. In front of it are five 3rd division men lying dead just where they collapsed, bullet ridden, as they gamely rushed the enemy gun. In several shell holes are rifles and equipment that have been left by the wounded men, so we know that the Fritz gun had reaped a heavy toll before it was silenced.[16]

At 8.20 am, the second stage of the advance began. The plan was for the 4th Division to leapfrog the 3rd Division, and the 5th Division further south to leapfrog the 2nd Division. The objective was now the Red Line, three miles ahead, but unlike the first objective, there would be no creeping barrage to protect the line

moving out towards the villages of Bayonvillers and Harbonnières, and along the valley running from Morcourt to Harbonnières.

The new attacking battalions started forward with bayonets fixed behind a slow-moving line of tanks. As the Victorian 15th Brigade began forward, they were cheered on by the 28th Battalion, who cheered again as British cavalry and artillery passed through their position. At the same time, the 4th Australian Division passed through the 3rd Division in artillery formation 'as steady as if on a peace manoeuvre'[17] and pushed on towards the Red Line. The 44th Battalion history notes:

> The 4th Division can be well proud of themselves for that day's work. They had marched for miles behind attacking infantry, through thick fog with direction and touch difficult to maintain yet they passed through the 3rd Division on time and free from the slightest trace of confusion, looking just as fit and confident as one would expect of any unit with the fighting record of the 4th Australian Division.[18]

As the Green Line had been about the limit of the protective barrage, the eighteen-pound guns that could be quickly hitched and moved needed to be brought forward as early as possible, even though their range and hitting power was limited. As the 44th Battalion settled in, 'Field batteries galloped through the "Green Line" and deployed their guns and opened fire within minutes, to the delight and ribald encouragement of the irreverent infantry.'[19] The horse-drawn eighteen-pounders then followed the infantry, providing mobile fire support where required.

The battalion cookers also arrived to serve the men a hot meal after the advance. Never before had cookers been so close to the front line in an attack, and the provision of hot food and tea was welcomed by the men. Once again, General Monash was keen to see the men were well fed, and their fighting morale and strength maintained.

Crossing the Green Line, the 15th Battalion at the northern end of the line near the village of Cerisy came under fire from a German machine gun hidden in a house on the outskirts of the village. A tank was called up, which fired into the house, bringing down the walls as the gunners fled out the back door. Fleeing with them were the crews of a battery of 77-millimetre guns, which were overrun and captured.

Across the Somme, Germans could be seen scattering up the slope, running for a trench line and cover. Elsewhere the Allied tanks moved 100 yards ahead of the infantry, who were advancing in artillery formation, in columns of lines. The tanks gradually moved forward, engaging German machine guns and duelling with German artillery, often at point-blank range.

As the 15th Battalion advanced and cleared the ridgeline to the right of Cerisy, it came into full view of the German battery over the river on the Chipilly ridge, which quickly destroyed the battalion's supporting tank. A young Tasmanian Gallipoli veteran, Lieutenant Bernard Shaw, was killed as he led his men past the tank the instant it was hit. Immediately, the battalion used the captured German machine guns to put harrowing fire on the enemy positions, quickly decimating the ranks of the German gunners and preventing them returning fire. By the time the battalion reached the Red Line they had one officer and seven men killed, plus three officers and thirty-three men wounded, including six gassed. They captured 350 Germans, two 77-millimetre guns, two *minenwerfers*, fifteen heavy machine guns and four light machine guns.

At the southern end of the line, the 15th Brigade found the advance difficult from the start, and were unlucky to receive the only real German resistance, apart from that at the northern 4th Brigade sector along the river. The 15th came under German artillery fire as they formed up, and the tanks supporting them pushed forward in an attempt to suppress the German artillery. One tank was knocked out but two others advanced, supported by the infantry, driving the Germans from the gun and capturing the crew. More opposition was encountered and overrun by the 59th Battalion on the extreme right as it went south of Bayonvillers, leaving the village to be cleared by the 58th Battalion with the aid of tanks.

In the centre of the line were the 8th Brigade, part of 5th Division, and to their left, the 12th Brigade of 4th Division.

The 8th Brigade was in the vast flat plains to the north of the Roman road where the country provided no cover and, fortunately, no defensive high ground. This gave them a straightforward advance to the east and, apart from a skirmish near Bayonvillers, it was only when they came to the outskirts of Harbonnières and the Red Line objective that they encountered serious resistance. Having all but one of their tanks knocked out, they succeeded in firing on and stopping a German battery of 77-millimetre guns escaping, with the crew fleeing and leaving the stricken guns by the roadside.

To their left flank, the Victorians of the 46th Battalion, 12th Brigade, encountered the head of the valleys running south from the Somme, first at Lena Wood, then Susan Wood and finally Jean Wood. Here they overcame scattered German resistance with the assistance of the tanks. To their north, the 45th Battalion found the steeper valley sides slowed their advance and diverted the tanks south to a point where they could cross the valley. They finally reached the southern end of the Morcourt valley and halted as British heavy artillery burst along the ridgeline.

All along the line, Germans were surrendering, filing back with hands high above their heads to be quickly ratted by the advancing Australians. A note in the 44th Battalion history makes an interesting reference to Germans being captured by Australians: 'The enemy surrendered in droves and it was noted that several of them were well aware of the Australian habit of frisking prisoners for souvenirs as in their posts the capitulating Germans had actually taken off their watches, emptied their pockets and lined their personal effects and accoutrements along the parapet of their trenches before the Australians arrived to spare themselves the indignity off being "ratted".'[20]

As the 48th Battalion approached the next village, Morcourt, accompanied by a unit of the Royal Horse Artillery, they found themselves looking down into a long valley filled with German billets, supply dumps and bivouac areas. The artillery quickly opened fire while the Australians entered the valley and cleared it of enemy opposition. Here they located equipment and discarded weapons, the Germans having fled to the east, abandoning everything. The 45th and 46th Battalions pushed ahead to the end of the valley and the Red Line, just east of Morcourt where it intersected the Somme.

Further south, the 48th Battalion joined with the 30th and 31st Battalions to continue the advance to the old Amiens line between the Roman road, south to the village of Harbonnières. Here German resistance was weak, consisting of in most cases machine gunners firing a few bursts then either making a hasty retreat or surrendering. In some places German machine gunners fought until overrun then surrendered, expecting mercy from men with scores to settle and revenge on their mind. The diggers rarely took prisoners in those situations. Private R. E. Barrie, DCM, wrote:

Machine gun fire began to take its toll as we left the copse, but following Captain Caldwell, we forged ahead. My cobber on the right, a chap named Mason, got his issue about a couple of feet from me and my blood boiled when I saw him fall. Every man who went down in the fire automatically spurred the survivors on to fresh efforts to reach the objective. Much to our surprise, the Germans suddenly stood up with their hands raised higher over their heads and going hard, we were on them in quick time. But for the levelheadedness of Captain Caldwell, things would have been unpleasant for them, as feeling against them was running high during the advance. One Fritz officer had in his holster a revolver which I souvenired, despite his protests.[21]

The Australians' training and trust in each other now provided an advantage. When a machine gun was seen, men would rush forward over short distances, covered by Lewis-gun fire which would engage the enemy machine guns. Yet again, individuals advanced with Lewis guns, firing from the hip in individual acts of bravery. Such was the case of Private E. S. Brown, who, after noticing a German gun firing on his advancing platoon, raced forward, firing as he went and shooting down three Germans as they attempted to flee. For this action he was awarded a Military Medal.

During the advance to the Red Line, there were many notable acts of individual bravery. Apart from the work of the tanks, it was the discipline and outstanding quality of the infantry battalions which carried the line.

★

At 9 am, the 4th Brigade advanced along the Somme, with the 13th Battalion tasked with capturing the right of the brigade's Red Line objective, the 14th in the centre and the 15th on the northern end by the river. As they advanced, and with the fog now dissipated, the 15th immediately started to take enfilading fire from across the river, particularly from the Chipilly ridge.

A German record by the 13th Field Artillery Regiment states, 'Now targets offered in confusing plenty,'[22] and 'other German accounts say that the [German] artillerymen on the northern heights felt keenly their inability to fire at all the targets offering.'[23] Bean also notes, 'During most of this phase, and of the next, the German artillery north of the Somme was the chief instrument of the enemy's resistance on the Australian front.'[24]

As the 13th Battalion history notes:

They would have had no more opposition than we, had the commanding Chipilly Spur been in the hands of the Third Corps of the Imperial troops as we had been assured it would be by 8.20am. That Corps had, on the 6th, been driven back 1000 yards on a frontage of 1000 yards losing an area just won by the 3rd AIF Division. After repelling the Tommies today (8th August), the German gunners and machine gunners slewed their guns around and dealt with the 4th Brigade and our tanks, knocking the later out, one after the other, by direct hits, easily obtained over open sights.[25]

Soon after, the 13th Battalion came under fire and fifty-seven men fell within a few minutes, such was the intensity of the German fire. By 10 am, after taking fire and heavy casualties from the Chipilly Spur, the 4th Brigade descended the last of three ridge-lines and crossed the Red Line.

In spite of these hardships, the men remained in good humour. The 13th Battalion history notes, 'Captains McKillop and Swinburne had treated the battle with such joy and coolness that they had infected their men, one and all, with their spirit. Never have men joked so and laughed so heartily throughout a long battle as did the 13th that great day.'[26] They were also rewarded for their good work, coming as they did on a mass of German stores, and 'an officers mess (with fresh grapes and eggs), two canteens with good pre-war cigars, a store of photographs and boxes of maps and a pay office where one man blew open a case with 25,000 marks in notes'.[27]

Nearby, the 48th Battalion had reached Susan Wood south-west of Morcourt, and halted for fifteen minutes to allow the 45th Battalion to move ahead and prevent bunching as an attractive artillery target. At 9.15 am, as they approached the Red Line, they sent the following message: '48th Bn HQ in vicinity of Susan Wood. No further casualties. Everything going well. Very little hostile shelling here.'[28] They then moved forward, bayonets fixed, crossed the Red Line at 10.55 am and continued leapfrogging and advancing towards the Blue Line, 1500 yards ahead, the third and final objective of the day.

The Blue Line was taken easily, and consolidation began soon after midday. Quickly runners were sent back, making the dangerous journey across land that was in German hands barely an hour before. One man, Private O'Loughlin, was shot in the leg while returning to battalion headquarters. Determined to get his message back, he began crawling over bullet-swept fields until, exhausted and suffering loss of blood, he delivered his report. He was awarded a Military Medal. Similarly, a party of signallers under Sergeant Davies established a telephone line across open country at great risk after the previous line was cut. The new line allowed every company to be connected to battalion headquarters, assisting also with the artillery fire support. For his bravery, Sergeant Davies was awarded a Distinguished Conduct Medal.

While the Australians advanced relentlessly along the line, another surprising and gallant action was undertaken by British cavalry and armoured cars. After the taking of the Green Line, Whippet tanks ranged far and wide, well behind the German lines, shooting up transport lines, German troop concentrations and battalion headquarters, and even disturbing Germans eating their breakfast. The British 1st Cavalry Brigade divided into three units and charged into the villages of Rainecourt, Framerville and Vauvillers, a charge that was chivalrous and heroic like those of days past. The cavalry and the Whippet tanks did enormous damage during the first day of the offensive, a fact that has been unrecognised for too long.

It was at this time that a squadron of British cavalry made for three railway trains that were shunting north-east of Harbon-nières. Two of the trains began to retreat east but the third one, a broad gauge train with a strange hump, was seen to belch smoke. The cavalry realised it was a large railway gun. As it too tried to retreat, it was strafed by a British aircraft and its boiler pierced, causing the train to lose power.

At this time, the 31st Battalion was advancing south of the Roman road on the right flank of the 8th Brigade, and soon came upon the railway gun with the back carriages alight. Lieutenant George Burrows and two sappers rushed forward and, as machine-gun bullets whipped around them, put out the fire and then shunted the smouldering carriages into another siding before repairing the line and moving the gun back to safety.[29]

★

The enfilading fire from the north of the river continued to hamper the advance of the 4th Brigade. Two guns firing from the wood above Chipilly and four more guns below the village knocked out a number of tanks and stalled the advance. Other tanks pressed into Cerisy, opposite Chipilly on the southern river-bank, flattening houses and driving Germans from the village. They were closely followed by men of the 15th Battalion, who went through the houses capturing several hundred Germans. But destructive fire came from across the river, again stalling the advance. The 4th were now on the Red Line but had, as Charles Bean wrote, 'By far the most difficult task on the Australian front'.[30]

At the southern end of the Australian line, Pompey Elliott's 15th Brigade was also having a difficult time securing Harbonnières, two miles east of Bayonvillers. The Canadians on the brigade's right had been held up at Guillaucourt and were unable to secure the Australian right flank. Instead, the brigade's 57th Battalion was required to lag behind to protect this flank. The Canadians had been held up due to the late arrival of the tanks and the destruction of many of them as the fog lifted. As a result, the northern end of the Canadian advance, across the railway line, did not take the Red Line until 4.30 pm. However, by the end of the day, the Canadians had advanced through to the Blue Line and had taken all their objectives.

By 12.30 pm, most of the area along the Blue Line had been consolidated and most battalions were dug in and secure by 3 pm. By the end of the day, all objectives had been taken. Along the front, the men rested, secure behind a defensive line that, given the disorganised state of the German army, need hardly have been constructed.

Like the Australians, the Germans were quickly digging in, with their line 800 yards from the Australian front. After sunset,

Australian patrols pushed out into no-man's-land, some sneaking right up to the German front line, where peaceful penetration and harassment continued. Others pushed towards the town of Proyart to gauge the enemy's strength there.

While the Australians dug in, other services came to their support. Quartermasters were ready with cookers serving hot meals. Some men were so hungry they tried to bribe the cooks with souvenirs collected during the day. The engineers were also hard at work in the villages, testing wells, fixing the buckets and repairing the windlasses and watering points that were established close to the line. They were also busy with the bridges along the Somme, repairing access roads, erecting signs and bringing up materials like barbed wire, screw pickets, picks and shovels. As an indication of this frenetic work, the 8th Field Company 'had sent in accurate reports on over 19 miles of roads and railways in the newly won ground by 4pm'.[31] Overhead, both the Royal Flying Corps and the Australian Flying Corps continued their aggressive patrolling and photo reconnaissance while also delivering ammunition by parachute.

In taking and consolidating the Blue Line, the Australians, and the Canadians to their right, had not only achieved their objectives for the day, but had also enhanced and confirmed their reputation as crack colonial troops. Similarly, the leadership of Monash and Currie, along with their divisional and brigade staff, engendered a new respect for their detailed planning and operational brilliance.

Much of the credit for all of this must go to Monash, for his precise, detailed and intricate organisation and contingency planning. As one digger said, 'it was a *tres bon* stunt',[32] a sentiment Monash would have no doubt appreciated, coming as it did from an impressed digger.

EIGHT

Pushing on from the Blue Line

While the Allies were digging in after their successful offensive on 8 August, things looked very different on the German side of the line. By the end of the day, the German army was in total disarray and unable to launch a counterattack on the well-defended Australian positions. Ludendorff was later to write that 8 August was 'the black day of the German army'[1], noting that in just seven hours the Allies had advanced on an eleven-mile front to a depth of nearly seven miles, and had captured thousands of prisoners as well as a massive haul of artillery and field guns, machine guns, stores and intelligence. The Australians alone captured 7295 prisoners, with the Canadians capturing a further 6000.

Charles Bean provided an interesting comparison of Allied and German strength at the beginning of the attack. He notes, 'In all, the Allies had concentrated 22 infantry divisions against 12, possibly 115,000 bayonets against 36,000, three cavalry divisions against none, 2650 guns against some 500, 450 British and 90 French tanks against none and 1900 aeroplanes against 365.'[2]

The Allied attack and success on the first day came as a complete surprise to the Germans. From early August, German field reports had noted the movement of vehicles, horse-drawn transport, guns and men from the back areas behind Amiens, and stories of tanks approaching the front were also mentioned in reports. However, as these tanks did not actually appear on the front line or make an attempt to attack, it was mistakenly reported they were trucks. Also, the Germans did not identify or report the increased presence of Allied artillery, which must have added to the German shock on the dawn of 8 August.

The main reasons for the German misreading of British intentions are varied, but the fact that Ludendorff considered the British army exhausted, beaten and short of supplies was high on the list. Along with this, an inaccurate picture had been delivered to Ludendorff as to the state of German defences, the wire protection and the fitness of his frontline battalions. In particular, reports avoided mentioning the low morale and depression of his frontline troops, which he knew nothing about. For all the failings of the day, German command did get at least six reserve divisions forward into the battle, when Haig and Rawlinson had estimated they'd only be facing five.

The suddenness of the attack, the speed of the Allied advance and the absence of useful intelligence about where the main advance was coming from all impeded the German response. As a result, there was a confusion of command. The roads were obstructed and crowded in the general retreat. Allied artillery and reinforcements moving forward had found themselves struggling through retreating German units heading east, many calling their comrades 'black-legs' for continuing the war.[3]

Ludendorff attributed the disaster of 8 August to 'the failure of the German soldiers' morale',[4] while other senior German officers attributed Allied success to the number of tanks they deployed. A history of the German 119 Infantry Regiment notes, 'Everything was affected by the fearful impression that the fire-vomiting iron dragons had made on artillery and infantry. A true tank-panic had seized on everything, and, where any dark shapes moved, men saw the black monster. "Everything is lost" was the cry that met the incoming battalions.'[5]

Others placed the reasons for Allied success elsewhere. A French officer claimed it was the mist, although this had not been present at recent successful attacks, including Hamel. Bean put it down to three factors: surprise, the tanks and the mist. While Ludendorff blamed the morale of his troops, Bean praised that of the Australians: 'this [German] infantry was attacked by Dominion divisions of which even those that had been long in the line were at the peak of their morale and training.'[6]

Back at Bertangles Château, General Monash was pleased with the day's success. He had again demonstrated his capabilities as general and the strengths of his Australians, but he remained mindful of Haig's broad wishes. Haig was keen to see an advance of twenty-five miles in which his three divisions of cavalry might at last break through and 'roll up the line'. He, like Monash, did not fully realise the rethink needed for this new mobile war, vastly different from static trench lines and a defined front. These commanders also overestimated the German panic. The days ahead would soon get much tougher as German reserves were rushed forward and resistance stiffened.

That night, General Rawlinson ordered his troop commanders to maintain the pressure and the advance, keeping the momentum on the shattered German line the following day. Confusion quickly prevailed, however, with Rawlinson deciding that the main advance would be in the Canadian sector, and that Currie would determine the start time and personally coordinate the Fourth Army. The role of Monash's Australian Corps depended, therefore, on the movement and deployment of the British north of the Somme and the Canadians south of the Amiens–Péronne railway. The Australians were instructed not to move until the British were at the edge of Bray, an impossible distance ahead with the Chipilly Spur still blocking their advance. Currie notified Monash that the advance would not begin until 10 am, but Monash notified his divisional commanders to have their men ready to go at short notice after 7 am.

To the surprise of the Australians, the night of 8 August passed calmly. Intermittent shelling broke out, but exhaustion overcame both sides. Defensive work needed to be done, and many of the hastily dug gun pits were joined up in one continuous trench line, providing some protection against an expected counter-attack. During the night, battalions reorganised, the men were fed, their weapons cleaned and their water and ammunition resupplied. Medical officers inspected minor wounds, sending men who needed treatment back behind the lines. As rollcalls were conducted, casualty lists were compiled and submitted. The 8th Brigade war diary notes, 'Casualties for 24 hours: Killed, two officer and seven OR's. Wounded eight officers, 50 OR's.'[7]

As the sun rose on 9 August, the day was clear and bright, and free of the ground mist of the morning before. At the southern end of the line, Pompey Elliott's 15th Brigade was eager to move forward. At first light, patrols from the 57th and 59th Battalions had pushed out as far as the old Amiens defence line and found it lightly held. Trains were heard withdrawing from Vauvillers, and 'the enemy appeared to be dribbling away in twos and threes.'[8] At 9.15 am, the Canadians requested the 15th Brigade protect their left flank, as the Australian 1st Division had been delayed in getting to the front line. The 10 am start was postponed until 11 am due to these delays in getting men into position.

After liaison problems with the Canadians, the 15th Brigade attacked Harbonnières, going around and through the town and breaking the German line. The advance was initially slow, moving forward only 500 to 600 yards due to German resistance, but after the artillery was called in, the advance continued and 'enemy resistance immediately broke down and those who did not surrender, ran.'[9]

The British 1st Cavalry Division, coordinating closely with the advancing infantry, perhaps did their best work in rounding up large batches of fleeing Germans who otherwise would have escaped. The armoured cars went even further afield, streaming up the main road past the Morcourt Valley. They shot down all kinds of enemy transport – staff officers in cars, drivers of motor lorries carrying supplies, scores and scores of horse-drawn vehicles – most of which failed to recognise them as British vehicles. The roads were soon blocked with dead animals and upturned vehicles. The armoured cars drove on, branching off the main road to Proyart, Chuignolles and other villages. They chased a lorry loaded with troops and killed nearly all of them. One armoured car pulled up in front of a hotel where a number of German officers were seated at lunch. It fired through the window and shot them down. Other officers and men were shot in their billets. For a distance of five miles beyond the furthest infantry outpost, the whole German organisation was hopelessly confounded while the Australian infantry on the Blue Line remained immune from counterattack.

Towards evening the armoured cars started to return homeward, but found great difficulty in getting back over the roads which their own efforts had almost rendered impassable. Until nightfall, they patrolled the roads immediately in front of the Blue Line. During the day they had fired 26,880 rounds of machine-gun ammunition and suffered only eight casualties, with four officers and four other ranks wounded. Though it was the only occasion on which they were employed throughout the war, this magnificent effort amply justified their existence.

At the northern end of the line, the 4th Brigade also reported, 'Enemy fairly quiet during the night.'[10] They too had called the roll and reported fifty-four killed and 239 wounded, testament to the casualties the four battalions had sustained from the artillery, machine-gun and rifle fire from the high ground near Chipilly on the north bank of the Somme. Dawn on the 9th revealed the Germans had brought up guns and shelled the village of Morcourt on the river. German aircraft were active early, bombing and machine-gunning the Australian trenches, but causing few casualties.

While the Australians were taking fire north of the railway line, the Canadians, with the assistance of four tanks, were surging forward. The Germans quickly swung their artillery off the Australians and onto the Canadians who, by 1 pm, had advanced two miles and were threatening the important German railhead at Rosières. Further pressure was put on the Germans with the arrival of four Whippet tanks.

Elsewhere and just to the north, British Mark V tanks were taking a battering. Firing from a shed on the north-western edge of Vauvillers, a German anti-tank gunner was able to knock out tank after tank, and the road became a line of smouldering wrecks. Effective mortar fire at least eliminated German machine guns in the village, the German gunners running forward with their hands held high.

By 2 pm, the 15th Brigade was relieved by the 2nd Brigade. Having been in the line only a few hours, the 15th withdrew to the Blangy area outside Amiens. Brigade headquarters moved out of what was previously a German divisional headquarters. Here they noted, 'Evidences of hurried flight were everywhere apparent and much material was secured in addition to very valuable information.'[11]

At 4.30 pm, an attack by the 7th Brigade's 27th Battalion began, the objective being a series of strongly held sunken roads south-east of Framerville. German resistance resulted in casualties, but by 5.30 pm, the battalion 'had captured the objectives on a front of 3000 yards, instead of the 1000 original intended'.[12] It was then they looked behind them:

And there was the 1st Division, in artillery formation, dotted over the ridge a mile behind. The waves in their regular patterns stretched backwards for thousands of yards, and sideways for miles. On they came. They passed over us. It was 20 minutes before the last wave went through. Their fresh faces contrasted with ours that were unshaven and grimy. They strode on, and on and on. Shrapnel eddied and flashed and puffed above them, bullets ripped through their formation. As one man fell, another stepped into his place, without slackening, without hurrying, outwardly calm.[13]

With them went the men of the 1st Division's 2nd Brigade, who had been rushed south. In Flanders, they had successfully held the Germans around Merris and Hazebrouck, and came puffed with pride after General Plumer had told them 'that there was no division, certainly in my [Fourth] Army, perhaps in the whole British Army, which has done more to destroy the morale of the enemy than the 1st Australian Division'.[14] They had been in reserve, but were now coming up from Amiens on a long hot dusty march to take over from the 15th Brigade.

The 2nd Brigade was soon attacked by low-flying aircraft and, south of Vauvillers, sustained high casualties from machine-gun fire on their front and left. While closing on their objective, they came under heavy artillery fire, which held up the advance. Close-quarter fighting ensued in a maze of old trenches. As the Australians closed in on the Germans, many of the enemy bolted and were shot down as they ran. By 6 pm the 2nd Brigade had taken their objective. Half an hour later, the Germans counter-attacked, but withered before the Australians' fire. This period was special for the 6th Battalion, as it marked the third anniversary of the initial attack on Lone Pine, but it had not been a good day; fifty-eight men were killed, with 177 wounded and three missing. The following day, they were withdrawn to support positions, and the 3rd Brigade passed through their position and continued the attack.

Back on the northern end of the Australian line, the problem of enfilading fire from the Chipilly Spur across the Somme remained. Rawlinson had pressed the commander of the British 58th Division to ensure the spur was cleared and the village taken, but repeated attacks had failed. In June, Monash had requested control and responsibility of the north side of the river and the heights stretching to the Bray–Corbie road, but this had been rejected.

Throughout 9 August, British assaults had been turned back. The 131st Regiment of the US Infantry was sent to clear Gressaire Wood, high on the top of the ridge, but they, too, had been halted after taking many casualties. The Americans were poorly equipped, had few Lewis guns and an inexperienced command.

The Australians across the river watched both the American attack and the 2/10th London Regiment's advance, and the toil the German machine guns took on these advancing lines.

By chance, two Australians, Quartermaster Sergeant Jack Hayes and his mate Sergeant Harry Andrews, had already been into Chipilly. Earlier in the day, Hayes, who was expecting 'Anzac leave' – a return to Australia for the men of the earliest contingents, who had left home in November 1914 – and Andrews decided to take a walk in the recently liberated areas along the Somme in the hope of finding souvenirs to take home to Australia. They had purposefully set out unarmed as they believed they'd need both hands to carry back the booty they would find. Crossing a small bridge to the north side of the canal, which ran parallel to the Somme, they were now about half a mile from the front line at Chipilly. As there was no firing above them on the spur, they proceeded east, crossed the river and moved nonchalantly along a narrow track. They had heard rumours that the battalion would be making a night attack on the village, and figured anything they could find out would be of value. They picked up two discarded German rifles and some ammunition, and cautiously proceeded. As they approached a chalk pit, they heard English voices behind them and turned to see English soldiers, yelling and waving for them to join them. This they did, more out of politeness than anything else, and then returned to the Australian lines and reported in.

The temporary commander of the AIF's 1st Battalion, Major Alexander Mackenzie, then suggested to his CO, Brigadier General Iven Mackay, that a small patrol under an NCO may be able to help the British secure the village. This request was initially rejected, as another British attack was planned that night following a heavy barrage of high explosive and smoke. Again the British attacked, this time with the Americans along the top of the ridge, and again the assaulting lines were scythed down. Witnessing this, Mackay quickly sent word to Mackenzie to send a small patrol under a couple of NCOs across the river 'to ascertain reasons for and if possible, to assist the attack'.[15]

Back across the narrow bridge went Hayes, Andrews and four privates at 6 pm. They reported to Captain Jack Berrell of the 2/10th London, who advised them not to go on. However, 'the village was enticing'[16] so the Australians, after spreading out to twelve paces, raced up the hill and across the open ground as German machine guns fired down at them. Making it safely to the edge of the village, they called on Berrell to bring up half his company. They too were fired on and men were killed, but Hayes and Andrews had split into two parties and began searching the village. Hayes then headed out across the open land above the village and advanced over a mile towards the very top of the spur. He circled around, coming in behind German machine gunners, who he and Andrews attacked. The Germans fled and disappeared into a dugout, leaving behind seven machine guns. Hayes quickly dropped a grenade into the dugout entrance, tempting the Germans out. One officer and thirty-one men filed out to be led away by the British.

While this was going on, the planned barrage for 5.30 pm had crashed upon Chipilly. Hayes and his mates were caught in the middle, but the smoke and dust gave them a new advantage. They circled round and came in behind the German positions, but not before Hayes had been blown off his feet a number of times by the exploding shells. As the barrage eased off and the smoke cleared, Andrews noticed Germans streaming up the hill away from the village. He quickly brought a German machine gun into action and, after this jammed, carried on with another gun.

Germans were now retiring back across the Chipilly ridge as two of Hayes' men, Privates Kane and Fuller, went on to capture more prisoners and two machine guns, which were sent back by Berrell. Advancing Americans appeared on the skyline and Hayes signalled them to advance, but the Americans mistakenly fired on the Australians, forcing them into cover. The Chipilly ridge was now clear, and though the British advance had stalled at this village for thirty hours, it was now in Allied hands due to a clever, audacious attack led by six Australians.

With the action over, Captain Berrell handed Andrews a note recommending the six Australians 'for their conspicuous work and magnificent bravery with me today'.[17] The small patrol of AIF men then took their leave of the Londoners, returning down the towpath and across the Somme to their battalion headquarters, arriving at 9.30 pm, along with twenty-eight prisoners, to report their action to Major Mackenzie. The six Australians were officially credited with capturing seventy-one Germans and nine machine guns and became legends within the AIF. Hayes was recommended for the Victoria Cross, but was awarded the Distinguished Conduct Medal instead, along with Andrews. The other four Australians, Privates Fuller, Kane, Turpin and Stevens, all received Military Medals.

Following this successful action, Monash again pressed Rawlinson to gain responsibility of the northern bank of the Somme. To this Rawlinson agreed, allowing Monash to now plan the defence of his left flank and push along the northern side, past Chipilly towards Bray and ultimately Péronne, with his area of responsibility now north to the Bray–Corbie road.

While the advance had been extraordinary, the planning that had led to success on 8 August was not sustained. Indeed, after the initial success, planning was hasty and uncoordinated, resulting in unnecessary casualties, especially in the loss of men and tanks. Lacking artillery support and tanks – most had been knocked out – as Bean says, 'the Australian infantry had to rely solely on clever and dashing use of their own weapons (including the Stokes mortar) in conditions in which even the cleverest troops could not avoid considerable loss. The two attacking brigades of the 1st Australian Division, fresh from the height of their success in Flanders, lost nearly 100 officers and 1500 men in three days.'[18]

The blame for these failures fell upon Rawlinson, Currie and Monash. Rawlinson allowed General Currie to determine zero hour on day two, and Monash had allowed subordinates to determine other elements that should have remained his decision. It seems everyone had been too busy patting each other on the back at the end of the first day to worry too much about the next, and the details of the further advance. In trying to coordinate a rapid advance across a broad front where the fighting was following the patterns of open warfare, it was extremely difficult to receive battlefield intelligence, consider strategic options and have these orders successfully passed forward. While signals were passed by field telephone, the contingencies were not fully allowed for, and this breakdown in communication also affected the Allies.

The Australian and Canadian advance, and the consolidation of enemy territory, was substantial. But the second day had not been as successful as the first, and the German defensive response was starting to be felt. They were soon to realise how vulnerable their position remained, and how easily their gains could be threatened.

NINE

Green Slopes
Above the River

With the Germans in retreat and disorganised, Monash came up with a bold plan to launch two advances on 10 August to cut off and bottle up the Germans in the area between Bray and Proyart. This involved the 13th Brigade (4th Division), made up of four battalions – the 49th, 50th, 51st and 52nd – north of the Somme, and the 10th Brigade (3rd Division) made up of four battalions – the 37th, 38th, 39th and 40th – south of the Somme.

The 13th Brigade was to push along the Bray–Corbie road from Gressaire Wood, which the Americans held after the Chipilly fighting, with the aim to advance 2000 yards then turn directly south to envelop the Germans in the village of Étinehem. Simultaneously, battalions of the 10th Brigade would advance 2000 yards along the Roman road on the south side of the Somme and turn sharp left, northwards, to envelop the Germans east of Méricourt-sur-Somme.

Monash's plan immediately drew criticism from both British and Australian staff officers. The Commanding Officer of the 37th Battalion, Lieutenant Colonel Ernest Knox-Knight, who was to lead the advance on the south side, left the Monash briefing grim faced, and his staff 'received their orders quietly but "with some amazement"'.[1] The battalion history notes, 'The colonel treated the matter very gravely, and showed by his manner, if not by his words, that he considered the proposed enterprise not merely risky, but rather foolish.'[2]

British tank commanders, however, were more vocal, stating they 'thought the job was mad'.[3] While the advance of the 13th Brigade and their tanks was covered by Gressaire Wood, the tanks and infantry of the 10th marching along the flat, exposed Roman road would be under German observation from the time they began their approach. Knox-Knight told the British tank commander, 'There'll be a train load of VC's waiting for us when we get back, if it's a success, but we won't want them if we get through with our lives.'[4]

Knox-Knight had a formidable challenge ahead. Monash's plan required three tanks abreast to advance along the Roman road; one on the actual road, the other two in the field parallel. They were to advance with as much noise as possible to panic the Germans and confuse them about the size and intention of the advance. As it turned out, the two outrider tanks could not traverse the fields beside the road due to shell damage and deep, wide trenches in the old Amiens defence line. Instead, it was decided they would travel along the road in a column of three, with three more tanks behind the 37th and 38th Battalions.

North of the Somme, Brigadier Sydney Herring of the 13th Brigade faced fewer challenges. First, he could assemble out of sight at the back of Gressaire Wood, which at the time was 'reeking with enemy gas and with the decomposing corpses of horses and dead Boches',[5] and then move forward without alerting the Germans. He would also be advancing along the major Bray–Corbie road that ran along the spur, with the land dropping off to the Somme on the right and the Morlancourt valley on the left. He, too, had to make an advance of 2000 yards and then a similar right-angle turn to head south across the rolling fields to the east of Étinehem, and down to the river where he would meet Knox-Knight's 37th Battalion across the river. Monash's plan was ingenious but risky.

On the night of 10 August, the 10th Brigade's commander, Brigadier General Walter McNicoll, spotted German observation balloons and delayed the departure until darkness could conceal his advance. This was one of the first times tanks had been deployed at night, and the tank commanders wanted to give their men the best chance of seeing exactly where they were going over the terrain. As there was no artillery support, except for strafes into back areas of the German front, these six tanks had much work to do, and being few in number they needed support and clear direction.

The advance of the 10th Brigade along the Roman road south of the Somme began as planned. In the lead were the three tanks, then the 37th Battalion, the 38th, three more tanks then the 39th and 40th Battalions bringing up the rear. The other battalions were to follow the 37th when it made the right-angle advance at Avenue Cross to turn north, and to follow through to the Somme. Here the 37th would form a new front line extending one mile south, with the 38th and 40th continuing the line to the Roman road and the 39th stretching back. Once this had been consolidated, the 10th Brigade would have enclosed an area 2.5 miles long and 1.5 miles deep in which many Germans – including guns, equipment and stores – would be encircled. Into this would go the 9th and 11th Brigades of the 3rd Australian Division to mop up.

As the 10th Brigade advanced past La Flaque at 10 pm, the guides and the tanks had only 900 yards to go before the left turn and the drive north. Behind the three tanks came the other battalions, stretching back two miles to Méricourt-sur-Somme where the 39th was formed up. Suddenly, a German plane flying very low along the line of the road dropped a bomb on the lead tank, turning it over. The plane continued dropping bombs on the exposed line of infantry. Immediately dozens of flares rose from the German line and illuminated the road as numerous machine guns sent devastating fire into the lines of men stretching back for over a mile. Bean describes the scene: 'Machine gun bullets now rained in torrents, sparking off the cobbles and outlining the tanks with a continuous glow.'[6]

Further, a fierce artillery barrage shattered the night and, along with the bombing and strafing by the German plane, the road was quickly strewn with Australian dead and wounded. Even the two battalions a mile in the rear came under this fire. Contradictory and confusing messages began passing up and down the line of the road. Word of the death of Knox-Knight was passed along; he had been hit by a fragment of anti-tank shell that had ricocheted off a nearby tree.

After the tanks halted, German fire slowed but, with the flares still illuminating the bare, flat landscape, any movement drew further fire. At about midnight, the commanders of the 38th and 40th Battalions formed a line, with the 38th parallel with the road, so they could extract the remainder of the 37th Battalion. By the time the 37th withdrew, they had 103 men killed and wounded, one quarter of their strength. While the withdrawal was underway, German aircraft continually ranged up and down the road, bombing and strafing the unprotected battalions.

Part of the advancing column included a heavily laden mule train, the men in charge being told they must, under no circumstance, allow their mules to get away as they were carrying precious ammunition. And indeed the mule drivers 'stood to their animals throughout',[7] displaying great courage and discipline in the face of carnage and death.

When the barrage first landed, however, a stretcher-bearer by the name of Jock Young had found himself sheltering in a narrow hole. Suddenly another man landed on top of him and then a third, a mule handler, still grimly hanging onto his laden mule. The battalion history takes up the story:

The man held on like grim death to the unruly beast, which threatened at any moment to pile in on top of the three.

'Let the blanky, blank, blank go.' Yelled digger number 2 to the man above him.

'I can't,' replied the mule driver. 'I've strict orders that it must not be turned loose. Have you any authority to countermand that order?'

'No, but I'll ask this b—— below me. Hey there! Digger, what rank do you have?'

'I'm a corporal,' said the half smothered Jock Young.

'Well you give this silly b—— authority to let this blanky mule go'.

'Yes,' said Young. 'Let the damn mule go.'

And away went the mule to the relief of all concerned.[8]

North of the Somme, the 13th Brigade found things a little easier. The brigade formed up with the tanks, the 49th Battalion in the lead. They headed east along the Bray–Corbie road before turning right as instructed, and down the slope towards Étinehem. The Germans started to fire on the tanks, but their fire was high and wild, and missed the advancing Australians. The Germans withdrew, falling back towards Bray. Then for about 1000 yards they fired more flares, forcing the leading company, under Captain Richard Tambling, to deploy. At one point, the leading sections came under German light machine-gun fire and one of the scouts, Private Hockey, snuck around the back of the post where he killed two gunners and captured another five Germans. After this, the battalion joined up with the 50th and dug in on their objective.

At daybreak on 11 August, the Germans struck back. The Australians' newly dug trenches, with their white chalk, easily disclosed their position to German aircraft and soon German artillery was firing around them. Losses quickly mounted, with forty-nine out of Tambling's company of 110 men becoming casualties.

During the afternoon, a 'line of men'⁹ was seen digging in. As it was not clear if they were Australians or Germans, no artillery fire was directed onto them. They were soon identified as Germans, but they made no effort to counterattack. The Germans also established a post on the northern side of the main road and captured a group of wounded Australians coming back. A number of attempts were made to free the Australians, but after more men were killed and wounded, the rescue was abandoned.

At this time, back on the Roman road to the south, the 10th Brigade withdrew and was replaced by the 11th Brigade, which immediately attacked, capturing 260 prisoners and thirteen machine guns after heavy and bitter fighting. Quickly they cleared the village of Méricourt-sur-Somme, and in the rear Cateaux Wood, which ran along the Somme.

Brigadier Herring brought together his battalion commanders and issued instructions for the clearance of the whole of the

Étinehem peninsula on the night of 12 August. The Battalion Operation Memo No. 2, dated that day, specified the 51st 'will attack and mop-up the whole of the southern area of the spur and then establish strongpoints on the lower ground covering the bridges and possible crossings of the River Somme. The 50th Battalion will operate on the left and establish a strong position covering the exits of Bray.'[10]

The attack went in 'behind an excellent barrage'[11] and, although the Australians were met with intermittent fire, the peninsula was secured on 14 August, with over 100 Germans captured. The two battalions, the 50th and the 51st, then linked up, but not before a party of Germans in a post halfway down the cliff turned four machine guns on them. These Germans were hard to dislodge, but when an attack went in the following night, with a supporting Stokes mortar bombardment, the German post was found abandoned. By this action, the whole area was cleared of enemy. In all, one officer and 174 Germans were captured along with twenty machine guns, one light trench mortar and five horses. Australian casualties were five ranks wounded.

With the clearing of the Étinehem peninsula by the 13th Brigade, all objectives of Monash's plan had been obtained and consolidated. The Germans had withdrawn to Bray, exhausted and beaten. The Australians now turned their attention to attacking Bray.

Meanwhile, at the very southern end of the line, the Canadians had taken Rosières, with the Germans pulling back as the AIF's 8th Battalion advanced. The next objective was the village of Lihons, sitting as it did on the top of a long, flat sloping hill. This was allocated to the 3rd Brigade, comprised of the outer state battalions as they were known (those from Western Australia, South Australia and Tasmania), with orders to follow the 2nd Brigade in the advance on the village.

As the Australians moved forward in the dawn mist on 9 August, German machine guns raked the advancing lines and casualties mounted. Two men quickly moved forward: Private Robert Beatham and his mate Lance Corporal William Nottingham. Together they attacked four German machine guns holding up the advance, killing ten in the gun crews and capturing a further ten Germans. They then laid down covering fire using two of the captured guns, allowing the 8th Battalion to continue their advance towards Lihons. (Two days later, Beatham was again in action, this time while wounded. He rushed a German machine gun, throwing bombs and silencing it, but he was riddled with bullets and killed. For this and other actions, he was awarded a posthumous Victoria Cross. He is buried nearby, in Heath Cemetery.)

However, on the whole, things were not going well for the Australians on the southern end of the line, and confused orders compounded a difficult situation. As the mist rose, the advancing troops became clear targets for the Germans along the line of the Framerville–Lihons road and, without tank support and with the barrage falling 800 yards to the rear, later described in one report as 'wretched, skimpy and without sting',[12] they struggled to push forward.

The 9th and 11th Battalions were tasked with seizing Crépy Wood and the Blue Line east of Lihons. Meanwhile, the Victorian 5th and 6th Battalions were to pass to their right or north of Crépy Wood. As they advanced, they sustained heavy casualties from the Germans along the Framerville–Lihons road and the wood itself, with German machine guns concealed in the tangle of old trenches and barbed wire.

Parties of Australians entered the wood, moving from shell hole to shell hole, one of them led by Lieutenant Hereward Gower, MC. (Gower had joined two weeks after the declaration of war, and had been wounded on the Gallipoli peninsula a few days after the landing.) Locating the guns, he worked around behind them, outflanking them and attacking. At one point he attacked a machine gun, threatening the crew with a Lewis-gun rod and forcing them to surrender, but soon after he was badly wounded.

A company from the 10th Battalion attacked through the wood again at 1 pm and was able to establish a new line on the eastern and northern edge of the wood. At 3.45 pm the Germans laid down a heavy bombardment on the wood, and two of the four posts were completely destroyed.

At 4 pm the Germans counterattacked, but only a few of them, laden with full packs and greatcoats, attempted the advance. They were driven off. Then at 5.30 pm, after a heavy barrage, the Germans again counterattacked with about 300 men. While they captured sections of 9th Battalion trench, they were driven back by the support platoons, leaving ninety of their dead in the wood. By the end of this attack, the 9th Battalion had captured ninety prisoners, eight 4.2-inch howitzers, thirty machine guns, two trench mortars and three field telephone systems. It was these captured machine guns that were to be put to good use in the days following.

As the 9th Battalion had mistakenly stopped short of its objective, digging in on the east of Crépy Wood rather than the eastern side of Auger Wood, the 11th and 12th Battalions of the 3rd Brigade were given the objective of the Blue Line. A gap had opened up between the 11th and 12th Battalions just north, however, which needed to be quickly filled. As the exhausted

9th Battalion moved to fill the gap, so did the Germans. Fighting quickly started, and the enemy was driven back.

During this fighting, a party of fifty Germans was encircled and trapped in a trench. Posting a Lewis gun to prevent them escaping, Company Sergeant Major George Walker found two men to help him. The three charged into the trench with bayonets, one being killed on the way, driving the Germans before them. The Australians threw a bomb into the crowded Germans, killing four, and the remainder surrendered. While a few escaped, Walker returned with twenty-eight prisoners, and by 9.30 am on 11 August, the gap had been filled. For this action, Walker was awarded the Distinguished Conduct Medal.

Also sent to fill the gap was Lieutenant Ernest Meyers, who moved with his platoon of about thirty men against Auger Wood to the north. Again, machine guns in the wood slowed their advance but these were slowly eliminated, leaving only a heavy machine gun manned by two Germans. They were picked off, the gun captured and the wood cleared. As the Australians emerged from the wood they came across a group of Germans, some 100 to 150 strong. Meyers immediately attacked with his remaining platoon and again drove the Germans back, taking thirty prisoners and re-establishing the line by setting up small posts 100 yards apart to fill the gap. Meyers had already proven his leadership skills, and was to finish the war with a Military Cross and two bars. After this action, the 9th Battalion was sent to the rear, but their casualties had been heavy: twelve officers and 166 other ranks.

One incident mentioned in the 9th Battalion history reveals the sense of humour, or perhaps cynicism, in response to the mounting Australian casualties. Before the advance on Lihons and the fighting in Crépy Wood, a private in the battalion had made a small fortune playing two-up. As was often the case, men could not bank winnings or lodge them anywhere safely so this private went into action with 10,000 francs, worth about £370, stashed in his pack. (Soldiers were paid five shillings a day at this time.) As he advanced, a 5.9-inch shell 'burst beside him and he was blown to pieces, bank notes and all. After the battle, his mates were loud in their lamentations that so much good money had gone up in the air, but no word of regret was heard for "poor old blank".'[13]

On 15 August, battalions from the 4th Brigade moved into the area of Crépy and Auger woods, and occupied the railway embankment at the southern end of the line recently vacated by the Germans. Colonel Douglas Marks of the 13th Battalion immediately sent out patrols to continue with nibbling and peaceful penetration.

On 17 August, the Germans laid a heavy bombardment on the two woods, 'where it seemed the enemy knew the exact position of our posts'.[14] As they advanced, the men of the 13th Battalion moved through the old overgrown trenches of 1916, where they found signs of recent occupation: beer, cheese and meals on the table, showing the haste with which the Germans had evacuated. Marks, fearing a German counterattack, spread his men thinly across the front, setting up listening posts and gun positions, and sending out patrols to stall German intrusion and counterattack.

At daybreak on 19 August, the 4th Brigade's line was again hit with a heavy German barrage. Marks quickly stood his men to, but the Germans attacked the 2nd Manchesters on the brigade's left, driving the Englishmen out of their trenches and pushing them back. These troops had relieved the Australian 6th Brigade, and were 'composed largely of raw soldiers, many were boys who had little war experience. The enemy (well informed as usual)

John Monash was promoted to lieutenant general on 1 June 1918 and given command of the newly formed Australian Corps, comprising all five Australian divisions. This photo was taken before his promotion, when he was General Commanding Officer of the 3rd Division, at his headquarters at Bertangles Château. *AWM E02350*

Camon, near Amiens, 5 May 1918. German arms and equipment captured by the Australian 15th Brigade at Villers-Bretonneux. The Australians' recapture of the town on 25 April was broadly celebrated and reaffirmed the effectiveness of Australian troops. *AWM E04818*

Australian soldiers inspect a German tank captured by the 26th Battalion at Monument Wood, near Villers-Bretonneux. After being bogged and abandoned on the battlefield, it was recovered in July 1918. *AWM E02877*

A group of French, American and Australian soldiers gathered in a trench at the International Post. The post was established at the junction of the French and Australian lines in the trenches near Monument Wood. The sign on the right reads 'International Post, Front Line' in English and French. *AWM E04910*

A high-velocity gun captured by the Australians near Morcourt during the offensive of 8 August. *AWM E02888*

Lieutenant Rupert Frederick Arding Downes, MC, addressing his platoon from 'B' Company, 29th Battalion, during a rest near the villages of Warfusée and Lamotte before the advance into Harbonnières, the battalion's second objective of 8 August. The sergeant on the left of the line, William O'Brien, was killed the following day. *AWM E02790*

Unidentified men of the 8th Brigade established in the final objective of 8 August. The men are occupying old French trenches. *AWM E02789*

Studio portrait of Lance Corporal Bernard Sidney Gordon, MM, VC, of the 41st Battalion. Gordon was awarded the Military Medal for action on 8 August at Hamel, and the Victoria Cross for further bravery during advances towards Fargny Wood. On the night of 26–27 August, Gordon led his section through heavy shellfire and single-handedly attacked an enemy machine-gun post, then cleared up a number of trenches. *AWM A05210*

Wounded Australians of the 15th Brigade standing over wounded German prisoners beside a British Whippet tank near Harbonnières on 9 August. *AWM E02880*

A German sniper killed in the Allied advance towards Bray, where the 9th Brigade experienced heavy fighting on 22 August. He had in his pocket a letter to his wife, telling her he was facing the Australians and wanted to get out of the area as quickly as possible. *AWM E03061*

Members of the 24th Battalion in a trench about 1.20 pm on 1 September, awaiting the lifting of the artillery barrage before the renewed attack that led to the capture of Mont St Quentin. *AWM E03138*

The gap in the tangled barbed wire at Anvil Wood through which some of the 53rd Battalion advanced on 1 September, facing heavy machine-gun fire. The packs of five wounded men can be seen near the bodies of two of the four men killed. *AWM E03149*

Portrait of Sergeant Albert David Lowerson, VC, 21st Battalion. Sergeant Lowerson was awarded the Victoria Cross for 'most conspicuous bravery and tactical skill' on 1 September at Mont St Quentin. *AWM P02939.037*

Studio portrait of Corporal Lawrence Carthage Weathers, VC, 43rd Battalion. Weathers received the Victoria Cross for an action on 2 September, undertaken while his battalion was clearing enemy positions north of Péronne. He was mortally wounded in action four weeks later, not knowing of his award. *AWM P05212.003*

Men of the 4th Australian Field Artillery Brigade having lunch beside their camouflaged gun, established in an open field, on 2 September. *AWM E03145*

Australian soldiers carrying a dummy tank, weighing about a quarter of a tonne, made to mislead the enemy. These were to be used the following morning, 18 September, in the attack on Le Verguier and the Hindenburg Outpost Line. *AWM E04934*

Troops of the 45th Battalion at their newly captured objective between Bellenglise and Le Verguier, in front of the Hindenburg Outpost Line, on 18 September. They are seen sniping the enemy retreating up the opposite hillside. *AWM E03260*

Studio portrait of Private James Woods, VC, of the 48th Battalion. He was awarded his Victoria Cross at Le Verguier on 18 September after capturing a heavily defended German post and holding it against counterattacks. *AWM A02640*

Portrait of Sergeant Maurice Vincent Buckley, VC, 13th Battalion. Buckley was also awarded the Victoria Cross for his actions at Le Verguier, where he rushed at least six machine-gun positions, captured a field gun and took nearly 100 prisoners. *AWM A05136*

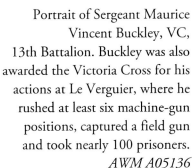

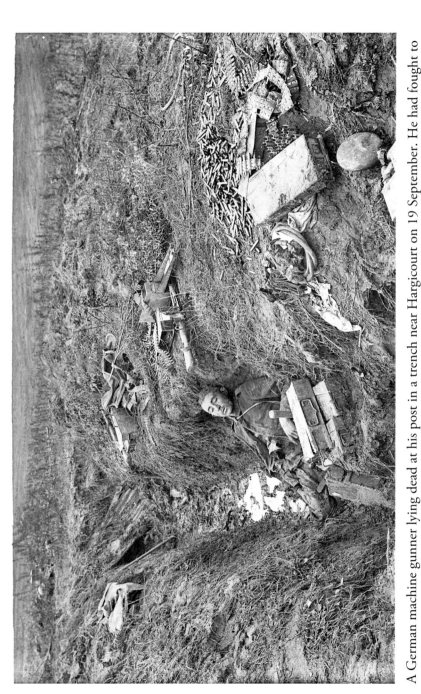

A German machine gunner lying dead at his post in a trench near Hargicourt on 19 September. He had fought to the last against the advancing Australian troops, as can be seen by the spent machine-gun cases. *AWM E03351*

Bodies of American troops laid out for burial. They were killed in the fighting near Guillemont Farm on 29 September, when the American 27th Division attacked towards the main Hindenburg Line and suffered many casualties. *AWM E04942B*

View showing the distribution of landmines in the wire near Ronssoy, which rendered useless many of the tanks assisting in the attack on the Hindenburg Line. These 'plum pudding' bombs formed part of a former British minefield. *AWM E04939*

The entrance to the St Quentin Canal tunnel near Bellicourt. This photograph was taken on 26 October 1918. *AWM E03655*

took advantage of the relief of the seasoned troops stationed there to make a cleverly executed and successful raid in broad daylight, under cover of a heavy barrage.'[15]

Sergeant William Boyes, MM, DCM, of the 14th Battalion, seeing the German attack, rallied some of the surviving Tommies and twice led a small group against the Germans now holding the trench, shooting three of the most prominent enemy soldiers. As the battalion history relates, 'When the enemy, strongly reinforced, swarmed back against his little party, Boyes, kneeling by a sandbag, held them practically singlehandedly at bay, playing on them with rifle grenades. Boyes was soon wounded when the Germans laid down a box barrage to cut off any assistance, but he survived and was awarded the DCM. A widower with a child, he returned to Australia in early 1919.'[16]

Having taken Lihons and the high ground, the Australians could see far and wide across the Canadian sector to the south, as far as Chilly and ahead to the German-held village of Chaulnes. Now the 2nd Australian Division was on the left of the 1st, astride the Roman road.

After the capture of Lihons, the Australians slowed their advance although they continued their peaceful penetration and nibbling, waiting for new orders in the wider offensive plans of Foch and Haig. The GHQ planners realised that German resistance was stiffening, and the old battlefields over which they were now fighting were creating a problem for the movement of tanks and cavalry. This vast area was strewn with overgrown trenches, rusty barbed wire and a desolate moonscape extending north to south in a band twenty to thirty miles wide. Given the success of the advance to date, the commanders wanted to keep the pressure on the Germans.

Foch wanted to take the Somme bridges near Péronne and, through General Rawlinson, ordered the Australians to push forward along the Somme on 15 August, an advance that would include the capture of Bray and Suzanne. Haig, meanwhile, issued orders on 15 August for a substantial offensive further north. This involved the British Fourth Army stretching on a front from the French army across the Roman road, up to Albert, and the Third Army from Albert to Arras. Over three days, the two British armies would advance on a thirty-three-mile front extending from Herleville, south of the Roman road, to Mercatel, 3.5 miles south of Arras, and push across the old 1916 battlefields to take Bapaume.

On 20 August, the Australian 3rd Division – made up of the 9th, 10th and 11th Brigades – moved to secure the northern side of the Somme and support the very southern flank of III Corps in the extensive British plan north of Albert. The 9th Brigade's 34th and 35th Battalions, with the 33rd in support, relieved the 13th Brigade east of Tailles Wood and along the Bray–Corbie road to a position north of Bray, to secure the northern flank of the Australian advance, always of concern to Monash and the Australian command. This attack was orchestrated in conjunction with the British 47th Division, which would be supported by tanks and a smoke barrage.

The three Australian battalions moved up the Bray–Corbie road to the start line. Here, lying on their tapes in the darkness just before zero hour, a heavy German bombardment fell among them. Miraculously, only six men were wounded. Then, at 4.45 am, the Allied barrage fell 300 yards ahead and the men rose, shouldering their rifles and moving forward in the mist, which was quickly thickened by dust and smoke. German machine guns fired briefly, but these were quickly overrun, as was a forward command post where the commander, his officers and forty men were captured. The 34th Battalion, however, lost its lieutenant, and twenty other ranks were killed and fourteen wounded.[17]

At 7 am, the lead battalion was ordered to move forward 'as the Imperial troops were reported to be retiring on the left flank, under pressure of an enemy counter-attack'.[18] In the 9th Brigade war diary, an entry on the 21st states:

Enemy counter-attack commences with the result that the English troops on our left (47th Division) and the 12th Division further north retreated before the enemy who was making only a half-hearted attempt to gain ground on their front. The enemy's attitude during this advance was one of hesitation. He was apparently surprised at the English withdrawal for no apparent reason and seemed to suspect it as being somewhat in the nature of a ruse to draw him in. A result of these operations was to leave the left flank of the Brigade entirely in the air as the English troops became very demoralised and disorganised during the course of the counter-attack.[19]

A 33rd Battalion officer, Captain N. Cains, reinforced the left flank and organised some of the British troops, who were then able to repulse a German counterattack on their position, inflicting 'very heavy losses on the enemy'.[20]

The men had been fighting all day and were badly in need of a hot meal. At midnight, the battalion ration limbers arrived 'in spite of heavy shelling and machine gun fire, to the men who had a hot meal whilst actually holding the enemy at bay'.[21]

On 23 August, the 9th Brigade's other battalion, the 36th, left Hazel Wood, crossed the Somme and tramped up the dusty road through the ruins of Sailly-Laurette, passing large parties of German prisoners walking westwards to the POW cages around Villers-Bretonneux. The 36th then marched past Gressaire and Tailles woods, where the faint smell of gas lingered. About midnight, they reached what was then the front line a mile north-west of Bray, where they relieved the 33rd in the trenches. They were told that, two days earlier, the British battalion on the left had withdrawn several hundred yards to the rear to take advantage of a better defensive position, leaving the 33rd's left flank exposed. Quickly posts were established to the left to connect up with the British troops. Eventually, the British troops re-established this front line after a short barrage and some tough fighting.

Shortly after midnight on 23 August, the 10th Brigade's 38th Battalion took over from the 39th, allowing them to move forward ready for the attack upon Bray. As the battalion moved towards the Bray railway yards, they were subjected to heavy shelling with high explosive and gas, and the men were forced to advance with their gasmasks on. At 2.30 am, a tremendous British barrage crashed into Bray and obliterated German defences, with only a few machine-gun crews surviving. One of these fired directly into the advancing Australians at twenty-five yards, but was quickly silenced by a Lewis-gun team, avoiding serious casualties.

German artillery responded, but as they were unsure where their own men were, they fired over the heads of the advancing 39th Battalion, cutting the telephone wires that had already been laid. This required some brave work by battalion runners and signallers, who dashed into the barrage to get messages through and to repair lines. Two privates, John Reeves and David Marsh, continually ran messages and returned with answers through the German barrage now falling in the rear.

During the night, the 37th Battalion was lined out in shallow posts holding an important section of the line. The young lieutenant, Lubin Robertson, whose platoon held one of these posts, knowing that a German machine gun and a British Vickers machine gun sounded very different when fired, decided to try and entice the Germans nearby into thinking it was a German post by firing the captured German machine guns in intermittent bursts into the houses nearby. At 4 am, a German approached their post. The men lay silent until the figure was right among them then they jumped up, frightening the life out of the man and capturing him. He turned out to be a machine-gun officer doing his rounds, unaware his guns had been captured.

Robertson and his men again baited their trap and waited. This time a party of five Germans approached the post, but upon being challenged, dived for cover. They were fired on and quickly surrendered. Next came a ration party of two men who were also captured. Such was their relief that they cried with joy on being captured, glad to be out of the war. When questioned, they mentioned that a group of twenty from their unit were also willing to surrender, but these men were not followed up, Robertson feeling this was a ruse to fire on the Australians.

The attack on Bray was supported by units of British cavalry, the Northumberland Hussars. At 8.45 am they had passed Australian positions on the Bray–Fricourt road and charged the German guns. Of the 150 that went out only twenty survived, as most fell victim to German machine guns or were bombed from the air. Riderless horses streamed back past the Australians, and it was a grim task for some diggers to shoot the wounded horses after this dashing failure.

On 24 August, Bray fell to the 10th Brigade, who had relieved the exhausted 9th Brigade. As they moved into Bray, mopping up and clearing houses, they found a massive supply dump mined with explosives and ready to be blown. The retreating Germans had had no time to fire these charges before their hasty withdrawal, so these stores fell into Australian hands. As the town had not been seriously damaged by Allied shellfire or in the fighting, the Australians were able to use the village houses for accommodation and administration.

By daylight, the 37th Battalion had moved east and were on the hill overlooking the next village, Suzanne. As dawn broke, a heavy ground fog enveloped the area, reducing visibility to ten yards and creating a dangerous situation for the Australians. Patrols were sent out and reports came back that the enemy were still retreating. As the fog lifted, men started sniping the Germans, firing into their backs. Others attacked a gun crew, putting it out of action.

The Germans could be seen withdrawing towards Ceylon Wood on the western outskirts of Suzanne. The wood was entered and searched by the 42nd Battalion. Meanwhile, the Tasmanians of the 40th Battalion pushed south-east towards the end of the peninsula and the village of Cappy. Here they captured twenty-nine prisoners and eight machine guns from a party of Germans who reported that, if attacked, they had been ordered to fall back on the main line of resistance in Suzanne.

To the north of the Australians around Bray, things were going well for the British divisions. The commanders of III Corps had decided to push on with the advance and take Maricourt, north-east of Suzanne, which commanded the northern slopes of the Somme.

The commander of the AIF's 3rd Division, General Gellibrand, also decided to push forward in four stages to the northern end of the next bend of the Somme at Fargny Mill, but word came from Monash, probably a direction from Rawlinson, that the 3rd Division must stop and allow the III Corps to take Maricourt before recommencing their advance.

As the 3rd Division's 11th Brigade advanced, with the British 58th Division on their left, it was reported that Billon Wood, the main defensive obstacle before Maricourt, had been cleared, but as the brigade's 43rd Battalion advanced, machine-gun fire indicated that these reports were false.

By dawn on 26 August, the 11th Brigade had taken the area south of Billon Wood and the 10th Brigade was on the north-western outskirts of Suzanne. Again the Australians were ordered to wait until the British 58th Division had taken Maricourt. Yet Australian patrols remained active, particularly patrols from the 37th and 39th Battalions who were pushing forward and across the top of Suzanne, continuing their advance eastwards.

At this point, the 37th was held up by Germans firing from Murray Wood on the eastern side of Suzanne. Lieutenant Stanley Le Fevre and Sergeant Cornelius Loxton went forward with a runner. They dashed into the wood, where they found a group of Germans and charged them with fixed bayonets, putting the enemy to flight. The runner was then sent back to order a Lewis-gun team to come up to consolidate the position while Le Fevre and Loxton remained to hold the position. The Germans had retreated to another post a short distance away, so Le Fevre and Loxton charged this post, killed the crew and captured their machine gun. This action allowed the advance of the battalion and the occupation of the wood.

While this was happening, one patrol under Lieutenant Robertson and another under Lieutenant Ayers attacked the main trench, dislodging several hundred Germans who then ran across the open ground towards Vaux Wood, which bordered the next bend of the river. The men were fired on by Australian rifles and Lewis guns, and many fell. The Germans continued their retreat eastwards, exhausted and disorganised. The historian of the German 120th Infantry Regiment later wrote, 'You could no longer call it a fight . . . The enemy brigades rolled up behind a mighty curtain of fire and ceremoniously crushed the motley assembly of German soldiers.'[22]

The Germans now fell back to Fargny Mill – a mill complex, which was the last of their designated defensive lines along the Somme – where they were resupplied with ammunition from the air.

By late August, the advance of the British Third Army south of Arras was proceeding while the Fourth Army, to the north of the Australians, continued to maintain pressure on the enemy. The 57th British Division, however, had suffered severe casualties and it was unable to capture Fargny Wood south-east of Maricourt. This task now fell to the 3rd Australian Division, who were advancing steadily through Vaux Wood on their way to Curlu.

South of the Somme, the 1st Australian Division was pushing towards Péronne. Monash, keeping a close eye on the advance of both divisions, ensured the flanks were secure and the advance was in tandem on both sides of the river.

To push the Germans from Fargny Wood and the mill complex on the river, the 41st and 44th Battalions of 11th Brigade had made a silent advance, first to Vaux Wood and then northwards into Spur Wood. At 4.55 am on 26 August, after fighting through Spur Wood, the leading company of the 41st Battalion emerged into open country, where they came into Fargny Wood and pushed forward to Fargny Mill. Here they were hemmed in by steep cliffs rising above them, the river and the Germans on the heights above.

At this time, a German machine gun that was enfilading the battalion was attacked by a Tasmanian, Lance Corporal Bernard Gordon. He had earlier been awarded a Military Medal on 8 August near Hamel and now found himself, along with his mates, in a difficult and dangerous predicament. After Gordon had led his section through heavy artillery fire and consolidated their position, he went out alone and attacked the machine gun. He killed the gunner and captured the post, which contained an officer and ten men. Gordon moved along the enemy trench, where he captured a further twenty-nine Germans and two machine guns. By the time he had finished this stunt, he had captured two officers and sixty-one other ranks and six machine guns. He was awarded the Victoria Cross and returned to Australia in January 1919.

While the exhausted 57th British Division once again continued its advance, capturing Flint Ridge above Curlu, the Australian 11th Brigade was relieved by the 9th Brigade. This brigade needed to divert men to the flanks as 'The English troops on our left have again failed to keep up with the barrage and our left flank is subsequently exposed.'[23] The 9th Brigade's war diary went on to state, 'The enemy is very strong in machine guns opposite our whole front . . . where he is offering very strong resistance.'[24] Their war diary further expresses their displeasure with English communications:

English troops do not appear to have sufficiently qualified signals personnel or sufficient organisation to maintain efficient communications between the frontline and Brigade HQ. Some English brigades rely solely on runners while we usually have telephones and Fuller phones, power buzzer and amplifier sets, pigeons, message carrying rockets, visual signalling, Lucas lamp and flag, success signals, flares, contact aeroplanes and trench wireless sets as well as runners.[25]

Meanwhile, the 10th Brigade from the 3rd Division had its rest cancelled, and was deployed to the right of the 9th to continue to clear the next peninsula eastwards. General Gellibrand then took responsibility of 500 yards of the British 57th Division's front at Fargny Mill. When the 35th Battalion advanced, however, they found the mill deserted and the Germans gone. Meanwhile, the 37th Battalion had cleaned up the remainder of the Suzanne bend and peninsula, and the river crossings established at Frise and Eclusier, which had been guarded by men of the 38th Battalion. During this time, Lieutenant Murie and some of his battalion mates had occupied a recently vacated large German dugout. Early the following morning, they heard noises from a separate section of the dugout and were amazed when four German officers, who had been asleep or holed up there, came out and surrendered.

On 28 August, the 38th and 40th Battalions formed skirmish lines and advanced eastwards towards Curlu. The 38th Battalion went straight for the village with the 40th in support, while the 35th Battalion wheeled around to protect their northern flank. Here the 35th took the Chapeau de Gendarme, a 'steep scrubby cliff',[26] capturing sixty Germans and eight machine guns.

After the capture of Curlu by the 38th Battalion, their advance continued towards Hem and, by 29 August, these battalions were closing on the village of Cléry-sur-Somme, an advance of 8000 yards from Vaux Wood in less than two days. This advance was extraordinary, given the German resistance and the resupply requirements to own this ground. It was here that the Somme turned south past Péronne, forming a natural defensive barrier for the Germans.

Meanwhile, the British Third Army to the north had continued their successful advance on Bapaume, and by 23 August had decided to break through with the New Zealand Division. This put pressure on Monash to push his men forward again, asking them to give their last ounce of strength and resolve.

The AIF's 3rd Division was now past Curlu and in sight of the high ground of Mont St Quentin, a formidable German line, the key to Péronne and the crossing of the Somme. Given their strategic importance, it was anticipated that both Mont St Quentin and Péronne would be strongly contested by the enemy. But first, Cléry-sur-Somme and the bridgeheads to the immediate west of Mont St Quentin and Péronne needed to be fought for.

TEN

Eastwards on the Roman Road

While these advances were made north of the Somme, the Australians were advancing and consolidating their position along the Roman road, south of the river. After the disastrous attack by the 10th Brigade on 10 August – in which Knox-Knight's 37th Battalion lost over 100 men, including Knox-Knight himself – the AIF 3rd Division's General Gellibrand was keen to maintain pressure on the Germans, and ordered the 10th Brigade to advance north and south of the Roman road, beginning with the 38th Battalion. This battalion, under Captain Francis Fairweather, MC, advanced across the flat, open plain devoid of cover on 10 August. After crossing the Proyart road, they came under heavy machine-gun fire from half a mile to the east and from the crossroads at Avenue Cross.

The advance of the 10th Brigade was also subjected to heavy artillery and machine-gun fire, particularly upon the 38th and 40th Battalions, after the 37th and 39th withdrew to safer positions. The two forward battalions dug in, but the going was tough due to the shortage of picks and shovels. With the help of the morning mist on 11 August, the 10th Brigade had completed a disjointed line which was again heavily bombarded, isolating the battalion headquarters. The bombardment continued throughout

11 August but, under cover of the mist, men of the 38th patrolled forward and eliminated a number of German machine guns that had targeted the Australians.

The work of the runners and signallers was especially valued during this time, though a number were killed and wounded. One brave man was Lieutenant Anthony Mills, who ran between the front line and battalion headquarters. As the 40th Battalion history states, 'The sight of this officer breaking all previous records across the open with machine gun bullets flicking up the dirt under his heels became a familiar sight . . . and on each appearance the odds were called and the bets made in our posts as to whether he would arrive. Odds were about 12 to 1 against.'[1]

An Australian patrol advanced north-east, south of Proyart, while another patrol moved up the road and into the village. Here they observed Germans fleeing west. A lone patrol by the 40th Battalion's Sergeant Ernest Billing, however, found that the trenches north and east of Proyart were held in force by the Germans. Before returning to his unit, Billing camouflaged himself in a pile of rubbish and sniped three machine gunners. The remaining gunners ran.

With machine-gun fire pouring into the 37th Battalion, one party of thirteen Australians rushed forward, but were wiped out to a man in their brave dash to take the guns. After witnessing this action the 40th Battalion's Sergeant Percy Statton, MM, from Beaconsfield, Tasmania, called on three men to follow him and, armed only with his revolver, rushed across eighty yards of open ground. The Germans were busy firing on the 37th, so Statton quickly entered their trench, shot two gunners manning the first gun and then rushed to the next gun. Here he shot the crew, with the exception of one man who came at him with the bayonet. Statton wrenched it from the German's hands and killed him.

The Germans at the two remaining guns had fled, only to be cut down by the battalion's Lewis guns. Suddenly, German machine guns in Robert Wood to the east of Proyart opened on Statton's small party, killing Private Lesley Styles and wounding Corporal Wilfred Upchurch.

For his bravery, Sergeant Percy Statton was awarded the Victoria Cross. The 40th Battalion was then relieved after they had taken casualties of twelve killed and sixty wounded, including two company commanders.

Orders went out to the Australian 11th Brigade to clear the area north-east towards Chuignolles on 11 August. The 41st Battalion advanced on St Germaine Wood, where a large number of Germans were defending both the wood and a quarry, from which heavy fire fell upon the Australians. Without Stokes mortars, they called for artillery support, and fifty shells were quickly dropped into the area. The German artillery then mistakenly dropped shells into these German positions, ignoring the flares fired by their own defenders. The battalion moved through the area, capturing 100 Germans and many machine guns while the Germans streamed back, fleeing for their life.

The brigade's 42nd Battalion had only entered the fight with 300 rifles, and this was to be the battalion's most grim and testing attack of the war. At one point Lieutenant Arthur Boorman, MC, led a small party of seven men and one Lewis gun. With their nearest support 300 yards away, they found themselves virtually surrounded, forcing the Lewis gunner to fire first up the road, then across the valley and then down the road. German troops 'were thick in Luc and Long Woods. Up the valley came several hundred with many machine guns, and on this front the 42nd, now holding a 2000 yard front with 250 men, fell back several hundred yards to behind the Proyart–Bray road.'[2]

By the time the 42nd were relieved by the British Army's Sherwood Foresters on 12 August, fifty per cent of the battalion had suffered casualties,[3] but they had achieved their objectives, to clear the areas north-east of Proyart towards Chuignolles.

Haig was keen to continue the advance, and had decided on two separate offensives. The first, to the south, was to occur at dawn on 15 August with the Fourth British and First French armies attacking Chaulnes, east of Lihons, and the area north and east of Roye. The second offensive, on 20 August, would see the Third British Army, with the addition of four infantry and two cavalry divisions plus 200 tanks, attack towards the large town of Bapaume north of the Somme.

The Australian part in the first operation was to provide the 4th and 5th Divisions to advance on the northern flank. On the night of 14 August, these two divisions moved up and relieved the 1st Division south of the railway. However, on 13 August, the planned attack was delayed a day, and on 14 August, it was delayed indefinitely. General Currie was unhappy about his Canadian troops advancing across the old battlefields, against thick belts of wire with high potential casualties. Instead, he wanted his divisions returned to the area they knew, the Arras front.

The AIF was then shuffled about the battlefield, with the 4th Division relieving the Canadian 1st Division at the southern end of the line on the 16th and, two days later, the 5th Division relieving the British 17th Division south of the Roman road. Meanwhile, the French to the south had continued their progress, advancing over one mile on a seven-mile front south of the Canadians, near Roye. Orders then came down that the Australians were to halt their advance and, except for continued nibbling and peaceful penetration, were to bring the line up ready for the next stage of the advance. The 2nd Division held a front of 3000 yards, with the 6th Brigade holding the line. Further south, the 4th Division held a line near Madame Wood, nearly two miles north of Lihons, advancing up old trenches. On 17 August, they occupied the German positions in Lihu Farm near Auger Wood.

Now, facing the next village, Herleville, were three Victorian battalions of the 6th Brigade – the 22nd, 23rd and 24th – with the 22nd spread across the brigade front. Around Herleville, the Germans held a series of trenches, including a sunken road, and orders were issued for an attack by these battalions at 4.15 am on 18 August. During the recent advance, the Australian battalions had been decimated, with the 22nd's three companies having thirty, twenty-four and thirty-six men instead of 250 each. Only 120 men could be mustered for the attack on a front of over half a mile and, of them, thirty had to remain to hold the front line in case of counterattack.

As soon as the men rose to advance, they were hit with heavy machine-gun and artillery fire. Twelve of the thirty men in 'D' Company went down immediately. Lieutenant Leo McCartin, MC, a draper from Geelong, directed his men to the objective and held on until he was relieved later in the morning. He was twice wounded in the attack and, in attempting to return across open country to report his position, was again shot. He made his report and again set out across the open country to get back to his men, but never arrived and was afterward found dead. He was buried in Heath Cemetery, but later fighting disturbed his grave.

After the 6th Brigade had pushed the Germans back 800 yards, the enemy began to fight back, as noted in the brigade's war diary:

'this occasioned grave resentment by the enemy who vigorously counter-attacked, driving our attacking force back and reducing our gains to five hundred yards.'[4]

The 6th Brigade was relieved on the night of 19–20 August by the British 32nd Division, who reinforced the line with two brigades, a much stronger force than the 1200 Australians who had held this dangerous section of the line previously.

The 21st Battalion, who had 'overran a German Headquarters, dumps, hospitals, heavy batteries and even railway trains', added that 'Souvenirs were plentiful.'[5] They were relieved and returned to the bank of the Somme at Daours. The men enjoyed a rest and clean clothes: 'all the fish had been bombed out long ago, but the swimming was good.'[6]

The Australians learnt two lessons from the attack: first, that aggressive patrolling needed to be continued until an hour before zero hour, as it was found that the Germans, in the night before the advance, were in greater strength than previously believed. Thanks to patrolling work this information was able to be included in further planning, saving the Australians a potential massacre later on. Second, the Australians realised they were not to underestimate the German defences, morale and the strength of their resolve, as their resistance had stiffened in the days following the initial advance. Even during this difficult and costly retreat, the Germans remained a tough and wily enemy.

Outside of Lihons, the 4th Brigade was fighting through the woods and holding a line of posts. The Germans bombarded the woods and the immediate rear areas, with a 5.9-inch shell smashing the 13th Battalion cooker and killing CSM Joe Meek, 'one of our bravest',[7] and wounding three men.

On the night of 18 August, the Australian 6th Brigade was relieved by the British. This movement was the prelude to two days of heavy shelling, which limited peaceful penetration and further nibbling. As the 13th's battalion history states, 'We had to sit under this unmerciful shelling. These days he [the enemy] spared neither front nor rear, but poured H.E. [high explosive] and gas shells into us day and night. The weather had been very hot and dusty, the traffic having cut up the roads and fields. Gas masks on top of this added to the discomfort.'[8]

By 21 August, news began to arrive along the Australian front of the success of the British and French attack, and the fallback of the Germans all along their line. At various times, German prisoners had mentioned that the German army was retiring to the Hindenburg Line. Despite this, the Allies still encountered staunch resistance by the Germans. On 23 August, when the 4th Brigade once again attacked Madame Wood, south of Vermandovillers, 'great was the astonishment of all to find the Bosche fighting as gamely as at any period of the war, several severe hand-to-hand encounters taking place, and every foot of trench being stubbornly contested, but those diggers who revelled in tough propositions were delighted, and the contempt they had recently begun to feel for Fritz changed to admiration.'[9]

Further north, closer to the Somme, the 1st Brigade moved up east of Méricourt-sur-Somme, with the 3rd Battalion located just south of the town in old trenches. Over the next few days, their advance would take them from north of Proyart, through Arcy Wood and Chuignolles, and on past Chuignes to form a line south of the river.

It was during this advance that the battalion came upon the massive German fourteen-inch naval gun hidden in Arcy

Wood that, along with the railway gun already captured near Harbonnières, had been firing on Amiens since June. Although it had already been spiked by the Germans, Monash said it would be 'the largest single trophy of the war won by any commander during the war'.[10] He added that, 'it was a matter of great regret to me that the cost of its transportation to Australia was prohibitive.'[11]

With the success of the Australian advance on the north of the Somme, by 23 August, the line now stretched from Herleville, west of the Froissy plateau south of the river, and onto the heights north of the Somme around Curlu. Bean makes an interesting point that at this time, 'for a day and a half, the [Australian] Corps held a front of 30,000 yards (17 miles).'[12]

Further north, the British III Corps had recaptured Albert, but its advance had been slow and Haig was forced to rethink his plans. He ordered two separate advances; first, the Third Army towards Bapaume, and second, the Australians to reach and pass the Froissy plateau and go for the bridgeheads on the Somme ready for the attack on Péronne.

Following the capture of the German naval gun and Arcy Wood, the 1st Brigade was to take Chuignes. Bean mentions that 'this attack, south of the Somme, though delivered by only two divisions, was one of the hardest blows ever struck by Australian troops,'[13] and the battalion history records that they 'fought with bull-dog tenacity, the individual bravery of the Diggers being quite outstanding'.[14] The casualties, however, were high, with the 3rd Battalion's 'C' Company suffering four officers and sixty ORs from the five officers and 100 men who went into the attack. Other companies of the 3rd Battalion also suffered high casualties in the taking of Chuignes.

Over the next four days, by revolving attacking companies within the 1st Brigade, the Australians were able to advance the line 2500 yards beyond Chuignes, including the taking of Cappy on the river. During the advance, the battalion captured four German officers and 155 men, along with six guns, fifteen machine guns and six trench mortars.

Further south, astride the Roman road, the 2nd Brigade started their advance. Here the Victorians needed to deal with St Martins Wood, thick with German machine guns, with good fields of fire across two open, small flat valleys (the Rainecourt and Herleville gullies) that crossed the road north to south at this point. The brigade attack went in on 23 August with the 4th and 5th Battalions, supported by the 7th, north of the Roman road, and the 6th Battalion, supported by the 8th, south of the road. The supporting twelve tanks were to go around the wood, with four of them passing through it in the hope of cutting off the enemy.

As the Victorians advanced, the German barrage came down behind the two leading battalions, falling instead on the two rear battalions who had to move steadily forward through a curtain of rising dust and smoke. In the 8th Battalion, about thirty men were hit, and the 7th Battalion had nine casualties.

As the Australians emerged from the smoke, closing on the woods, German machine guns fired on them, but men ran forward, immediately attacking the guns or directing Stokes mortars to suppress this devastating fire. The tanks also played an important role, with one tank commander reporting twenty German machine guns in just 100 yards of front, and how, 'after a desperate fight',[15] he could eliminate them or drive off their crews.

North of the road, the 5th Battalion, and on their left the 4th Battalion, kept pushing forward, but two machine guns firing along the line of the road held up the advance on the south side. The 8th Battalion had been temporarily demoralised by their high casualties and they and the 6th Battalion, who were now leaderless, were quickly organised by Lieutenant William Joynt. He led a bayonet charge on the German machine guns in St Martins Wood, capturing the wood along with eighty prisoners. Then, at Plateau Wood nearby to the south, Joynt attacked again with the remnants of the battalions, forcing the further surrender of German gunners. In the days after, he was severely wounded and evacuated to England, where he saw out the war. For his leadership, Joynt was awarded the Victoria Cross.

On the same day, a little further south, the 16th Battalion was held up in their attack on Madame Wood. As the battalion advanced towards the small village of Vermandovillers, north of Lihons, in support of the British 32nd Division, they secured their objective, but the British on their right were held up by German machine-gun fire, which quickly threatened the 16th Battalion's flank. The attack evolved into a bomb fight, with the 16th's bombers and the Germans fighting over a trench block.

Lieutenant Lawrence McCarthy arrived to see what was holding up the advance and, after being told of the delay, he realised the only thing to do was directly attack the guns. With his mate, Sergeant Fred Robbins, DCM, MM, McCarthy charged across open ground and into the first section of trench, where he came upon a wire entanglement blocking the trench. First he shot a German sentry and then, racing on, captured the first machine gun by shooting the gun crew that was enfilading the Australian trench fifty yards away. McCarthy continued his mad charge along the trench. Around a bend, he came upon a German officer rallying his men, so McCarthy shot him. He raced on, capturing three more enemy machine guns and inflicting more casualties.

With Robbins on his heels, McCarthy made contact with the 16th Lancashire Fusiliers briefly, but continued to the last trench. Herding Germans into a sap, he hurled the last of his grenades among them, and soon a white handkerchief appeared above the trench and forty Germans surrendered. Behind them lay fifteen dead. As he entered the trench, the surrendering Germans closed around him and relieved him of his revolver, but, after patting him on the back, they filed back into captivity. By this audacious action, McCarthy had seized 500 yards of trench line and captured about fifty Germans. McCarthy was awarded the Victoria Cross, and returned to Australia in December 1919 after getting married in England.

Back to the north, with the capture of Chuignolles by 5.30 am on 23 August, the 1st Brigade moved forward with the support of twelve Mark V tanks. Soon, however, machine-gun fire was coming from the large wood to the east of the village, and the Australians had to withdraw as heavy Allied shelling pounded the German positions. On the right, the 4th Battalion followed five tanks as they moved forward with the barrage. The German artillery response fell behind them and, with the support of the tanks, the Australians were able to 'follow closely to the barrage and thus complete surprise and quick dealing with the enemy enabled the advance to continue'.[16]

By the early afternoon, the 3rd Battalion passed through the 1st Battalion. To maintain the advance, they called for a barrage as they moved south-east from Marly Wood. They were quickly resupplied by carrier tanks bringing up small-arms ammunition, grenades, flares, Stokes mortar bombs, sandbags, wire, screw pickets and picks and shovels. Tanks also contributed to the success with the war diary noting, 'great help was given to the infantry, again providing that the tank when well supported by the infantry, is an invention much dreaded by the enemy.'[17] The casualties for the 1st Brigade, however, were six officers and eighty-three men killed, eighteen officers and 433 men wounded, one officer and seventy-two men gassed and twenty-eight men missing. In a separate attack by the 2nd Brigade, immediately south of Proyart, they suffered four officers and seventy-nine men killed, twenty-one officers and 343 wounded, eight officers and 399 gassed and nineteen men missing.

While the Germans' resistance was increasing, they were also taking high casualties. The Australian attacks south of the Somme had decimated three German divisions, troops that had been told they were facing tired Allied soldiers. The historian of the 87th German Infantry Regiment reported that these 'tired' troops were instead 'Great strong figures with dash and enterprise' and, referring to the success of Australian peaceful penetration, he added, 'these Australians do not give the impression of a worn out Division.'[18] Some German troops held defensive lines briefly; at other points the Australians were momentarily stalled, some German reports stating they were driven back. For the German 232nd Regiment, 23 August was 'the most fateful day of the whole campaign',with the historian of the German 28th Infantry Regiment lamenting, 'The fight was too bitter for taking prisoners.'[19]

In the advance on the village of Cappy, the 12th Battalion formed up in a gully east of St Germaine Wood, and from there they followed the 1st and 2nd Brigades into the attack. Zero hour was at 4.45 am and, within ten minutes, a German barrage of 5.9-inch shells was falling in the gully, causing about fifty casualties. At 1 pm, the Australians moved into a position north of Chuignolles but were seen by the enemy, who subjected their ranks to severe machine-gun fire from Long and Marly woods. At 2 pm, the Allied barrage came down. This allowed Long Wood to be attacked, and parties of enemy were mopped up. Fire was still coming from nearby Marly Wood and when it was cleared, fire immediately began from the next wood, Gareene Wood, which was quickly encircled, with seventy Germans captured.

The Germans were now falling back to Cappy, taking heavy casualties as they fled. Some Germans found shelter in a house, but this was attacked by Lieutenant Edward Norrie and an NCO, who, 'firing through the window of a house into a crowd of Germans penned there, captured 37 and two machine guns'.[20] By evening, the Australians were close to the village and exploring the old trenches, which would allow them cover as they moved east. The following, day, 24 August, was quiet as patrols went out, testing the enemy and looking for dead ground and cover from which to continue their advance.

During this day, a 12th Battalion officer found a trench running from the south-east corner of Gareene Wood in a north-westerly direction that would provide cover. Taking his company into the trench, they encountered a bomb block, and here they engaged the enemy. The company quickly pushed the enemy back 150 yards and consolidated their new position along a line just east of Square Wood, across and around Gareene Wood and down further to the northern side of Chuignes. It had been a good couple of days but, again, the casualties were high.

★

By the close of 25 August, the Allies had secured a great victory. In the north, the Third Army had driven the Germans back to Loupart Wood on the edge of Bapaume and, further south, the Fourth Army had advanced from Albert eastwards towards Pozières and across the fateful battlefields of the 1916 Somme campaign. Over these days, the Allies had captured 8000 prisoners, 2000 of whom were taken by the Australians. Haig now abandoned his methodical tactic of advance, suggesting instead that each division be given an objective which they must pursue, independent of the advance of their neighbours on the flanks. He concluded, 'The situation is most favourable. Let each one of us act energetically, and without hesitation push forward to our objective.'[21]

While the AIF's 3rd Division continued their advance on the north side of the Somme, cutting off the retreating Germans and pushing east, the 1st Division also continued moving eastwards south of the river.

By this time the Australians had been heavily involved in fighting for over two weeks and, even though short breaks behind the line had been offered, the infantry and artillery units were exhausted. Monash knew this, but was keen to push his men to the limit, towards the Somme bridgeheads and the heights of Mont St Quentin, and with the aim of clearing Péronne of the enemy. Rather than setpiece attacks, he wanted aggressive patrolling and the concentration of artillery firing on back areas and German lines of communication.

To progress the attack, Monash advocated peaceful penetration. This meant utilising the old trench systems, in particular communication trenches which radiated back and provided ideal protection. The Germans, realising the vulnerability in their line, established trench or bomb blocks which halted the ease of this advance, resulting in savage bomb fights and hand-to-hand fighting.

In an example of what could go wrong with this less centrally coordinated approach, the 12th Battalion, with the support of the 11th, pushed up the communication trench north of the Chuignes gully and through what was referred to as Canard Wood, 'gaining bend after bend of the trench to a point, 1100 yards due east of the start'.[22] They were mistaken for Germans by a company of the 11th Battalion, and were fired on and shelled. Fortunately, the 9th Battalion had pushed the enemy from the river flats, beyond Cappy, to prevent fire coming from that quarter.

Nevertheless, the pressure put on the Germans through the combined force of the infantry, artillery, tanks and aircraft was paying off. Late on the night of 24 August, the Germans again fell back to a new line along the edge of the Olympia Wood and Fontaine road. But the Germans were subjecting the Australians to shelling by high explosive and gas, possibly to expend their stock of shells rather than allow them to fall into the hands of the advancing Allies. On 25 August, the 10th and 11th Battalions relieved the exhausted 9th and 12th Battalions, and after a delay, they moved forward again at 6 am the following morning. By the evening of 26 August, the 10th Battalion was between Frise and Dompierre-Becquincourt on the south bank of the Somme. In this advance, 'captures in prisoners or material were necessarily small on account of the elusive nature of the enemy defences, but the operation was carried out with only one man killed and five men wounded, while of the enemy, a much larger number were killed and wounded and two prisoners taken.'[23]

Further south, the 2nd Brigade advance continued, although the Australians on the Roman road had slowed after heavy shelling, particularly with gas, had left them in no condition to keep moving. At the southern end of the line, the French had replaced the 4th Division, which added to Monash's strength. He now sought to drive forward with two divisions, the 2nd and the 5th, to overcome the impediments to his advance. Haig cancelled these plans, however, instead focusing the Allied effort on the advances further north by the British Third and Fourth Armies. The Australians needed to proceed slowly and wait, but they wouldn't have to wait for long.

ELEVEN

Mont St Quentin: What Presumption

By the end of August 1918, the Germans had been pushed back sixteen miles from their line of 8 August, having suffered serious, irreplaceable casualties and lost a massive amount of weapons, stores and transport. From north of Arras to south of Chaulnes, they had suffered defeat and retreat, and were now desperately trying to hold a line north of the Somme stretching up through Rancourt and Bapaume, and on to Arras. In the Australian section of the line, the Germans' fragile defence was east of Cléry and up to the ridgeline stretching north-east to Bouchavesnes-Bergen and south to the Roman road.

Events were escalating quickly, and the German strategic future was looking grimmer by the day. In the north, the Canadians had driven through to the Hindenburg Line east of Arras and the French, Americans and even the Belgians were starting to manoeuvre into stronger positions north and south of the Australians, ready to continue the offensive. The old battle-fields of the Somme with their iconic, bloody placenames again came into contention as the Allies advanced: Albert, 22 August; Thiepval, 24 August; Mametz Wood, 25 August; Delville Wood, 27 August. On 29 August, Bapaume fell to the New Zealanders and the rolling Allied storm continued unabated. Now Haig was keen to see the advance move north into the First Army's front, and ordered the transfer of artillery and men to assist this offensive.

To add to their woes, the German army was disorganised, exhausted, demoralised and hungry. Letters from home revealed the impact of the Allied submarine blockade and the desperate hunger of the civilian population. Men had also been combed out of civilian jobs and conscripted, women were forced to work and the loss of two million men left wives without financial support and reliant on meagre government pensions. As news of the shortages on the home front filtered through, it severely undermined the morale of the German army.

In the Australian sector, Rawlinson was heeding Haig's wish to slow the advance, confused as to whether the Germans were reinforcing their front or retreating. Rawlinson's Fourth Army would 'mark time and wait for events elsewhere'.[1] But Monash, even with his exhausted and drastically reduced battalions, still wanted to force the pace. He could also point to Rawlinson's order that, 'Touch must be kept with the enemy,'[2] and used this as his excuse for continuing aggressive patrolling. Above all, Monash believed in his AIF, their spirit, their invincibility, their 'reserve of striking power'[3] and their hunger for victory and glory.

Monash was also keen to include two innovations in artillery practice, introduced to him by the 5th Division's General Talbot Hobbs and the 3rd Division's General John Gellibrand, themselves artillery officers. The first innovation was to include smoke shells in a ratio of one to five to cover the advance of the infantry in an attack. The second was to allow battalion commanders to control and direct artillery batteries for their own immediate purpose. These changes would allow for Monash's next advance, which would involve the taking of Péronne and the strategically important Mont St Quentin. However, he still needed Rawlinson's permission.

Rawlinson well understood Monash and his pride in the AIF. He also knew that the battalions were severely depleted and needed rest. When Rawlinson raised this, Monash's response was that, 'It was no longer merely a question of earmarking certain divisions for a specific operation; but of planning many days ahead, the rotation in which the divisions were to be employed in a continuous series of operations.'[4] General Hobbs had also pressed the need for rest of his exhausted battalions, but Monash later wrote, 'I was compelled to harden my heart.'[5] He even went as far as confiding to General Gellibrand that 'casualties no longer mattered',[6] a surprising admission since his evolving strategies usually looked to save lives.

By 29 August, the Australians had closed on Péronne, had isolated a pocket of Germans on the south side of the Somme opposite the town and, after taking Cléry-sur-Somme, were now poised to turn south and attack Mont St Quentin and Péronne. Here was the great opportunity for Monash to strike, with only the river, and possibly Rawlinson, standing in his way. Péronne was a great strategic prize, the laurels of which would go to his all-conquering AIF and the credit of success, of course, to him.

The following day, Monash met with Rawlinson to seek permission for the attack. Monash later wrote that Rawlinson, after hearing in detail Monash's plans, said, 'So you think you are going to take Mont St Quentin with three battalions! What presumption. However, I don't think I ought to stop you! So, go ahead and try! – and I wish you luck.'[7]

The immediate problem for Monash was getting his battalions across the Somme. Between Corbie and Cléry-sur-Somme, the Somme meandered in an east–west direction, but at Cléry-sur-

Somme it now turned north–south, with Mont St Quentin and Péronne on the eastern bank. Most of the bridges had been blown up by the Germans, but Australian engineers had succeeded in repairing some, and building pontoon crossings and small single-file personnel bridges across the river marshland, which required causeways, and the Somme canal. Monash had originally proposed crossing the canal at Omiécourt-les-Cléry, but the Germans had partially blown up the bridge there. So desperate was the German commander to ensure the bridge was completely destroyed that he offered an Iron Cross, money and a good stretch of leave to the man who could finish the job. While a small party tried, they did not succeed.

Another problem for Monash was the German machine guns on the high ground to the north-east. They needed to be eliminated, as did the last German resistance in Omiécourt-les-Cléry. As a result, Monash delayed the attack for one day, then ordered a safer crossing of the Somme canal at Feuillères, requiring a two-mile march through Cléry-sur-Somme to the start line.

At 3 am on the morning of 31 August, the attacking battalions of the 2nd Division's 5th Brigade established a battalion head-quarters near Cléry-sur-Somme, and meetings of company commanders were held. Of the four battalions to attack Mont St Quentin, the 19th Battalion was on the right, attacking across the slope towards Uber Alles and Gott Mit Uns trenches; the 17th in the middle, attacking straight up Mont St Quentin; and the 20th on the left, attacking across the face of the hill towards the village of Feuillaucourt, north of the mount. The plan was that the 6th Brigade – the 21st, 22nd, 23rd and 24th Battalions – would push through the 5th Brigade on Mont St Quentin and 'thrust deeper along the crest'.[8]

Meanwhile, the 7th Brigade, holding the line opposite Péronne, would be relieved by the 15th Brigade, along with the rest of the

5th Division, who were to then attack Péronne and drive through to the hills beyond Doingt. In the north, the 3rd Division, having worked along the northern bank of the Somme, would push north-east up the Bouchavesnes ridge to protect the 2nd Division flank. To their north, the British 58th Division of III Corps would advance towards Rancourt. Monash's plan had now evolved into a flanking attack through Cléry-sur-Somme, as the hoped-for bridges and causeways could not be constructed and maintained under German artillery fire.

A major issue in this grand plan remained the condition of the men and their reduced battalions. On 27 August, Monash, addressing his divisional commanders, had stated that each attacking brigade was 'to be kept in the line till it had reached the limit of its endurance'.[9] Beyond the three brigades designated to directly attack Mont St Quentin, the whole Australian Corps – infantry, gunners and the vast support staff and supply line – remained exhausted. The war diary of the 17th Battalion, who were in the middle of the attack, noted, 'the men were so fatigued and sleepy that even officers almost fell asleep standing up.'[10] One of the company commanders even fell asleep while being briefed for the 5 am assault. Monash's disregard for the state of the men was deeply resented.

The attacking battalions were also severely understrength. From a full strength of 1000 officers and men, the 17th Battalion was down to eighteen officers and 357 other ranks, the 19th Battalion had about sixteen officers and 200 men, and the 20th Battalion had eighteen officers and 302 men. Companies, usually consisting of 250 men, were down to fifty to seventy men.

As the minutes ticked away to zero hour on 31 August, few officers and men felt they had any real chance of success in the assault ahead. They knew that the objective, 2400 yards ahead, was a difficult one, and Mont St Quentin was a formidable fortress well known for its strong defensive position, its strategic importance and the fact that it was defended by elite Prussian Guards. Facing a numerically superior force that was dug in and protected by artillery, trench mortars and hundreds of machine guns, the future looked grim. Indeed, Bean wrote, 'The task ahead was in some ways the most formidable ever faced by the Australian infantry.'[11]

The men had not had a hot meal in two days, and were surviving on dry rations and anything they could scrounge. They were, however, given a small rum ration, procured from headquarters after an order went back; the commanding officer himself had warned the men not to return without the rum. The 17th Battalion history adds, 'Then two more runners were sent back by an alternative route with a similar order.'[12] As hoped, each of the three pairs of runners came back with rum jars.

Around this time it was decided that should the advance be held up, 'the company concerned should simply rush the position, making as much noise as possible.'[13] Captain Ernest Manefield of the 17th had suggested the advancing men 'yell like a lot of bushrangers'.[14]

At 3.30 am, the four companies of the 17th Battalion left their forming-up position and advanced to the assembly area in Park Wood. Initially, heavy fire was encountered from the wood, but the battalion had few casualties, as 'the tactics agreed upon [of yelling] had the effect of causing the enemy to surrender freely.'[15]

The barrage opened at 5 am along the whole front, with eighteen-pound guns putting down the main barrage while the heavier guns undertook counter-battery work. The main barrage fell nearly a mile ahead of the advancing troops, as it was believed that the enemy trench lines and strongpoints needed to be engaged rather than having a creeping barrage in front. The bombardment fell along the arc of the German Gottlieb Trench, around the bottom of the slope, then half an hour later moved to the next defensive line higher on the mount. Meanwhile, the heavy artillery pounded the summit and likely German strongpoints and targets along the two sloping flanks.

With the 17th tasked to attack the mount directly, they started their advance astride the Péronne–Cléry-sur-Somme road, quickly running into German posts and machine-gun positions, 'but the troops when they saw them, charged with a yell and the Germans, obviously astonished, hardly attempted defence; they simply passed through the advancing lines as prisoners.'[16] This rapid advance raised the morale of the exhausted diggers, driving them on, and they yelled as they raced towards the German line. Though the German defenders were all volunteers from the elite 2nd Prussian Guard, with orders to hold the hill 'to the death', they had only arrived in their position an hour before. Surprised and quickly overrun, they were soon retiring in large numbers back up the hill or were taken captive.

Prisoners in large numbers soon became an embarrassment. Stupefied by the rapidity of the advance, many Germans did little to defend their position and merely surrendered without firing a shot. As men were needed for the advance, there was a shortage of Allied escorts; prisoners were simply ordered to the rear, leaving their machine guns unguarded where they lay. Captain Herbert Allan of the 17th remarked:

I saw hundreds of prisoners streaming down in our direction from Mont St Quentin, and I remember thinking that it reminded me of the mob leaving the Sydney Cricket Ground after a football final. I 'chatted' to one of my NCOs who was moving back with prisoners and told him we were all wanted forward. He replied 'Have a heart Sir! I've got a General here. Take a look at the beautiful spurs he's got. If I don't take him back, some of those blasted base-wallahs will get them'. So I let him go.[17]

The Australians' attacking spirit was seen in the dash of Lance Corporal Olaf Stranlund, a labourer from North Sydney, who, alone, raced across fifty yards of exposed ground and, though shot in the ankle, took a machine-gun post, killing the crew. Nearby, Sergeant James Rixon, in a similar lone dash, attacked a machine-gun post, killing three gunners and capturing the rest.

Australian troops threw themselves on the ground and fired into the backs of the retreating enemy, then charged on to rush the next trench. Many of these trenches contained the fleeing enemy, who had run till they were unable to maintain the pace, before waiting to be captured, breathless and frightened. Initially there was little retaliatory fire from the Germans, but once the barrage passed the German defenders, they opened on the thin, advancing line of the 17th Battalion from Park Wood on the Australians' right flank.

Realising the danger these machine guns posed, Captain Herbert Allan led 'A' Company to clear the wood. They moved forward in small groups as machine guns cut into their ranks, taking immediate casualties. They pressed on, clearing Park Wood and the small village of Halle, but were then fired on from Prague and Florina trenches. Allan withdrew his men to Galatz Alley to form a strong defensive flank for the brigade.

To the right of the 17th, the 19th was advancing towards the German trenches lower on the hill. They had crossed the Somme on hastily made single-file bridges, but they were briefly shelled as they formed up on the eastern bank until Australian guns subdued the German artillery. For the first stage of their dash, behind the barrage, the 19th had few casualties. Once they started on the sloping ground south-west of the mount, however, they came under fire from Anvil Wood on their right and the German trench systems at Galatz and Agram Alley. The 19th quickly overran the German front line, taking many prisoners, but also sustaining casualties due to the shallow trenches and accurate sniping by the enemy.

At 5 am, the 20th Battalion had attacked on the northern flank. They went forward 'at the quickest possible pace in order to cover the 800 yards between the jumping off line and the barrage line'.[18] The battalion war diary notes, 'During this rush across, considerable opposition was encountered, but so high were the spirits of the troops, that they speedily overcame same, and when the enemy saw that our troops really meant business, they surrendered themselves readily in order to avoid coming to close quarters.'[19] The battalion had no difficulty following the barrage and securing their objective, including the village of Feuillaucourt. They were now able to connect with the 17th Battalion on their right who were, in turn, able to connect with the 19th on their right.

By 4 pm, the Australians' position was consolidated. The intelligence officers had verified they were on their objectives, and carrying parties came forward. At this time, a carrying party arrived at the 18th Battalion line, consisting of twelve men delivering 6000 rounds of small-arms ammunition and twelve boxes of grenades.

Meanwhile, the 17th Battalion was taking heavy fire from the brick wall that surrounded the western side of the mount, and they stopped their advance until this obstacle was dealt with by the artillery. It was at this point that the 19th linked up with the remnants of the 17th on their left, finding cover in Elsa and Leus trenches with other isolated parties in Agram and Save trenches.

At 7.30 pm, the enemy assembled and counterattacked, but this attempt was broken up by Stokes mortar, artillery and Vickers fire, causing the Germans to disperse. The Australians were in precarious positions, however, with their flanks open, in exposed, shallow trenches below the Germans and running out of food, water and ammunition. They were also continually sniped at, making movement of the men difficult and dangerous. By the end of the day, fifty per cent of the 17th Battalion (eight officers and 151 other ranks) had suffered casualties.

Nonetheless, Major Lesley Fussell, the Commanding Officer of the 17th Battalion, reported to 5th Brigade Headquarters, 'Seventeenth well on objective. Enemy barrage on the western flank slopes of Mont St Quentin gradually shortening and not very heavy.'[20] In the advance, the officers had moved ahead of their men, waving them on and inspiring them with their dash and leadership. At one point, Lieutenant William Flood's platoon was held up by a machine gun so he ran forward alone, killed two of the gun crew and, with the aid of his platoon, captured twenty-two prisoners and the gun. Young Lieutenant Frederick Croft, realising the danger to the battalion's flank, organised his men and, after consolidating his position, was able to drive back several determined German counterattacks. With Croft was an original Anzac, Sergeant Magnus McKay, who assisted in the organisation of the platoon, often exposing himself to dangerous fire to ensure his men were safely and strategically spread out.

No contact was made with the 20th Battalion on their left, however, and the Germans quickly counterattacked under a barrage of 77-millimetre guns, mortars and machine-gun fire. The 17th were quickly overrun, losing all of their officers, and the order was given to withdraw to a trench system eighty yards below the road. This line was defended by eight Lewis guns and two Vickers guns, which were able to beat off five enemy attacks, leaving many dead. Soon prisoners began coming back, with the 20th Battalion having captured 600. The prisoners were sent to the rear under minimal sentries, who were themselves often walking wounded, as men were desperately needed in the line and could not be spared. The war diary of the 18th Battalion, who had been waiting in reserve, states, 'Prisoners seem of a very solid stamp though many are youngsters . . . very superior looking individuals – but never-theless common HUNS. They are absolutely tongue-tied and seem very little inclined to give information.'[21] One captured German officer chatted easily with the Australians, telling them that a well-known Melbourne polo player was one of his best friends. Another prisoner told how he was conscripted while holidaying in Germany, and when he met the Australians he said, 'Well I guess I am glad to be here.'[22]

At 9.10 am on 31 August, the 18th Battalion was ordered forward to the east of Cléry-sur-Somme in support of the 17th Battalion, but were heavily shelled. German artillery were bracketing all likely targets along the line of advance for the reinforcements along the river, the railway and the main road. Further movement forward for the 18th became difficult. They were forced to remain exposed for the night, but ration and ammunition parties were guided in. For their brief time in the line, the battalion had two officers and sixteen men killed, and a further three officers and fifty-seven men wounded.

Now high on the slopes of Mont St Quentin, with vastly diminished numbers, exhausted and short on ammunition and bombs, the remnants of the 5th Brigade were strung out in a thin line. Gradually Germans began to infiltrate their line of posts on the eastern side of the road and get behind them. Unable to see their nearby mates, the 17th began to trickle back across the road to Elsa Trench. There was still no contact with the 20th Battalion on their left, so two young lieutenants, George Small and John Richardson, set out to link up with them, but they were both killed by a German mortar bomb. As the German shelling increased, two companies of the 18th Battalion, who were now able to move forward, were rushed to the 17th's left flank, just in time as the enemy launched a sudden counterattack on the struggling remnants of the 17th. Though low on ammunition, they fired into the advancing lines of Germans and held their ground.

It was while the 17th was tenaciously holding on that the 20th Battalion took enfilade fire from Feuillaucourt to their north. The 3rd Division, who were meant to push up to protect their flank, was late, having been stalled in their advance. Now finding themselves in a dangerous and precarious position, the 20th Battalion's commander, Major McDonald, moved his men carefully down the slope to a new position a few hundred yards further back, towards the river. The new line formed a salient, with the 20th and men from the 18th holding the line in the north, the 17th still facing Mont St Quentin in Elsa Trench below the summit, and the 19th with men from the 18th holding the right flank in Park Wood and on the outskirts of Halle.

Along with their frontal attacks, the Germans were now reinforcing their line. Enemy troops were seen advancing in twos and threes and settling in a newly dug trench on the sloping face of the hill. At this time, a young forward observation officer arrived at Brigade Headquarters looking for targets, and this new German position was pointed out to him. An Australian officer suggested high explosive, but the artillery man called for shrapnel. Somewhat put out, the Australian officer bet the artillery man that there would be no dead Germans as a result of the shrapnel, but an inspection of the trench the following day found twenty-one dead Germans and one wounded. As he noted, 'Let none question the hitting power of the 18-pounders of ours.'[23]

The second major line of attack on 31 August was to the north of Mont St Quentin, against the villages of Feuillaucourt and Bouchavesnes. Here the Australian 3rd Division, with the 9th, 10th and 11th Brigades, were supporting the British 58th Division to their north, with the attack on Marrières Wood beginning at 5.10 am. The 9th Brigade's 33rd Battalion advance began at 5.40 am towards Road Wood, where they were quickly stopped by heavy machine-gun fire. This held up the advance of the two leading companies, so Private George Cartwright stood up and fired at the troublesome gun. He then moved forward under fire, threw a bomb into the gun pit and captured nine Germans and their gun. From his lines his mates cheered, and rushed forward into the wood in the wake of Cartwright's gallant attack, for which he was awarded the Victoria Cross.

The 33rd Battalion was now bombing its way towards the Bapaume–Péronne road, at the northern end of the 1916 Spur. Here they came across six German field guns lined along the road and attacked them, driving off the gunners, then crossed the road to the command quarry beyond. Within the quarry, they forced the surrender of a further forty Germans. Just to their right, three battalions of the 10th Brigade were also making for the road and they too came under heavy machine-gun and artillery fire as they pushed towards Zombor and Inferno trenches.

It was here that Monash, fearing enfilading fire on Mont St Quentin from the Bouchavesnes ridgeline, gave an order to advance regardless of casualties, as he'd earlier confessed to Gellibrand might be necessary. By this time, the 10th Brigade's 40th Battalion had pushed across the road. They fought with bomb and bayonet, and 'with great dash and determination against superior numbers'.[24] Many Germans ran, and the Australians captured thirty-four prisoners. The battalion history notes, 'A large percentage of the prisoners wore the ribbon of the Iron Cross.'[25] The Australians advanced another 400 yards to Quarry Farm, but were again forced back.

In German records, this counterattack was seen as proof that 'even good Australian troops were by no means invincible if strongly attacked'.[26] Lower down the slope, at Feuillaucourt, the 20th Battalion was also being pushed back to the road. For the Australians, the order was to straighten the line ready for the renewed attack the following day.

Back in Monash's headquarters, all were celebrating a successful advance. The Germans had expected an attack from the west, directly towards the high ground, or from the south near Péronne, but because the line of advance had been forced to move through Cléry-sur-Somme rather than across the Somme, Monash had attacked from the north. This movement had confounded the defence. The rapidity of the attack, and the fact that a creeping barrage had not warned the Germans of the timing and direction of the attack, had also left them unprepared. They were confronted by a yelling, bayonet-wielding, determined group of Australians, and even their elite troops were overrun, despatched or sent back as prisoners. Many were found in trenches up the slope, breathless and exhausted, too tired to move and too afraid to speak. Bean notes, 'Ahead, along the whole face of the front, Germans were running back.'[27]

The consolidation continued in Gottleib and Elsa trenches. Though they also remained exhausted, the Australians were elated with their success. So, too, was General Rawlinson. When he heard the news, back near Amiens, he said, 'It was indeed a magnificent performance.'[28] He later called it 'the finest single feat of the war'.[29]

The congratulatory message from Rawlinson to the 2nd Division read:

> The capture of Mont St Quentin by the Second Division is a
> feat of arms worthy of the highest praise. The natural strength
> of the position is immense, and the tactical value of it, in
> reference to Peronne and the whole system of the Somme
> defences, cannot be overestimated. I am filled with admiration
> at the gallantry and surpassing daring of the Second Division
> in winning this important fortress, and I congratulate them
> with all my heart.[30]

In one reported exchange between Monash and Rawlinson, the conversation went as follows:

> Monash: By the way, we are on top of Mont St Quentin.
> Rawlinson: I don't believe it.
> Monash: Come and see.
> Rawlinson: You have altered the whole course of the war.[31]

The Germans were also astonished. One German report noted, 'It all happened like lightning, and before we had fired a shot, we were taken unawares,'[32] while another noted, 'Hardly had the alarm of battle been heard than the relived troops of the 81st [German Regiment] poured right through the company immediately followed by the Australians. A wild confusion and bitter mêlée.'[33]

In Australia, the news of the Mont St Quentin success was widely known. In Queensland, the *Warwick Examiner and Times* stated, 'It was a feat which astonished the British Army almost as much as the enemy . . . The capture of Mont St Quentin will rank as one of Australia's most brilliant achievements. Although fighting for several months without respite, they are still in irascible form.'[34]

By nightfall on 31 August, a line had been established and consolidated on the eastern side of the Somme, from the riverbank south of Halle up to the village of Feuillaucourt on the Bapaume–Péronne road. The summit of Mont St Quentin, however, was still in German hands, and further fighting the following day would be needed to finally secure it.

During the night, ammunition and rations were brought up, thanks to the brave and determined work of the runners, who all day had risked their lives delivering messages back and forth across the open, exposed landscape.

One such runner was Private William Anderson, who volunteered to lead in the ration parties with food and ammunition for the brigade. On the way up the slope, the trenches were shelled, so after telling the carriers to find shelter, he moved ahead through the barrage, finally making contact with Lieutenant Flood. He then went back and carefully led the ration party into the rear of the 17th Battalion's position, delivering the much-needed supplies. For this gallant act, young Anderson was Mentioned in Despatches.

As darkness settled over the battlefield, it must have been a disheartening and restless night for the remaining German defenders. One thing they knew for sure was that the Australians would be back tomorrow.

TWELVE

Taking Péronne

The success of the attack on Mont St Quentin on 31 August was a welcome surprise to Generals Haig, Rawlinson and Monash. It was also something of a dangerous surprise to the Germans, who had expected to stall an Allied advance by holding the western bank of the Somme for four weeks. The French, who had not long before faced the Germans at Péronne during the March offensive, had allowed two weeks just to cross the Somme and secure the eastern bank. The Australians did this in a day, securing a strong defensive position on the eastern side, and opening up the northern ramparts of Péronne and the outpost villages to the east towards the Hindenburg Line. While the mount itself had not been taken, nor the northern flank along the Bouchavesnes ridge secured, a strong start had been made and German counterattacks had not succeeded in driving the Australians back.

Through the night, the Allies made plans for the resumption of the attack, particularly onto the mount and the high ridge to the north. After much discussion and some change of plans, zero hour was fixed at 6 am on 1 September, with the 6th Brigade's 23rd and 24th Battalions attacking along the same lines as the 17th and 20th the day before. Their objective was the back side of the woods on Mont St Quentin. The 3rd Division was also to continue their attack to the north, and to secure a line to the east of the Péronne–Bapaume road and push towards Allaines.

Meanwhile, the 5th Division, with the 14th and 15th Brigades pushing south-east, was to clear Anvil Wood and St Denis, and close on the Péronne ramparts.

As dawn broke and the men ate a hurried breakfast of bully beef and dry biscuit washed down with cold tea, they mentally prepared for the day of fighting ahead. Though exhausted, they were keen to take on the demoralised enemy and see glory bestowed on the AIF.

Well before zero hour, the battalions started moving out. The 23rd Battalion was running late in getting to its jumping-off trench, and was then held up by machine-gun fire from further along Florina Trench and a barricade of wire. After one attempt failed, Private Robert Mactier, a farmer from Tatura in Victoria, leapt out of the trench and attacked the first gun. With grenades and a pistol he overcame the first post and threw the gun over the parapet after leaving its crew dead. He charged to the next trench and killed the gunners before charging a third post. Again, Mactier overcame the gun, but was forced out into the open because the trench was blocked with wire. When he was attacking a fourth machine gun, he was killed. Through Mactier's action, the battalion was able to get to their start line and continue the advance. Mactier was awarded the Victoria Cross, one of eight given for the fighting at Mont St Quentin and Péronne.

While the 6th Brigade's 23rd Battalion was getting to its start line, the 14th Brigade, after crossing the marshland and a narrow section of river across a fallen tree trunk, advanced past Florina Trench. The 53rd Battalion attacked on the left between the mount and Péronne, the 54th on the right, and the 56th would follow the 53rd and then pass around the east side of Péronne to reach their objective – the hills to the east. As they moved forward, misty rain fell, partly obscuring their advance and silencing their passage. The 54th Battalion history mentioned the fitness and excitement of these battalions, fresh from a month's rest and keen to be part of the glory of the advance.[1]

The 53rd Battalion on the left knew of the likely opposition from Anvil Wood, given the numerous guns within and the thick wire entanglements before it. The wood had formed a dangerous flank previously, and machine-gun fire had enfiladed the advance of the 17th Battalion the day before. An attempt was made to clear a path through the wire with cutters, but this proved too slow and the casualties were high. The Australians fought their way along Johannes Trench, with the Lewis gunners standing up, exposed to fire over the wire, taking out German machine guns. Two machine guns remained, but they were rushed, and the German gunners killed and wounded.

Suddenly, at the north-west corner of the wood, a German 77-millimetre field gun started firing at the advancing Australians point blank, inflicting casualties. At this moment, Private William Currey, a wireworker from Leichhardt in Sydney, rushed the gun, killed the crew and captured the gun pit. This and other acts of bravery during the fighting saw Currey awarded the Victoria Cross.

To the right of the 53rd Battalion, the 54th was having similar problems. The battalion had formed up 700 yards from the German line. One NCO, Jack Evans, 'ran along the top of the trench and he bawled out, "Fix bayonets and load up", and then he came back still running, "Up boys and at em. Keep going. There is no objective".'[2] The men ran through the wheat stubble, the machine-gun bullets whipping the ground around their feet and tearing into their ranks as they ran forward in artillery formation, in single lines of five to twenty men. Ahead, bullets struck sparks off the dense thicket of barbed wire which ran across their front, protecting the first German trench line. The men tore at the wire and the pickets hindering their advance, and some rested their Lewis guns on the 'knife rests' and fired into the German trenches only thirty yards ahead and at the fleeing Germans before them, who were racing back to Péronne. Sergeant Bill Wilson desperately searched for gaps in the wire that German patrols would have used, knowing full well that German machine guns would be covering these gaps. Upon finding a gap, he called for his men and bellowed out, 'Form a Line. Charge',[3] and carried the attack in and over the German trench.

Nearby, other brave actions were underway. As the 54th advanced into machine-gun fire, Corporal Alexander Buckley, a farmer from Gulargambone, NSW, rushed a machine-gun post with a mate, shot four gunners and captured a further twenty-two. Further along the same trench, Corporal Arthur Hall, a station overseer from Nyngan, NSW, was also held up. He, too, charged the machine gun, killing the German gunners and capturing fifteen enemy. Moving ahead, he discovered an unguarded plank bridge across the river, allowing his battalion to cross. Corporal Buckley also found an unguarded bridge, but was killed while trying to cross.

In Anvil Wood, 200 Germans had been formed up and were ready to march back to Péronne when two Australian privates burst out of the trees and threatened their officer. Facing a bayonet, the officer told his men to drop their rifles as the two privates took the surrender, marching the 200 Germans to the rear. Soon after, a German gun that had been abandoned was brought into action by a signaller, Ronald Crank, and his mate Lance Corporal Cecil Weatherby. Crank's DCM citation reads,

'When an enemy field gun was captured, this man helped another to work it, and brought fire to bear on the enemy, who were assembled in a quarry and inflicted severe casualties, compelling them to disperse.'[4] Crank did the same two days later in the streets of Péronne when, with Private Arthur Hopkins, and with shells bursting all around them from a German battery in Bussu Wood, he fired ninety rounds at the enemy.

Not all Germans were so easily captured. Lieutenant Williams of the 56th later wrote:

> The German positions must have swarmed with machine guns, and Fritz, being a past master in the tactical handling of these, took a heavy toll on the advancing infantry. Near Anvil Wood, our company came to a halt in a sunken road. Here I saw two German machine gun posts, each with their entire crew lying dead around their guns. The German machine gunners could be fairly ranked with Leonida's Spartan Three Hundred, as they fought by their guns to death.[5]

Despite the German resistance, the battalion had now cleared the wood and moved forward across the open expanse of the sloping hill towards Péronne. Under intensive fire, which killed a number of Australians, they made it up into Elsa Trench where the remnants of the 5th Brigade, notably the 17th Battalion, were huddled among their dead.

It was now 7 am and the attack had only been underway for an hour. On the left of Mont St Quentin, the Australians overran Varna Trench across the hillside near the communal cemetery, but they began to take heavy fire from a quarry higher up the hill to the right. At this time, Lieutenant Edgar Towner, in a narrow sunken road just twenty-five yards across the main road, turned a captured machine gun and two Vickers guns onto the Germans, who were preparing to counterattack, causing heavy enemy losses and taking out five of their machine guns. He also fired on machine guns higher up the hill, which were directing fire onto the advancing 24th Battalion on the left flank as they entered Feuillaucourt, forcing them to scamper in small groups across the exposed land. This movement and the effective use of captured enemy machine guns, along with the siting of Towner's own guns, allowed the advance to continue. For his fine leadership and bravery, he was awarded the Victoria Cross.

As the 24th advanced forward of Varna Trench, they were still taking intense fire from the quarry, which was bravely defended with twelve machine guns firing from along the rim and stick bombs landing among the approaching Australians. An attempt was made on the quarry by Sergeant Wignall and members of his platoon, but this was driven back. Sergeant Albert Lowerson, a farmer from the Myrtleford district in Victoria, called on a group of men to follow him and charge forward, and he overpowered the German gunners and captured the twelve guns along with thirty men. This had followed a number of heroic actions over the preceding weeks, and Lowerson was awarded a Victoria Cross. His action cleared the left side of the summit and pushed the Germans out into the open country to the east and into Plevna Trench. German losses were extremely heavy, and 'the large number of enemy dead bore grim testimony to the effectiveness of our shooting.'[6] The 24th Battalion's casualties were five officers and forty-three other ranks killed, and three officers and eighty-eight other ranks wounded.[7]

After an intense British bombardment, the Australians advanced along the right side of Mont St Quentin, driving the

Germans from Radomir Trench – the remains of which can still be seen today – and further back, 400 yards on the far side of the summit. Mont St Quentin was finally captured and cleared.

Further north, the 11th Brigade had pushed the Germans back to Allaines and the Scutari–Broussa trench line. This advance saw the capture of the slopes leading up to Bouchavesnes, securing the Australians' left flank on the north side of the canal. It was here that the 41st Battalion attacked eastwards from the start line along the road, high up on the Bouchavesnes ridge on a 1000-yard frontage. The 41st quickly took fire from Allaines, where an estimated 700 Germans were, and were forced back to Yassa and Kassa trenches. While they captured over 200 Germans, they had casualties of five officers and over 100 men out of the 400 who went into the attack. Just to their north along their left flank, the 42nd Battalion advanced to Quarry Farm, capturing eighty Germans and eight machine guns. The 42nd was on the northern-most flank of the Australians' advance, with the British III Corps on their left, which at the time had taken their two objectives and were now half a mile ahead of the Australian front.

While the main objective had now been secured, on 2 September, the Australians continued their advance to the north-east with the British 74th Division on their left flank. Of the 3rd Division, the 43rd was now the only battalion still in the line, the 41st and 42nd having been relieved the previous night. The task of the 43rd was to clear Graz Trench, which ran parallel to the unfinished Canal Nord, and Scutari Trench, which arced around further east. The Australians cleared Scutari Trench and pushed the Germans into a small complex of trenches, hemming them in. The Germans fought back, stalling the Australian advance.

Needing to break this deadlock, Private Lawrence Weathers, an undertaker from Snowtown, South Australia, rushed a fork in the trenches and bombed the German gunners, killing their commander. Returning for more bombs, he again charged the Germans, this time with the assistance of some mates, and captured 180 Germans and subdued the post. Weathers was killed on 29 September in the Australian attack on the Beaurevoir Line, leaving a wife and two sons. He was awarded the Victoria Cross posthumously. During their time in the line, the 43rd Battalion suffered four officers and forty-two other ranks killed, and eight officers and 116 other ranks wounded. They captured about 250 Germans, mainly Prussian Guards, and forty machine guns.

While the 3rd Division pushed through Anvil Wood, Monash ordered the 14th Brigade to pass further south to cross into Péronne and secure it. Before 7 am, men were beginning to arrive beyond the walls of the town and along the ancient moat that surrounded it. Two bridges remained: one on the road from Cléry-sur-Somme into Péronne, and a small footbridge further south. One of the first to this wooden bridge was Corporal Buckley from Gulargambone and some mates from the 54th. Finding the bridge unguarded, they attempted to cross but immediately a German machine gun opened on them. Lieutenant McArthur and then Corporal Buckley were killed.

The main bridge to the north, however, was still intact. As the Australians approached, a German sapper appeared with a plunger in his hands ready to fire the charge. He was quickly shot, but it's possible that a bullet hit the plunger, as the bridge disappeared in a huge cloud of white smoke. When the smoke had cleared, a group of Germans, led by an officer, surrendered by throwing their weapons into the canal. At this time it was found the canal was only six feet deep and could be traversed with planks and waste timber, allowing the battalion to quickly file across. It is believed the explosion caused panic among the Germans in the town, with many abandoning their machine guns and heading east.

Back at the wooden footbridge, German machine-gun fire precluded any crossing. The Germans wheeled up a field gun, which also fired on the Australians huddled under cover, and a number of men were killed and wounded as shells fell among them. There was no way forward.

After crossing by the exploded bridge, Captain Downing, the officer commanding the 54th Battalion, sent Lieutenant Charles Small and a group of men to eliminate the German field gun and machine guns covering the footbridge. As they approached it, they were fired on by a group of Germans up on the ramparts, but when fire was returned these Germans also surrendered. Next Small's men worked their way around the back of the defenders and, within twenty minutes, the door was open for the Australians to enter the town.

As the Australians cautiously entered the shattered streets of Péronne, they were in unfamiliar territory; street fighting was not part of their experience, and the rubble and shattered buildings offered perfect cover to snipers and machine guns. Machine guns were well sited, allowing set fields of fire onto designated 'killing grounds', with other machine guns providing interlocking fire and protection. However, even though many of the Péronne defenders were from elite units, they were also exhausted and demoralised. They feared for their starving families and realised the end of the war was close. With little to fight for and even given the strength of their defence, many simply surrendered en masse to the advancing Australians. In one incident, an Australian sergeant discovered a group of Germans in a cellar drinking coffee. The German officer invited the Australians to join him and asked if the sergeant would mind if they finished their coffee before surrendering.

The Australian battalions pushed on through the town to the southern boundary, where the marshy land of the Cologne River divided Péronne from Flamicourt. Across a lagoon was Péronne's railway station, where a German field gun fired on the Australians. In the railway yard, a large group of Germans were marching four abreast but Vickers and Lewis gunners across the river quickly dispersed them. As the Australians advanced, they overtook retreating parties of Germans which, in turn, prevented German machine gunners firing into the oncoming ranks. After clearing the last corner of the town, the Bretagne area to the north-east, the Australians fell back, leaving only fifty men to occupy the town, a dangerous decision given hundreds of Germans were at that time being collected and ordered back within a couple of miles of Péronne.

Meanwhile, the 15th Brigade's commander, General Pompey Elliott, not wanting to be left out, personally led his 58th and 59th Battalions to the destroyed bridge and proceeded to cross it himself. However, he lost his footing after stepping on a loose piece of steel and fell into the Somme. Here the river was deep and he had some difficulty getting himself out, but the signallers had a field day spreading the news of Pompey's discomfort and embarrassment. Soon after, it is said, he continued his advance trouser-less and in a borrowed greatcoat, though others say with just his shirt.

As he stood dripping on the bank, Elliott directed a post to be established immediately on the eastern bank to push patrols into Flamicourt. The junction at this point of the Somme and the Cologne rivers introduced a range of difficulties for the Australian advance. Both rivers were wide and marshy, a maze of reeds and swamp grasses at times spreading 500 to 1000 yards between sides that were steep in places, meaning it was impossible to walk or swim across the area. Crossing points became crucial and, while Péronne had been accessed and largely cleared, the marshland crossing points were still heavily defended by the Germans. As well as destroying some of these points, the Germans had heavily barbed-wired tracks, which were effectively covered by hidden machine-gun posts, and attempts to cross by the 54th were quickly stopped by machine-gun fire. The 15th Brigade war diary notes, 'All endeavours by patrols to effect a crossing found the enemy alert, and brought heavy machine gun fire and the patrols often suffered heavy losses.'[8]

At this time, a 59th Battalion patrol under Lieutenant Pentreath was working along the railway line, and crossed the damaged railway bridge and made for the station area that was the strongpoint of German resistance. As he advanced along the bank, he discovered a German post which he attacked, shooting the German officer who 'invited the party [the Australians] to surrender'.[9] He removed the explosive charges on the nearby footbridge but was confronted by machine-gun fire, and his advance stopped.

Meanwhile, the 54th Battalion had seized Radegonde, a small section of Péronne about one mile south-west of the centre, and were closing on Péronne from the north-west. By 11.30 am on 1 September, both the 58th and 59th Battalions had two companies across the river.

By dusk on the second day, the advance had slowed, although good progress had been made in securing most of Péronne. Monash now decided to rest his exhausted troops and provide a pause in the advance.

No sooner had he issued orders than he was asked by General Alexander Godley, who was temporarily in command of the British III Corps, to provide flanking support for the advance of the newly arrived British 7th Division. This required Monash's 7th Brigade to move through the 6th on the mount and push east along Koros Alley towards Aizecourt, and the 14th further south. The planning was rushed; there was little time to get fully prepared, and no time for reconnaissance.

At 5.30 am on 2 September, the 7th Brigade's 26th Battalion moved forward from near Elsa Trench, crossed the Bapaume road and headed towards the heavily defended Koros Alley, a series of trenches extending east–west along the Mont St Quentin ridgeline. Immediately they came under intense machine-gun fire, 'such as the 7th Brigade had not experienced even at Pozières',[10] and were driven back, with a number of officers killed and wounded. They remained sheltering from the heavy fire until dusk. Other companies were more successful in their advance. On the left flank, forty men, under Lieutenants McHardie and Lawson, pushed past their own barrage and caught a group of Germans in Kurilo Alley, parallel to Koros Alley, where they captured 1000 yards of trench.

Advancing on the 26th Battalion's left flank was the 25th Battalion. After the men emerged from Mont St Quentin Wood they were met by intense fire from a strongpoint 400 yards ahead in Brunn Trench, running north–south and crossing Koros and Kurilo alleys. Sergeant William Anderson, with a small party and a Lewis gun, was able to clear the German post holding up the advance. Meanwhile his brother, Corporal Samuel Anderson, also took the initiative and crawled forward with a small party to continue the attack. They stormed the strong German position in a crater, but the Germans fled, leaving behind seventeen machine guns and two small trench mortars.

The 25th moved along Lugos Trench and found themselves above and behind the Germans firing on the 27th Battalion, who were below and to the left, pushing towards Haut Allaines. The 25th raked the Germans' backs with fire as they fled, relieving some of the fire on the advancing 27th. At this point, about 100 Germans surrendered while others fled to the rear. The left company of the 25th chased the Germans, who threw away their weapons and equipment and raced to the Aizecourt road, the objective for the Australian advance past Brunn Trench. The Australians halted and spread out, consolidating the line of the Aizecourt road, but it was found that Darmstadt Trench to the right was packed with Germans.

While the Germans were attempting to establish a line of resistance, the average German soldier was not up to a hard fight. During the previous night, German officers had collected remnants from various units and tried to form them into a strong defensive line, but the relentless nature of the Allied advance had broken their defensive resolve. A retirement was ordered back to a new arcing defensive line between Moislains in the north and Bussu, west of Péronne and further south. This retirement was orderly and calm behind the British sector to the north, but described in German reports as 'a rout'[11] ahead of the Australian front.

Further south, at Péronne, at 3.45 am on 2 September, the 15th Brigade commanders had met and planned the next stage of their attack. It was decided the 54th would mop up Péronne with the assistance of the 58th, while the 60th would clear the dangerous village of Flamicourt and Chair Wood. The 59th, meantime, was to take the high ground between Flamicourt and Doingt as a prelude to the advance south-east to attack the latter and the trenches east of the river.

By early morning, though, the 15th Brigade was having problems advancing. At 8 am, the 58th Battalion was heavily shelled, first by the Germans and then by their own artillery firing shrapnel. They were also under fire from German machine guns located in two-storey buildings, firing down streets from the eastern corner of Péronne. The 60th reported difficulties crossing one of the ruined bridges, as they had come under intense fire and gas shells. North of the town near St Denis, the 59th were facing heavy fire from enemy reinforcements, sustaining serious casualties. In the confusion, remnants of a number of battalions were mixed up while the 14th Brigade was taking fire from the back of Mont St Quentin Wood because the 2nd Division had not advanced along the spur.

By 1.30 pm, Péronne had been cleared, but the situation remained precarious. The Commanding Officer of the 58th Battalion, Major Harold Ferres, reported that he was now at the extreme end of the town and digging into the banks of the moat. He also reported heavy shelling for fifteen minutes, with 5.9-inch shells and gas from the direction of Doingt. Seventy reinforcements had arrived, but he needed more. In summary, he reported, 'Our left flank is very exposed, machine gun fire very heavy . . . and the position we are holding is enfiladed from almost every direction and I consider it impossible to push forward.'[12] Unbeknown to him, the German High Command had ordered the retaking of Péronne and Mont St Quentin, if only to delay the relentless advance of the Allies towards the Hindenburg Line, which was just fifteen miles to the east.

By late on the afternoon of 2 September, reports were coming in that Flamicourt was unoccupied, as Germans had been seen trickling south-east towards Doingt. When a patrol approached, however, German machine guns again laid a heavy fire down the road and the Australians withdrew. Consolidation now began, with the 57th Battalion ordered to guard the river crossings, the railway bridges and entry points on the east of the town. Meanwhile, the 55th Battalion was to strike north of St Denis and push towards Darmstadt Trench running north–south into the open country beyond Péronne. This area was also very dangerous, as it was covered by well-sited German machine guns and defensive positions.

North of St Denis, the 53rd was ordered to advance, but was also pinned down. Fire was coming from a section of the ramparts in the Bretagne area of Péronne, which had still not been completely cleared, and these German guns were able to traverse and enfilade the slope towards Mont St Quentin and the open field before St Denis. This fire left a disjointed front line and led to increasing casualties. As Bean notes, 'The mistake of not taking all the risks to clear Péronne had been dearly paid for.'[13]

Recriminations now flew about, with Monash blaming delays in start times and the lack of determination in General Hobbs, who was in command of the 5th Division, and General James Stewart, Commanding Officer of the 14th Brigade. Perhaps Monash was forgetting the exhausted state of his men and their successes of the previous two days.

For the attack on St Denis to succeed, the German machine guns on the ramparts at Péronne still needed to be silenced. An artillery bombardment was planned from 5 am until 6.40 am on 3 September, before this remaining section of German resistance would be assaulted by the 54th Battalion. Before this could happen, battalions in St Denis and the nearby sugar factory and brickworks needed to be recalled, in particular Lieutenant Waite of the 53rd. When he couldn't be contacted, Private Currey, who had done such good work at Anvil Wood, offered to attempt to contact him across dangerous open fields. Currey immediately came under intense and concentrated fire, and was gassed and had bullets rip through his gasmask, but while he was unable to reach Lieutenant Waite's position, he was able to call to him to get in, which Waite quickly did.

In the confusion orders were misunderstood, and the infantry attack did not eventuate. The 54th did not arrive on time, and the 56th was hit hard by German retaliatory shelling. With the dawn light breaking and the river mist rising, the German machine guns on the ramparts, which had been reinforced during the night, now sprang into action. The 55th Battalion sustained casualties both from the reoccupied sugar mill and batteries in the nearby woods, which fired directly into the Australian lines.

Responding to this fire, Major Ferres of the 58th took his men across a bridge and into Bretagne, where they attacked the houses and rubble piles hiding the German guns. Lewis gunners engaged German machine guns, distracting them while a patrol attacked from the rear. Germans were hunted out of houses and through gardens, where running fights occurred. When five machine guns were seen firing from the top of the ramparts, Lewis gunners and riflemen fired on them, putting them out of action. Some of the Germans now fell back into St Denis Wood, while others were captured in a ditch by the fort where they'd been hiding.

The Allies' position was finally being consolidated. With Péronne cleared and the last Germans driven from the ramparts and Bretagne, plans were finalised for taking Darmstadt Trench. Here the Germans were hopelessly mixed and disorganised, and when the attack came in, they withdrew, first to Silesie Trench then to the woods north of Doingt. The 57th pushed on and took Mannheim Trench with little opposition, then established a line north of Doingt, sending patrols into the town. While the men of the battalion were exhausted, they maintained pressure on the enemy line, with patrols pushing forward to remain in touch with withdrawing German units. By 5 pm, the line was well to the east of Péronne, running from Bussu in the north to Doingt and then across the river to Mesnil in the south. Finally it was time for a rest.

North of the Australians, the British and French were also pushing forward. The Germans were pulling back their troops and only lightly defending positions to slow the Allied advance.

By 4 September, Flamicourt was cleared, and by dawn on 5 September, the Australians occupied the high ground to the east of Péronne and the long Mannheim Trench. Patrols pushed through Doingt and down the road towards Mesnil. By 4 pm, the 8th Brigade had pushed through the woods at Bussu and consolidated the new line. As the advance continued, supply dumps were established and engineers worked hard on roads and bridges.

Meanwhile, the Germans had begun their withdrawal to the Tincourt–Nurlu Line, destroying everything as they went – wells, trees, houses and bridges – much as they had done in February and March 1917, on the retreat to the Hindenburg Line at Bullecourt.

Perhaps the Australian attack on Mont St Quentin and Péronne is best summed up in the passage of a letter home by Corporal Arthur Hall, VC:

We went into the stunt about 400 strong and took the town and over 700 prisoners. We were told afterwards that Foch had given the Aussies a fortnight to get the town properly and we did it in two days. They had not known about the wire and when the generals looked at the ground afterwards, they said 'Almost impossible' . . . One felt at Peronne as if he was doing something towards winning the war and it is certainly something that will not be forgotten by anyone who took part in it.[14]

THIRTEEN

The Hindenburg Outpost Line

The success of Mont St Quentin and Péronne was one thing, but Monash was now faced with a dilemma, partly of his own making. He needed to continue the pressure and the advance, but he knew his men were past exhaustion, and the whiff of mutiny hung in the air. Monash also needed to rebuild the Somme bridges, remake the roads and restore the railways that were crucial for resupply. Rawlinson also knew of the men's fatigue, but as he looked eastwards to the long lines of smoke from burning buildings, he realised he needed to keep up the pressure on the retreating Germans, who were leaving a devastated landscape in their wake. There was much to do, but few who could do it. Sleep was more important than consolidation, but it needed to wait.

The big prize was the Hindenburg Line, some fifteen miles to the east of Péronne and stretching north–south for some eighty miles from Arras to Laffaux, near Soissons on the Aisne River. However, before Allied troops reached the line, Rawlinson laid down four objectives for them, moving steadily eastwards. The first, about four miles to the east of Péronne, took in Estrées-Mons, Cartigny and Nurlu; the second, Vraignes, Tincourt and Liéramont; the third, Vermand, Jeancourt and Épehy; and, finally, the Hindenburg Outpost Line through Le Verguier.

At 2 pm on 5 September, the 3rd Pioneer Battalion, an engineering unit, moved off with the 42nd Battalion from Cléry-sur-Somme in warm weather, past the shattered remains of Mont St Quentin and out into the green countryside. Their first objective was the Green Line, which they expected to quickly take, and the second was the Red Line. At dusk, they took up a defensive line 1500 yards east of the mount and moved off again at midnight. Progress was slow due to the darkness of the night and the wire, gun pits and trenches that littered their way. The Pioneers struggled through a wood and, on emerging on the far side, reformed their line and moved on to the Green Line, which they reached at 3 am. There had been little evidence of the Germans apart from some very light and random shelling that fell behind them. They lay down in the clover to await the advance to the Red Line scheduled for dawn.

At 4.30 am on 6 September, the men moved forward in a light mist behind the scouts who entered Buire, still occupied by the enemy. The Pioneers were not infantry trained, which showed when heavy fire came from Buire Wood to the north of Tincourt. Unsure of how to suppress this fire, the Pioneers charged the wood, killing all but one of the Germans there. The exhausted 42nd Battalion helped clear Buire Wood, but were then held up by shelling and machine-gun fire, with strong opposition coming from Tincourt. This died down after 10.30 am, when the pressure of the Australian advance forced the Germans to fall back and evacuate. The town was left burning, which provided an unexpected smokescreen. At this point, the Pioneers and the 42nd were relieved by the 41st and 44th Battalions. Meanwhile, light horse patrols pushed well ahead, sometimes two miles behind the German forward posts.

To the south, the 8th Brigade force, made up of the 29th and 31st Battalions, pushed forward to the third objective with only light resistance, collecting on the way shiny patent leather helmets, which 'could be picked up in good numbers above Bussu. These helmets belonged to the Prussian Guard Regiment who had been put to flight and compelled to leave much gear behind them. Souvenir hunters took advantage of the opportunity, and added these helmets to their already extensive collections.'[1] The 41st Battalion history notes, 'It was a lovely summer's day and most unwarlike in appearance; no trenches, few shell holes and the woods in full leaf, not that stripped naked appearance generally associated with battlefields.'[2] The 44th Battalion also advanced at dawn, 'crossing open country strewn with the debris and abandoned equipment of the German army'.[3]

'Ratting', theft, was by this time a perfected art, with the Australians masters at it. An 'unofficial patrol' from the 44th Battalion intercepted a column of German prisoners being marched to the rear by the British 173rd Brigade. The Australians simply moved through the ranks of the Germans, with one later writing, 'My cobber and I decided that these Tommies would not be alive to souveniring as they had just come from Salonica so we followed them up and fanned all the prisoners we could get. Altogether that day turned us in thirteen watches, three field glasses, one very small pistol, a pocket full of rings, one oversized accordion and a pocketful of the dandiest cigars possible.'[4]

Advancing by virtual route march, the 44th encountered scattered opposition on the road towards Roisel, but the first real resistance came as they approached the town, where machine guns and field guns fired over open sights. This was quickly bypassed, though, as battalions moved either side of the village, which was then shelled. The Germans pulled out but left sixty wagons, two howitzers and ten machine guns. To the south, the Germans also withdrew from Hervilly, allowing the Australians to take their third objective.

On 14 September, the first battalion strike broke out.[5] The 59th Battalion war diary only records that, 'when the Battalion moved off, "B" Company and a few men from "A" Company refused to go forward.'[6] The exhausted 59th, having been promised a rest, had been ordered back to the line again. Bean relates, 'three platoons refused and their officers supported them.'[7] The men said they were tired of making up for British troops' failures, and that their exhausted state had not been made known to the High Command. While the incident fizzled out and the men returned to duty, it was a clear warning to Monash about what would happen if he continued to push his men.

It was now that the order came down from Haig, via Rawlinson to Monash, that all the British troops along the line were to rest. Monash called a halt and used the time to bring up guns and supplies, consolidate the ground taken and relieve tired battalions.

The key question for the Allies was where the Germans would establish their main defensive line in one of the three old British lines. It was generally accepted that the British reserve line, the next one along the advance, would not be chosen. Perhaps the Germans would choose the old British front line or, further east, the British outpost line through Villeret, east of Le Verguier.

Despite the halt to the advance, pressure needed to be kept up on the Germans through peaceful penetration and aggressive patrolling. Patrols reached Vermand, through which ran the old British reserve line, with the Germans holding Vendelles and Hesbécourt further north. It was now found that German resistance was stiffening, and the posts encountered were stronger. This was the German forward zone, which was strongly held to give the German command time to construct a defensive line of fortified posts behind wire through Le Verguier and to lay tank mines, erect searchlights and machine guns, and bring up field guns ready for the expected attack.

Haig was keen to know German strength, defence intentions and morale, but pressure remained on the Allies to exploit their success before the Germans could consolidate behind the seemingly impregnable Hindenburg Line. Canadian General Byng, along with the French, was keen to press the advance, but found the Americans, whom they had factored into the offensive, were not yet ready.

The Australians were quietly maintaining their advance. Monash realised that the German defences ahead were not the scattered and disorganised temporary lines they had encountered since Péronne, and would instead require a setpiece battle. On 8 September, the 10th Brigade relieved the 41st and 42nd Battalions of the 11th Brigade, who returned to Doingt for 'a fortnight's dinkum spell after six weeks of strenuous activity and crowded incident'.[8] This was part of Rawlinson's broad plan of rotation, to bring fresh brigades into the line and to allow his men to rest, but not before they had 'thrust within striking distance of the Hindenburg Line'.[9]

On 10 September, the 1st and 4th Divisions came into the line to push beyond Hesbécourt and into Vendelles and Jeancourt, and carry the final advance to the Hindenburg Line. A patrol of the 2nd Battalion found Jeancourt deserted and set up a machine-gun post to secure the eastern side of the village. No sooner had they done this than a group of Germans, marching in ranks of four, came up the road. The Australians waited until the enemy troops were close and then fired into the party, who suffered heavy losses.

Further north, at 5.30 am, the 4th Battalion resumed their attack on Hill 140 south of Templeux-le-Guérard and, with the aid of a supporting barrage, drove the Germans back. However, the Australians were now exposed on an easterly-facing hillside with the mist rising. German artillery and machine guns from Templeux, and further east at Hargicourt, fired on the Australians and many men were killed. The Germans then counterattacked, driving the 4th Battalion back and capturing ten men. By the time the Australians reformed on their start line, they had casualties of five officers and ninety-eight men. Meanwhile, the 2nd Battalion on the right cleared two German posts and moved the front forward, south of Jeancourt.

For all the success of the advance, however, the Australian battalions continued to take casualties. On hand were the brave and determined stretcher-bearers, whom Edward Lynch writes about:

Another little wood over on our right. Six of our chaps run into it. Enemy shells land in it in a roar of flame, dust and smoke. The little stunted trees begin to leap skyward under the bursting shells. Four of our men come flying out, yelling hard, and pointing to the wood they've just left.

Two bearers run for the wood carrying a stretcher. Without a pause they charge straight into the jumping, flaring hell that but a few minutes ago was a peaceful little green wood. Fair into the awful shell bursts the two bearers run. Now they are moving through smoke, flying earth and screeching shell fragments. We watch two brave men going to their doom in an endeavour to rescue a couple of wounded men who are by now probably dead.

A shell is right on to the bearers! The great explosion seems to leap from under their feet!

'He's got 'em!' And the two bearers are thrown yards by the shell burst.

'They're goners!'

No, they're on their feet, finding their stretcher. On into the wood they go. Straight on into the terrific shellfire. It's impossible for men to live in there. The bearers disappear deep into the shell-tossed wood and we give them up.

'Here they come!' Like two drunken men they stagger out of the smoke, reeling from side to side, but between them carrying their stretcher, a wounded man on it! We see the bearers place him on the ground some distance from the wood.

'They're goin' back in again!'

'Cripes, but that's guts if you like!' And sure enough the two bearers are going back into the wood, going back running!

We see them enter that inferno of roaring, crashing flame, both flung down by the force of the explosion of a mighty shell, see them rise and stagger on a few yards only to be blown to the ground again.

Now they are lost to sight behind a wall of belching smoke, stabbing flame and shattering roar. We've forgotten the advance, forgotten the Fritz, forgotten all in our anxiety for two brave men. There comes an emotionally cracked call of, 'God! They're coming out!' And two blotches take shape in the smoke, and the dim figures of our two bearers stagger and lurch out of the smoke, grimly hanging on to their stretcher. They've got their man! Their second man! Clear of the danger they carry him and gently lower the stretcher. Bearers as gentle as they are brave. We've seen something to think about in the past few minutes.[10]

At the southern end of the line, the 4th Division advanced 2000 yards. As they pushed towards Le Verguier, the 4th Brigade encountered thick diagonal bands of barbed wire, which required the officers to use their compasses to maintain direction. As the Australians closed on the outpost line, both Rawlinson and

Monash realised the Germans were preparing to make their stand at the old British main line, which ran from Épehy in the north, through Hargicourt and on to Le Verguier in the south. This was an important realisation, as it confirmed the only way forward was with a setpiece attack, and it initiated the planning and considerations for the coming week of attacks and the coordination of, for Monash at least, his five divisions.

As the advance slowly progressed and the distance extended, communications between the advancing battalions, their immediate headquarters, brigade and divisional headquarters became crucial. The 44th Battalion history makes special reference to the runners:

Australian runners reached an extraordinary standard of efficiency. If a message was handed to a runner on a dark night with instructions to deliver it to a certain unit 'exact whereabouts unknown, but probably at so-and-so,' it is certain, if that unit was within miles of the indicated spot, that the message would be delivered. In the darkness, among the outposts, amid mud and wire, memory does not register a runner ever returning with a message undelivered. A truly marvellous record.

The same with the signallers. If by any improvisation they could establish necessary communication between two points, it was done. With flags, lamps or telephone, if one way was impossible, the 'sigs' ingenuity could be depended upon to find some other method of 'carrying on'.[11]

Over a cup of tea at Monash's headquarters, Rawlinson, Monash and their staff planned the next stage of the offensive, settling on 18 September as the day of attack. At this time, the whole of Rawlinson's Fourth Army, along with the northernmost units of the French army, would attack on a front of seventeen miles from Gouzeacourt in the Third Army sector in the north, down to Holnon near St Quentin in the south. This would bring the Allied front within striking distance of the Hindenburg Line.

In the centre of the Allied line, the Australian 1st and 4th Divisions, each on a 3500-yard front, would advance and take Bellicourt and Bellenglise, with four brigades made up of sixteen battalions designated for the attack. It was decided that the first objective would be the old British main line ('Brown Line'), the second the outpost line ('Red Line') and the third, if the opportunity presented itself, the Hindenburg Outpost Line ('Blue Line'). The hope was that, in taking the Blue Line, the ridge at Bellenglise would provide a high point for observation for a great distance behind the German line, including the village of Bellicourt and the entrance to the St Quentin Tunnel.

In planning this battle, Monash had a good artillery allocation, but he had only been allocated eight tanks, four for both divisions. He cleverly had the engineers build dummy tanks that could be manhandled by men inside and left in view of the Germans. He also had no aircraft to drop ammunition and smoke bombs, as forty aeroplanes had been damaged in a storm. This all placed great pressure on the Australians. Monash had battalions well below strength, many with only twenty officers and 400 men; he had reduced companies from four to three, and now had three platoons per company. Monash worried that many of these men, who had been serving since November or December 1914 and were eligible for Anzac leave, would return home, particularly after shipping was found for 800 experienced officers and men, with other ships becoming available. He also had his generals in his ear about casualties, exhaustion and the potential for mutiny within his battalions.

On 17 September, Monash had another concern: the capture of Lieutenant Colonel Thomas Marsden, the Commanding Officer of the 5th Machine Gun Battalion. Marsden had gone out to check the safety angle of his machine guns ready for the next day's barrage and had been seen to leave the support lines between the 13th and 16th Battalions and wander towards the German front line. Here he was challenged by a German officer who called on him to surrender, which he did, faced as he was with a line of rifles squarely aimed at him. In his pack were the orders for the following day's attack, including start lines and objectives, and the barrage map, both of which were extremely valuable for the Germans.

The day before the attack, the 48th Battalion of the 12th Brigade moved up to their start line. On the way in, they were bombed from the air and were forced to 'move around shell holes and very dead Fritzes'.[12] Each man carried, in addition to their weapon, five sandbags, five Mills bombs, and either a pick or shovel. Advancing with them were four stretcher-bearer squads, two 3-inch mortar teams and a section of Vickers guns. The men were in high spirits and 'sang lustily during the evening'.[13]

The 48th were part of the 4th Division advance of 1200 yards across a number of valleys along the River Omignon, where they were to capture Dean and Cooker trenches on the first objective. They would then be leapfrogged by the 45th Battalion, who would advance to the Red Line.

On the night of 17 September, battalions all along the line moved forward to their start line. The weather was wet and miserable, and men shivered in their cold, damp clothes as they lay in hastily dug, waterlogged dugouts. The 13th Battalion history notes the discomfort of the men as they waited: 'Some lay down in the rain; others stood up. It was a long lonely hour; not a word spoken above a whisper, no comforting fag or pipe; and the pelting rain. It seemed as if zero would never arrive.'[14]

The Germans didn't seem to observe the assembly of the troops, and little hostile shellfire fell along the line. Some men were fortunate, like the 10th Battalion whose Commanding Officer, Lieutenant Colonel Maurice Wilder-Neligan, found them huts to spend the night in. Others were served a hot breakfast close to their start line and given a nip of rum to warm them up. In the 13th Battalion line, 'at 5.15am all stood up and faced enemy-wards, felt the pins of their bombs, and saw that their bayonets were firmly fixed. "One Minute" was soon whispered.'[15]

At 5.20 am the barrage came down in a dense line 150 yards ahead of the waiting troops. This barrage was heavier than at any time previously, plus there was a heavy machine-gun barrage of 200 Vickers guns fired on fixed lines and 'the roar rose to a crescendo'.[16] Monash, knowing there were not enough tanks to commit to an attack, wanted to give the men the most protection possible. At three minutes, the barrage made its first 'lift', now falling 200 yards further on. The rain gave way to a morning mist, which provided good cover. Initially, enemy fire was sporadic, and there were few casualties.

The advancing Australians ran forward, using the heavy fog, thickened by smoke, to negotiate dense barbed-wire entanglements and then outflank the Germans. Some officers used compasses to maintain direction, and scouts worked to keep battalions connected. Everywhere the men 'wondered when they would stumble on Germans',[17] and it was often the sight of a line of helmets above the parapet of a trench that gave the first indication of the enemy. Everywhere, enemy posts were overrun and prisoners sent back. Fighting through a wood, Lieutenant Wally Graham glanced up from his map to see a row of German heads, all wearing red banded caps, pop up from behind a log. Just as he drew his pistol, a line of hands shot up in surrender 'as if by clock-work'[18] and these men were sent to the rear as prisoners.

The advance continued. Isolated German posts were overrun as the 1st Brigade consolidated in Hargicourt. The eight tanks had, in most cases, arrived late due to the wet, slippery ground, but once in the fight were quick to crush the thick belts of barbed wire and take on German posts. A tank commanded by Lieutenant Rupert Anstice Rafferty, and directed by compass, trundled to the south of Cambrieres Wood and drove straight through the creeping barrage into the enemy lines. Though fired on, it crushed several enemy posts in the flank positions of the British 2nd Brigade. The 48th Battalion history notes that, after their tank had veered off, a dummy tank was dragged up to the start line by a reluctant mule. However, 'unfortunately, the mule made for a heavy belt of wire, where the "tank" immediately became inoperative after the fashion of tanks.'[19]

On the southern end of the line, Brigadier General Ray Leane's 48th Battalion had advanced 1000 yards with few casualties, and took numerous prisoners along the way. On the north of Dean Copse, Private Robert Wells, DCM, in a single-handed attack, captured two enemy posts and seven Germans while Private James Binnie fired his Lewis gun on an enemy position and eliminated it. He also fired on retreating Germans, cutting them down. For his actions, Binnie was awarded the Military Medal, as were many others who performed acts of bravery in the advance. One of these acts occurred in Dean Copse, which was entered by Corporal Sid Massey. After a quick recce where he located a machine gun, he led a small party forward under fire, destroyed the post and captured the gun. Nearby, Private Reuben Pinto leapt into a section of trench and captured fifty Germans. Further on, several deep dugouts were entered and the enemy, driven into corners, was forced to surrender. Some who escaped through the back entrances came under artillery fire and also surrendered. In this section alone, 189 Germans were captured, including eleven officers.

In planning for the attack, the Australians had wanted an earlier start and a faster pace for the advance, believing they would catch the Germans napping, which in fact was the case. The British had wanted to start later and move more slowly, which resulted in the Australian flank being exposed. Soon after zero hour it was found that the British 2nd Brigade on the right flank were failing to maintain the aggressive pace of the 48th. Second Lieutenant William Parry of the 48th crossed into the British sector and led the 2nd Royal Sussex Regiment forward, deploying these men to take the junction of Cooker Trench and protect his flank. He returned to his men and led them forward, whereupon the Germans fell back from Cooker Trench and ran to Parker Copse.

Here, German officers attempted to reorganise their men into a defensive line, but Privates John Rochford and Henry Tucker deployed their Lewis gun on the German position with devastating effect.[20] The deep dugout was attacked with grenades and the German battalion commander, six officers and sixty other ranks were captured. Similar aggressive actions continued all along the line. At one point, Corporal Thomas Price turned a captured German machine gun on a large party of Germans falling back across open ground and cut them down. Prisoners were rounded up and many were mere boys, frightened and demoralised.

As the Australians advanced, however, German resistance and the number of machine guns increased. In the centre of the front, the 13th Battalion, now advancing along a ridge, was taking fire from Le Verguier. It was here that Sergeant Gerald Sexton (his real name was Maurice Buckley) sprang into action. His exploits are explained in his battalion history: 'Sexton advanced, his Lewis gun at his hip, slung from his shoulder, far ahead of the rest of the company, firing, he killed the stubborn crew who continued firing to the last.'[21] Germans emerged from a dugout and manned their trench, but Sexton fired along the line of the trench, killing many and forcing others to surrender. He then ran alone into a clump of trees where a machine gun had slowed the 13th Battalion advance; Sexton killed more Germans there, and sent others running back as prisoners.

Running down the slope, the 13th Battalion suddenly found themselves under fire from two German field guns and four trench mortars. Getting past them was now impossible. But Sexton once again appeared. The battalion history records:

It was like a tonic to him. His eyes flashed, he rushed like a whirlwind towards them, jumping a trench and tearing his clothes free from the barbs which threatened to hold him back, firing short bursts as he rushed, killed the gunners at the field gun and sent the others scurrying into their dugouts. Two machine guns opened on him as he dashed across the flat, but did not deter him from the new trench he was running at, and in which he killed 12 who hesitated to put their hands up. He now ran back to the field gun and fired down the dugouts until he heard cries of 'Kamarad'. 'Come up then', he called out, and, as they made their exit, he sent them back, 30 of them including a battalion commander.[22]

By 6.30 am, the 13th Battalion was on the first objective, the Brown Line, and was digging in.

The second objective was the Red Line. After a two-hour break, the Allied barrage again came down, crashing along the

German front. The battalion diary notes, 'the barrage was now more accurate on our front, and all were in tremendous heart because of such great success so far.'[23] The halt, however, had been too long, and had enabled the Germans to pull back the field artillery and bring up more machine guns. This response resulted in heavier German fire from Collins Copse. Into this copse rushed Lieutenant Harry Baker, who located the enemy gun, bombed it and returned with twenty prisoners. Soon after, he led a party to clear out an enemy trench and then, again, rushed a German gun, firing his pistol and bringing in more prisoners. For these actions, Baker was awarded the Distinguished Service Order.

The 45th Battalion, who had suffered heavy casualties from the barrage during their advance, now moved through the 48th Battalion and came under German shellfire as they raced towards their second objective, Ascension Farm. Here they founded disorganised German posts and took several hundred prisoners.[24] It was at this point that Lieutenant Colonel Noel Loutit was wounded, an officer famous for his advance on the first day at Gallipoli. However, the shellfire then all but ceased, and it was found the Germans were trying to withdraw their guns. As they tried to hitch them up, they were fired on by the Australians, and horses and men were killed and the guns captured. The 45th quickly dug in on their objective, 'which offered a panorama of the dense barbed wire entanglements and trenches of the Hindenburg Line'.[25]

In *Somme Mud*, Edward Lynch of the 45th Battalion graphically details the advance: 'Enemy shells are falling thicker now. Every now and again a fleeting shower of machine gun bullets is sprayed over our advancing line. Men are falling here and there.

Stretcher bearers are busy.'[26] His description of the Germans is also evocative: 'On we go, capturing more and more Fritz; cringing, crawling, cowardly fellows, those we meet now. Poor broken-spirited beggars, they've had the pluck knocked out of them. Many of them are just kids; poor, frightened, skinny little codgers of fifteen to seventeen, a pathetic sight in their big, round, silver-rimmed spectacles. Clad in men's uniforms that flap all over their under-nourished young bodies, there's nothing of the man about them except the rifle they've flung away.'[27]

Nearby, the 13th also advanced up Ascension ridge, 'taking farm after farm by the normal tactics against half-hearted resistance'[28] and collecting prisoners. They swept into Coronet Post on the summit, which had a dozen machine guns mounted on the parapet with their crews sheltering in dugouts, and captured eighty men. The 15th Battalion history relates the story of a German sergeant major who was very annoyed when captured; having served throughout the war, he had just been approved for a commission, and now this promotion would not be coming to him.[29] These battalions consolidated on the east side of Ascension ridge, with the Germans sniping as they dug.

On the northern flank, the 1st and 3rd Battalions were held up with fire coming from Villeret. The 3rd Battalion captured the northern part of Cologne Farm and went into Ferret Trench, which was attacked by Sergeant Tom McMillan and two men. Imagine their surprise when the three of them 'found it full of Germans, but putting on a bold face on their surprise, they hurled in their bombs. The whole trench full surrendered, whereupon all the Germans in the valley fled to the rear.'[30]

The 9th Battalion, to the left of the 13th and 15th, was also at the second objective. They had attacked with the 10th Battalion after an initial fight at Grand Priel Wood, advancing in artillery file with the creeping barrage lifting 100 yards every four minutes. Taking fire from Villeret, their tank, which had finally arrived, swept around the village. It was quickly hit as it went into action, but cheered by the men as it continued firing, allowing the village to be taken. At this time, the Germans were also firing on two dummy tanks and tried for two hours to knock them out. This allowed the 3rd Brigade to take Villeret, the Red Line objective, on schedule at 9 am. After, the barrage lifted and they reached the third objective, the Blue Line, before 10 am. Monash had called this 'The Line of Exploitation', meaning an objective that wasn't mandatory, but could be taken.

After reporting their progress to divisional headquarters, an intelligence officer was sent up to check the 3rd Brigade was actually on the objective, so surprised were the commanders that the Blue Line had been reached so quickly. The officer arrived and was satisfied, stating 'that the divisional commander was delighted with the result of the operation'.[31]

A story is told in the 9th Battalion history about two Germans who decided they would make a stand. Sergeant Porter told them to surrender, but when they refused, he called out to Lieutenant Earwaker, 'Can you speak German?'

'Why?' replied Earwaker.

'There's a couple of Germans here and they won't come out of their trench when I tell them to.'

'Why don't you shoot them?' responded Earwaker.

'I can't kill them in cold blood.'

Earwaker went to the Germans' post and told them in German to come out, and when they did not, he jumped into their position and pushed over their machine gun. They told him they wanted to collect something from their dugout. Earwaker, pointing his pistol at them, motioned them back and went into their dugout by himself, only to find many stick grenades.[32] Keeping his wits about him probably saved his life.

The new front line was now a mile from the Hindenburg Line, but needed much work to be consolidated. It had been a good day, although the 9th Battalion had one officer and nine men killed, and a further four officers and thirty-nine men wounded. They had captured 200 prisoners, as well as three field guns, eight howitzers and forty machine guns, a worthwhile day's haul.

By 10.30 am, the right of the 1st Division was consolidating on their Blue Line objective overlooking Bellicourt and the St Quentin Canal. From the ridgeline, they could look down on the village and see the glistening water in the canal and the tunnel entrance nearby. Behind was open green landscape for miles with Germans moving about among the trenches and wire of this formidable defensive line. Australian patrols now went past the objective, heading down the slope towards the canal through Quarry Ravine and Quarry Knoll. Leading the patrol, Sergeant John Bentley, MM, DCM, a linesman from Casino, NSW, and a Gallipoli veteran, came upon a German officer trying to organise his men. Bentley charged the officer and shot him, bayoneted one or two men and captured most of the party, with some fleeing, and repeated this action soon after, capturing another seventeen prisoners. At Quarry Knoll, a second patrol captured 200 Germans, who abandoned a field battery and their headquarters that contained important documents and code books.

At the northern end of the Australian front, the 3rd Battalion had fought through Hargicourt and were moving through

Malakoff Farm towards their objective. At this point, the line of advance changed slightly and the left-hand company under Lieutenant Cecil Clifton, wanting to keep contact, continued into the British area where his men cleared a German concrete strongpoint holding up the British advance. Here, Corporal John Roberts, after the loss of his officer, led the men forward 'with great skill and gallantry',[33] capturing a number of German machine guns that were holding up their advance.

Everywhere the Australians were advancing onto the third object-ive, the one Monash had designated for exploitation purposes only. While the Australians were consolidating, the 74th British Division was only just ahead of its second, and not scheduled to advance again until 1 pm. Their delay concerned the Australians as they now had an exposed northern flank, making further advances dangerous. To add to their woes, the 74th were shelled by their own artillery and fell back further to the second objective at Rifle Pit Trench.

Through the afternoon, the Australians continued the attack on the remaining strongpoints still holding out. The order came to wait for a bombardment at 11 pm and then to attack again at dawn. Hot food was sent forward and mule teams carried water, ammunition and bombs right up to the front line, coming up while the German artillery was distracted and disorganised. For a few hours, the men were able to rest and the fighting died down, with both the Germans and the Australians exhausted.

At 11 pm, heavy rain teemed down, making the advance in total darkness difficult and strenuous. West of Bellenglise, the Australians struck thick belts of barbed wire. Here they were heavily outnumbered by the defenders, but attacked with the bayonet and quickly seized both trench lines and dugouts, taking hundreds of prisoners[34] who were at the time sheltering from the barrage and the rain in deep dugouts. The Germans had left their machine guns unmanned up on the parapet, and as the battalion history states, 'the men of the 46th couldn't believe their luck.'[35] There now existed a gap between the 46th Battalion and the nearest Australians, the 4th Brigade on the left, but by 1 am, the Blue Line was secured and consolidation began. It was here that a German officer remarked to Major Frank Couchman, DSO, 'All I can say is you are some bloody soldiers.'[36]

The 48th then arrived, along with four Vickers guns, to secure the right flank as the British attack had failed to make the object-ive. The British commander at this point insisted his men were on the objective, but General Ray Leane, not convinced, sent bombers down and along Pen and Entrepot trenches to secure his flank.

There is a graphic description of the 14th Battalion attack, written by Lieutenant Edgar Rule in his book *Jacka's Mob*, which occurred after the battalion was pinned down by intense German machine-gun fire. Rule writes:

He [Tom Griffith] yelled out as he started bombing up the sap 'Have a bloody go at them'. This pulled me together . . . and I started to advance. We had to reach to support trench . . . with 40 yards to go when these guns opened again. I looked around and my heart sank. On account of the lead flying, we all got down flat on the ground. Bullets were kicking up the dirt all around us. I heard a man yell just beside me, and then he lay quiet. I was just on the point of ordering a bolt, when one of the boys with a Lewis guns crawled up alongside me, and in a second had opened fire along the trench, and to our surprise he silenced the Huns. A little further along another of the lads took his cue and opened fire, and after each burst, these gunners would yell, 'Now's your time to rush them'. We all up and ran for dear life towards those Huns, yelling like lunatics.[37]

The battalion history states, 'The advance to Ascension Wood showed the Australian infantry at its best; little bodies of men, singularly or in pairs, dashing forward amidst the bullet-swept slopes, dropping to ground for cover, and then making another dash forward with that skill and cunning which probably distinguished Australian troops beyond all others in the war.'[38]

With the Australian attack having driven the Germans back to the first real defensive line, the Hindenburg Outpost Line, the night was lit with star shells and flares. Needing to ascertain the German front line and the enemy strength on their right flank, a patrol from the 48th Battalion consisting of Lieutenant Robert Reid and two privates, James Woods and Walter Reid, set out to find the Royal Sussex Regiment. There was now a gap of 500 yards between the Australian front line and the furthest advanced post of the English line. The patrol made its way down the trench and suddenly entered a German machine-gun post of thirty men. Private Woods later described what happened in the trench:

We moved as quietly as we could and suddenly came to a traverse. I heard voices and the next moment by the light of a flare, I caught sight of a German helmet . . . The next thing there was a challenge in German and I could see the Hun with his rifle and bayonet pointed at the officer's stomach. Up went his hands, there was nothing else he could do . . . So I shouted at the top of my voice, fired off my rifle as quickly as I could reload and made the Jerries believe that it was an attack in progress. Luckily for me they panicked and went for their lives. They left four or five machine guns and then the officer and I attended to a number of them hiding in a dugout. We threw bombs down the steps, and those that weren't killed, they didn't try any funny tricks after that.[39]

The Germans having fled, Lieutenant Reid then ordered Woods to hold the post while he went back for reinforcements. Meanwhile, the Germans, realising there were few Australians involved, decided to counterattack. Woods mounted the parapet to watch for German movement, but suddenly became engaged in a desperate lone defence: 'I was there for two hours alone. The Boche tried several attacks over the top, but I managed to keep him off with bombs and by using his own machine guns against him. The only thing that did worry me was when he began to shell the position with gas shells. Our own artillery, not knowing of course that there were any of our men there, also began lobbing over gas shells.'[40] Just as the enemy came on again, Lieutenant Reid returned with some other men. He wrote, 'Full thirty men were pitted against this one lad when I returned with reinforcements.'[41] This group of about ten men held the post for nearly five hours until ordered to retire. The Germans then retook the post, but the Australians returned, and after the Germans were shelled by the Allies, the AIF were able to drive back the Germans and consolidate this important post in the line. For his bravery, Private Woods was awarded the Victoria Cross and Lieutenant Reid the Military Cross.

Other acts of bravery and determination were witnessed all along the line. Individuals and groups desperately fought for control of sections of trench, reorganising the men and providing covering fire and counterattacks. The Germans continued to attack the weak right flank over open ground, and the Allied advance here was decimated. Each time the Germans were forced back, the Australians took over sections of their trench and, by dawn on 20 September, they had secured several hundred yards.

The day passed in relative peace as each side consolidated their positions and prepared for the next stage of the attack. At this time, General Leane inspected his forward trench line and questioned a captured German officer, 'How was it that so few of the 48th had taken so many prisoners in such excellent positions?' The German officer replied, 'The Australians are so brave and so quick, that it is impossible to stop them.'[42] On 21 September, the 48th Battalion was relieved by the Lincolnshire Regiment and returned to Tincourt for a well-deserved rest.

Also on 21 September, a company of American troops relieved part of the 48th Battalion now situated in a dugout known as 'Harrod's Stores'. The Americans had marched to the front line in a column of fours, having never been in the line and not knowing how far they were from the enemy. Three Australian officers and four NCOs remained behind to help the Americans become acclimatised to the defensive position and life in the front line. One of these NCOs was wounded by a keen American, who challenged him with 'Who goes there?' and then fired and wounded him before he could answer.

In the 11th Battalion, Captain 'Wally' Hallahan, who had just been recalled from leave in London where he had become engaged, was killed. Being a 1914 Gallipoli original, his leave for Australia had already been approved and, had he been married, he would have been on a ship for home rather than fighting his last battle. Then, as the 11th Battalion was coming out of the line on 24 September, an enemy aircraft bombed the column and hit a party of officers, killing two Gallipoli originals: Captain Darnell, the Commanding Officer, and Lieutenant

Archibald. As the battalion history states, 'Thus the battalion's last major action of the war, a cruel twist of fate sees so many men, having fought from Gallipoli to the final hurdle in late 1918, cut down.'[43]

By dawn on 20 September, the Australians had captured the Blue Line, a feat not achieved along any other part of the line. The British were still a mile back on the second objective and their attempts to reach it overnight had also failed, leaving the Australians to retain the 48th to protect the flank. Bean notes, 'The victory was greater than realised then or afterwards by the higher command.'[44] He also notes, 'In reporting to Haig, Rawlinson mentioned that German officers said that their men would not now face the Australians.'[45] Before Monash could advance to the Hindenburg Line, however, he needed the British IX and III Corps to advance their line and secure their position and his flank along the Blue Line. Not only had the British failed, but they now turned to Monash for Australian help to secure 500 yards of their front.

Though Monash agreed, the position presented him with another problem. That afternoon, the 1st Battalion was to be relieved, but when the order came through rescinding this relief, the men of the battalion loudly complained. The new order was so resented by the men of Captain Steen's company that they refused to move, as they believed 'they were not getting a fair deal' and 'were being put in to do other people's work'.[46] This had been a common complaint over the preceding years, when British units had not kept up with Australian flanks. As a result, Australian battalions needed, as they said, 'to make good their neighbours' failures.'[47]

While the unexpected success in taking the Hindenburg Outpost Line was celebrated, new problems were surfacing in the Allies' position. And as the weary battalions trudged back to their billets at Tincourt and along the Somme, few would realise or even dare to hope that they had already fought their last battle.

FOURTEEN

Taking the
Hindenburg Line

With the Germans now behind their final defensive line, and
with little between them and the German border, their fighting
resolve was stiffened by the apparent impregnability of their line
and their desperate state of defence. Yet to the north, the French
and the Americans had attacked in the Argonne Forest, Haig's
First and Third Armies had penetrated six miles at Cambrai and
on the Ypres Salient, and Plumer's Second Army, with Belgian
support, was preparing to recover lost ground. Everywhere the
Germans were under pressure and, at the highest levels, command
and control were breaking down.

The fight for the Hindenburg Outpost Line was therefore still
raging when the next challenge arose for the exhausted Allied
armies. Haig, Rawlinson and Monash naturally wanted to keep
the pressure on the enemy, but there was serious pressure on
Haig, in particular, not to fail nor sustain high casualties. For
all the threats and intimidation from London, Haig believed a
further offensive could win the war, though as ever there was no
guarantee of success. Before him was the most formidable defensive line in history, defended by a resolute, well-equipped and
well-supplied enemy, but it needed to be overcome if the war was
to be concluded in late 1918. If the German army could hold this

line, even for a few weeks, the coming of winter would end major operations for several months, and allow time for Germany to negotiate a peace on more favourable terms.

Haig and Foch saw the breaching of the St Quentin Canal, north-east of the mount, as part of a much broader attack north and south against the bastion of the Hindenburg Line. While this twelve-mile section of the line would be attacked by Rawlinson's Fourth Army, to the north the British Third Army would advance and, to the south, the First French Army would also move forward on a six-mile front. Within the Fourth Army was General Sir Walter Braithwaite, a Boer War veteran who had been dismissed as Chief of Staff of the Mediterranean Expeditionary Force, but achieved success as a divisional commander on the Western Front. It was Braithwaite's IX Corps that protected the Australian 5th Division's right flank while the notorious III Corps still remained on the 3rd Division's left flank.

General Rawlinson was quick to see the potential of a rapid advance, and even before the capture of the outpost line, he had started planning the assault on the Hindenburg Line. Rawlinson relied heavily on Monash, as he needed the Australian Corps to undertake the main thrust at the St Quentin Canal. The canal ran underground through a tunnel for 6000 yards, forming a 'bridge' over the top, which was strongly defended by the Germans as it was considered a likely target for attack. Monash, of course, realised Rawlinson needed the AIF, and used this leverage to secure two fresh American divisions, the 27th and the 30th, whose numerical strength was double that of an empire division. While the Americans were keen and outwardly brave, they were still poorly trained, badly led, undersupplied and inexperienced, even after sixteen months in the war. On the upside, Monash had seen them in action at Hamel and Chipilly, and believed that if he could assist them with 'any technical guidance which they might lack',[1] he would be confident they would prove satisfactory on the day.

Monash set to work while the battle raged for the outpost line. This planning 'proved at once the most arduous, the most responsible and the most difficult'[2] that he was to undertake during the course of the war. At this time Monash, like his men, was exhausted, and a request by him to Rawlinson in early September for a few days' leave in Paris was rejected. He had lost weight, his skin was hanging from his face and his uniform was baggy. With no time to exercise, he had abandoned his daily walks, though he continued a series of mild exercises with dumbbells in the morning. He was also continually interrupted by visits from politicians, journalists and military groups seeking advice, but he remained focused and motivated, realising that victory was in sight.

Monash now grappled with a number of obstacles to the attack. He had initially hoped that the outpost line would be taken so he could replicate the straight start line that he had found effective for the 8 August offensive. However, apart from the Australian objectives through to the Blue Line taken by 18 September, there were still German strongpoints at the northern end of the line, not the least around Guillemont Farm west of Bony. The British objectives, to the north and south of the Australian Blue Line, were still in German hands and, as the clock ticked towards the planned day of the attack, 28 September, a series of assaults against these strongpoints had failed. If these were not captured by zero hour on 28 September, further complications and compromises would be thrown into the equation.

Monash first needed to get troops across the open terrain from a half to one mile from the Hindenburg Line, and then assault the 'bridge' above the tunnel, an area heavily defended by well-sited machine guns, trench mortars, artillery and clusters of land-mines. Next, he needed to assault the two defensive lines in the rear: the support line that ran from Le Catelet south to Nauroy and, behind this, the reserve line in front of Beaurevoir and Montbrehain, sometimes known as the Beaurevoir–Fonsommé Line. These lines formed part of a 'whole series of defences, with the numerous defended villages contained in it, [forming] a belt of country varying in depth from 7000 to 10,000 yards, organised by every possible means into a powerful system, well meriting the great reputation attached to it.'[3]

Securing these objectives entailed first an advance by the Americans of 4500 yards to the Green Line immediately east of Gouy, then the Australian 3rd Division would go through the Green Line and capture the Red Line east of Beaurevoir, another 4000 yards beyond. Towards the village of Vendhuile, the British 12th Division would then protect the northern left flank. Further south through Bellicourt, the American 30th Division would advance and be leapfrogged by the Australian 5th Division, who would then move east against the next two German defensive lines.

However, the Australians handed over their section of the Brown Line to the Americans on 24 September, as the Americans hadn't advanced beyond it towards the Blue Line, and the British III Corps had still not attained their objectives, remaining 1000 yards further back. The day before the planned 28 September start, an attempted attack to secure this Brown Line failed mis-erably, leaving many Americans stranded out in no-man's-land. While the Americans had followed the barrage, they'd failed to mop up, and the Germans had come out of their dugouts behind them and quickly cut them off. Artillery could not be used against the Germans, as isolated groups of Americans remained some-where out in front.

As a result, Monash suggested the attack be delayed for one day. Haig responded that this was not possible, as the attack was part of a major offensive and would need to go on as planned. A decision was made at Fourth Army HQ that the Americans should attack an hour before zero hour and connect with the barrage as they crossed the Brown Line. While there were few options available, the general feeling was that this was a compromise with little hope of success. The great fear for Monash was the casualties he would take in crossing the 'bridge' at the St Quentin Canal and, given the dramatically reduced battalions of the AIF, and their exhaustion and the mutinous spirit of the ranks, he had a lot on his mind.

Monash believed the American troops' aggressive spirit and keenness would make up for their lack of experience and training, and, with the Australians closely following their advance, they would be able to puncture the line then break through and consolidate. He broke down the subsequent advance into two stages. First, under a creeping barrage, the men were to seize the main Hindenburg Line defences on the earthen mound along the top, and then spread out north and south on the other side of the canal and attack the support line, moving forward in open warfare conditions to then attack the reserve line. Second, they were to consolidate and enlarge the bridgehead using the Australian 3rd and 5th Divisions, pushing forward with the available tanks.

Most of the Australian battalions were, while Monash was planning, back along the Somme, or in camps and bivouacs to the east of Péronne. The 39th Battalion had been camped in Handel Copse refitting and training, with every opportunity given over to sport and recreation. They undertook musketry practice with German weapons, particularly machine guns, and at 'the end of a fortnight, the troops had recovered sufficiently from months of fighting to enable them to go into action again'.[4] On 27 September, the battalion moved forward along roads congested with troops, wagons and artillery, and found themselves in old trenches near St Émilie for the night. Here they were surrounded by artillery positions, and it was a noisy and dangerous location due to counter-battery fire. The following day, ammunition, grenades and rations were distributed, and the men were briefed on the details of the attack. Ahead, they were told, was the American 30th Division, which would set out from behind the start line (the Brown Line) that ran through Guillemont Farm, and take the Green Line to the east of Bony and Le Catelet.

On 26 September, battalion commanding officers of the 8th Brigade had attended a conference to hear details of the planned assault on the Hindenburg Line. The next day, the 30th Battalion, which was to be the reserve battalion, moved forward to the Hervilly area. Here 'the Brigade allowed the Bn. [Battalion] to be bathed and to obtain a clean change of underwear instead. This was of great value, and enabled the men to go into action as fresh and clean as possible.'[5] On the night of the 27th, the battalion moved forward, but progress was slow, as it was a dark night and the roads remained congested. Arriving at their bivouac, they found no accommodation and spent the night in the open, with the weather 'very cold'.[6] The following day, 28 September, rain fell, making life a little more miserable, but as the 30th Battalion war diary notes, 'all rank were in very good spirits, and while it is recognised that the operation is rather a ticklish one, all felt confident that it would be brought to a successful conclusion.'[7]

Zero hour was planned for 5.50 am on 29 September. Rawlinson and Monash had assembled over 1600 guns, including 593 heavy guns and howitzers, and 1044 field guns of various calibre, which on the Fourth Army front was to fire one million shells. Apart from a high ratio of smoke, 30,000 mustard gas shells were included in the mix. The Germans had first used mustard gas a year before on the Menin Road, but this would be the first time the British had used it in the war. There were also tanks allocated to the American advance, including the American 301st Heavy Tank Battalion, which put in thirty-four British tanks with American crews.

On 28 September, the 38th Battalion marched to Ronssoy Wood through the fields of devastation left in the wake of the German withdrawal. The hope was for the battalion to take a well-earned rest overnight, but they were disturbed during the early hours by a heavy bombardment of high explosive and gas, and aerial bombardment.

At 5 am on 29 September, the men rose, had a warm breakfast and tea and prepared for the big 'stunt'. They had been briefed the day before and understood the operation: first following the Americans to the Green Line, as the two American divisions were waiting on their tapes and were tasked with taking the Catelet–Nauroy Line east of the canal. The 2000 men of the American 106th Regiment with the support of tanks would advance, on a 4000-yard front, 5000 yards into the German line and secure the Green Line. At 9 am, the Australians would cross their start line and move forward with the idea of leapfrogging the Americans and pushing forward across the bridge. This would open the way for the Australians to advance towards the Beaurevoir Line, spreading out and into the area behind the formidable Hindenburg Line to a distance of about three miles. With them came the other attacking Australian brigades, which all formed up well within German artillery range.

Between 6 am and the time the Australians moved forward to their start line at 7.15 am. The 38th Battalion was subjected to a heavy gas attack, which caused many to be sick and made the advance in gasmasks uncomfortable and difficult. The battalion advanced from south of Ronssoy along the Bellicourt road to Guillemont Farm, where they were to link up with the tanks allocated for their attack. Arriving at a higher altitude, the men were able to remove their gasmasks and breathe in the clear morning air and briefly enjoy the sunshine and warmth of the new day.

At 7 am, the 40th Battalion moved forward. Advancing from Ronssoy, they also came under German artillery fire with high explosive and gas as they passed through an eighteen-pounder battery line. As they topped the ridge, they immediately saw how the Americans, who were meant to be securing the Brown Line 1200 yards away, had been faring. As the 40th Battalion history notes, 'The first glance indicated disaster, for everywhere the Americans could be seen, wounded and unwounded, streaming back, some falling from enemy fire as they came.'[8] Six of the tanks had been taken out by mines. It was a pity the tank crews could not read German, because the Germans had even erected warning signs in front of them.

At 8 am, the 38th Battalion moved forward in artillery formation past the guns lined up to support the American advance. A German artillery spotter plane circled above, dropping signals to direct fire. The battalion history notes, 'For quite a while this "devil" hovered above, being fired at by machine gunners from all points until at last it was hit in a vital part and crashed to earth amid cheering of many troops.'[9] As the battalion advance continued to Pot Trench, machine-gun fire was coming from Bony, and as these guns should have already been eliminated questions were being asked about the American advance. As the

38th Battalion war diary noted, 'it was apparent that the mopping up parties of the Yanks had not done their work properly.'[10] To compensate for this, 'A' Company was ordered to push forward and clean up. They advanced in half sectional rushes from shell hole to shell hole, but 'the MG fire became exceptionally heavy and heavy casualties were suffered.'[11]

At this time, Americans began to trickle back through the Australian line. When questioned, they could provide no information, did not know where they were and, with the loss of all their officers, did not know where to go nor what was to be done. Now, as lines of dead Americans were starting to be discovered, the real cost of this shortcoming in planning was being realised. Also apparent was the failure of the tanks, with many of them burning and out of action.

The intensity of the German machine-gun fire was forcing the Australians to ground and hampering attempts to keep contact between the advancing companies. 'A' Company was now ahead and out of sight, so a small patrol led by Captain Charles Peters, MC, carefully moved forward, finding the company headquarters in a shell hole about 100 yards east of their position, and discovering their lieutenant was dead. Soon after, the 'A' Company commander, Captain Francis Fairweather, MC and Bar, was shot by a sniper in the neck as he looked over the edge of the hole. His death shortly afterwards was, the battalion history states, 'a severe loss to the Battalion [as he was] one of the unit's most capable officers, a cool, level-headed soldier, and a fearless fighter'.[12]

The Australians were beginning to wonder where the bulk of the Americans were, and how far had they progressed forward. At 12.30 pm, a message conveyed that they were spread along the Green Line, the first objective, but that, much like the earlier failed attempt on 28 September, in their enthusiastic advance the Americans had failed to mop up German dugouts and trench lines. They had been warned that this was crucial as the Germans had an intricate system of trenches, dugouts and underground passages, and could move troops below ground level. As a result, Germans now emerged to fire into the backs of the advancing Americans and also cut them off from the Australians, who were tasked with consolidating their positions and continuing the advance.

The Australians also began taking fire from the unmopped-up positions and from accurate German shelling, leading to many casualties. The 38th Battalion's advance was also slowed by thick belts of uncut wire, with cleverly sited gaps that were covered by machine guns and snipers. An artillery barrage was called for, including smoke, which was quickly laid down to enable the battalion to continue. They advanced to South Guillemont Trench, which had been evacuated by the enemy and into which Australian and American troops found shelter. Here they were also able to link up with the 41st Battalion on their left. However, the weather turned wet and cold, and the spirits of the men fell until 9 pm when hot food was brought forward and, later, cigarettes and matches.

As they needed to press forward with the attack, orders were received at 4.30 am on 30 September for the 10th Brigade, of which the 38th was a part, to push up Claymore Valley towards Bony, a tiny village within the Hindenburg Line. The Germans had manned the Hindenburg Line to the western side of the canal to defend the bridge, forming an arcing defensive salient that protruded towards the Allies.

By 9.50 am, the 38th held a position on the crest of the hill above Bony, giving them extensive views into German territory, particularly the Hindenburg system of trenches to the east of the tunnel. A telephone line was soon established to battalion headquarters, allowing important artillery information to be sent back on enemy dispositions and movements.

An attempt was made at this point to advance down the slope, but German machine guns covered the hillside and a patrol sent out was forced to return. The following morning, 1 October, a patrol from 'C' Company, 38th Battalion, now down to twenty men instead of the usual 250 men, pushed around to the north of Bony, but were fired on by determined German posts. One patrol of the 39th Battalion was decimated. At 2.30 pm, orders were received to advance the line north-east, taking in the process the northern tunnel mouth.

The 38th was now sent back into support and, seeking a place to rest, found a huge German dugout, which was part of the Hindenburg defensive system. The battalion history notes, 'These dugouts were wonderful caverns, deep and concreted and able to accommodate whole battalions. Here felt as safe from shell fire as if hundreds of miles from the line. The only danger which at first presented itself was the possibility of being mined, but a careful examination by engineers dissolved this fear.'[13] The following day, the 38th were relieved and fell back to their billets in Ronssoy, where a hot meal and a good rest awaited them.

The 39th Battalion had also set out from Ronssoy on 29 September, but were surprised to quickly come under intense machine-gun fire even though they were still 1000 yards from the start line. Unable to advance, the 39th moved into Dog Trench along with companies of the 38th, south-west of the fortified Guillemont Farm. Here the battalion found leaderless, confused yet willing Americans in what the 39th Battalion history described as 'a scene of complete chaos and disorganisation'.[14] The 40th Battalion notes a similar situation in a trench they entered:

> The scene in Willow Trench was appalling. Great numbers of wounded and unwounded Americans were huddled in the trench. Their rifles and machine guns lay beside them. They made no attempt to use them and the enemy were attacking. A wounded man would crawl across the open and drop into the trench on top of the others, and an unwounded man would run back, jump into the trench, and lay there sobbing at the unexpected horror and hopelessness of it all.[15]

Now held up in the trench with little information about the American advance, Lieutenant Colonel Robert Henderson, DSO, the 39th's Commanding Officer, went forward, but he was shot in the head by a sniper and died instantly.

The location of the Americans was still a mystery, and now heavy fire was holding up the advance. This tenacious German defence was unexpected, given the low morale and the poor fighting record of the enemy since the 8 August advance, and their readiness to surrender. Now determined resistance was seen in heavy and accurate artillery strafes and counterattacks forming up. Keen to get information about the American front line, the 39th received orders after midday to send patrols forward into the ruins of Guillemont Farm. As they moved forward cautiously, they drew fire from the farm and were forced to ground. After dark, the battalion advanced into Guillemont Trench but it had been a disastrous day, with one officer and seven other ranks killed, plus forty wounded.

At 11 am on 30 September, an order arrived to move the 39th Battalion into Guillemont Crescent to join the 38th and 40th Battalions. Here the trench was found full of American dead and wounded, many having lain untreated for thirty-five hours. The 39th Battalion Regimental Medical Officer, Captain Lesley Allsop, made a forward aid post close to the farm ruins and worked directly, mostly on American wounded, to get men back and into treatment. In this way, Allsop saved many lives, and earned the respect and gratitude from all about him.

As dawn broke on 1 October, the 39th Battalion's third day in the line, it became quickly apparent that the Germans had vacated Bony and fallen back behind the tunnel mound. A patrol moved through the village, where they bombed a few cellars, and continued their advance to the high ground 500 yards to the north. This allowed the 38th Battalion to come up on the right flank and the 40th on the left to consolidate a new forward position. At 6 pm that night, the battalion was relieved by the King's Own Yorkshire Light Infantry and returned to their bivouac near St Émilie. Though they did not know it as they drank their hot soup and cocoa, this was to be their last fight, the end of a strenuous and bloody chapter in the battalion's history. It was not as successful an operation as the men had hoped, largely due to the failure of the Americans in the attack, but the battalion was proud of its contribution to the AIF's history.

Elsewhere on this broad front, further south near Bellicourt, the 5th Division's advance had been slightly more effective.

On 29 September, the first day of the attack, reveille for the 29th Battalion was at 5.15 am followed by a hot breakfast at 6 am. At 7.15 am, they moved off for the advance through the American 27th Division who at the time, according to the plans, were completing their attack on the Green Line east of Nauroy. Moving along the 'Black' road, the 29th immediately encountered fog and smoke, which made it difficult to move in formation and keep touch with nearby formations. Arriving in Villeret, the battalion reorganised and continued forward at 8.40 am. At 9.30 am, they crossed the Brown Line and passed to the eastern side of Bellicourt just after 10.30 am, 'where our four tanks were found intact'.[16] Here they also found American troops streaming back as enemy fire increased in intensity from the front, both flanks and even the left rear,[17] in particular from Cabaret Wood Farm, a German 'tank fort'. The Allied tanks were also taking fire, with three quickly knocked out by German 77-millimetre guns in Nauroy Wood. These guns were soon after silenced, 'the gun crews being either bayonetted or shot',[18] but the intensity of machine-gun fire coming from Nauroy forced the battalion to consolidate on the German support line.

Another of the 8th Brigade's battalions, the 30th, had also moved forward, but quickly came under German shelling and, in the fog and smoke, difficulties were encountered keeping touch with the supporting battalions. Although there was concentrated machine-gun fire, the battalion suffered few casualties thanks to the lack of visibility. As the 30th advanced to the south of Bellicourt, a German anti-tank gun firing from a wood on the outskirts of the village knocked out five tanks before they could get to a position to deal with the machine guns. When four more tanks advanced towards Nauroy, they too were taken out by the anti-tank gun. Two fighting patrols were sent out to deal with the gun, after which the battalion established two posts on the east side of Nauroy. By the time these were handed over to the advancing 29th Battalion, the 30th had more than fifty casualties. But, as the battalion war diary notes, 'the men had gone through a heavy day's fighting [but] the operation had so far not been successful as regards the objectives set down.'[19]

The 8th Brigade continued their advance up the ridge and through the Catelet–Nauroy Line. At this point, three of the four battalion tanks were hit from a carefully sited tank fort. An Australian officer raced back to the final tank, which was still out of sight in the lee of the hill. The officer tried to convince the tank commander to remain out of sight until the tank fort had been dealt with, but the commander responded, 'I must go on, if there is a chance. And I know there is a chance.'[20] The tank advanced another thirty yards before it was hit and burst into flames. 'A door opened unsteadily and the officer, wounded, blinded and blazing from head to foot, fell out on the ground. "Shoot me please" he pleaded. Somebody shot him.'[21]

The 29th Battalion now started to take enfilade fire from the left rear and the German strongpoint at Cabaret Wood Farm, forcing them to halt for a few hours. They were still several hundred yards behind the Green Line, the American objective.

The 32nd Battalion, led by Major Blair Wark on the right, was finding their advance easier, particularly when they found the British 46th Division, who had probably achieved the most successful and gallant attack on 29 September. Under Major General Gerard Boyd, the 46th, part of the British IX Corps commanded by General Braithwaite, had the difficult task of crossing the V-shaped water-filled cutting south of the canal tunnel entrance and then scaling the steep eastern bank, which was covered by numerous German machine guns. Although the canal was not deep, the men used a range of flotation devices, including 3000 life jackets taken from cross-channel steamers. They succeeded in crossing the water with the support of an intense barrage and smoke. They also captured the beautiful Riqueval Bridge, which crossed the canal, before German engineers could destroy it, and which once secured could then bring across tanks, supply wagons and horses.

The action of the British division allowed the 32nd Battalion to now push forward through the outskirts of Nauroy, on the other side of the canal, clearing the village as they went and collecting fifty prisoners. They were followed by the 30th Battalion, who completed the mopping-up and secured the line.

The 32nd Battalion continued their rapid advance, mopping up the village of Étricourt and parts of Magny-la-Fosse, and joining up with the British troops who were coming up on their right. It was during this time that Major Wark repeatedly led his men forward, capturing German field guns, clearing up machine-gun posts and sending forward patrols; one patrol went through Joncourt, three miles ahead of the Australian front line, before turning back to establish a line near Étricourt.

The 8th Brigade now consolidated their line, but fire was still coming from their left flank, an area that was the responsibility of the 15th Brigade.

In the 15th Brigade sector immediately to the north, the advance was led by the 59th on the left and the 57th on the right, with the 58th Battalion in reserve. Initially, the dense fog and enfilade fire on the 59th Battalion's left saw it skew to the left and, when it reached the Hindenburg Line, it was hundreds of yards out of position. To fill the gap, the 58th Battalion moved up, and the 57th and 58th then moved forward together. By the end of the first day, the 32nd Battalion of the 8th Brigade had advanced 5000 yards beyond the assembly point while the 59th had barely crossed the same line.

Within the 5th Division front, the 5th Pioneer Battalion also had a big day. The pioneers had taken hard lessons from 8 August and saw a repeat performance in the demanding construction of roads and the clearing of obstacles to push the attack forward. The battalion was so close to the advancing front line that men had to drop their tools as they took fire near Bellicourt and resort to the rifle to take the fight to the enemy. They took six officers and 154 Germans prisoner, but by the end of the day had seven officers and fifty-seven other ranks as casualties.

It was at this time, within the 5th Division's advance, that word was received of a gruesome find in the mouth of the northern tunnel entrance. Initial reports spoke of a German 'corpse factory' where dead and dismembered bodies were found in large vats, presumably as part of a process for rendering cadavers to fat. In fact, the scene was the result of a terrible accident, where a large delayed-action shell had pierced the roof, travelled through ten feet of earth and exploded in a kitchen where men were probably assembling for dinner. Parts of one or two had been blown into the cauldrons used to prepare the food, and here they were found. Charles Bean visited this site and understood its true purpose, but the British propaganda machine had already reported the scene in the pages of the international news press.

By the end of 30 September, the 5th Division's advance had not proceeded a great deal from the night before. The line of advance and the line of German resistance had been defined, however, and the Americans had been collected and sent back. Now firm plans could be drawn up to redefine battalion and brigade boundaries, and plan the next setpiece battle.

To the north, the 3rd Division was still finding its advance towards Le Catelet held up by the fire from the village, and Gouy and Bony remained serious problems. The Germans were resisting, holding their ground and even counterattacking, something not seen over the past two months.

The Americans' inexperience and casualties in this attack would be discussed and written about until the end of the war. The Americans were not prepared for open warfare conditions and, along with the fog and the disorganised and haphazard advance, this meant that by the time the Australians prepared to leapfrog them at the Green Line, the American divisions were still far in the rear, floundering about leaderless and confused.

The failure of the Americans not only resulted in their troops being shot from behind and the slowing of the Australian advance, but also in places groups of German prisoners, who were being taken back by American escorts, were liberated and rejoined the fighting ranks of the enemy.

The American divisions suffered disproportionate casualties; some 1500 from the 27th Division and even higher casualties from the 30th Division. General Read, commander of the US Second Army, agreed with the broad criticism of his divisions' failing, pointing out that 'lack of experience was the chief failing . . . and their tendency to lose the remarkably close touch with the combatant units that all British headquarters maintained.'[22]

Late that day, Rawlinson wrote, 'The Americans appear to be in a state of hopeless confusion and will not, I fear, be able to function as a corps, so I am contemplating replacing them . . . I fear their casualties have been heavy, but it is their own fault.'[23]

FIFTEEN

Montbrehain:
The Last Attack

As 1 October dawned, the objectives set two days before had not been reached. The struggle, the fighting and the casualties just to clear the Hindenburg Line must have been daunting to both General Monash and his AIF divisions, particularly given the ease of the advance after the initial offensive on 8 August. Now, eight weeks later, and so far into German territory, the enemy were offering stiff resistance and even staging counterattacks. How impossible it would have seemed that, within less than a week, all five divisions of the AIF would be withdrawn from the line and their fighting over.

The Americans were sent to the rear, and the advance was to proceed without these brave but inexperienced troops getting in the way. Now the AIF 3rd and 5th Divisions had much to do. To increase control over each brigade's sector and to orchestrate a moderate advance, General Hobbs, Commanding Officer of the 5th Division, adjusted each brigade's line of advance east of Nauroy, with the 8th Brigade on the right to capture the Sugar Factory and establish a line on Mill Ridge, the 14th in the centre to take the Lamp Signalling Station and the high ground around it, and the 15th on the left flank to capture the tough objective of Cabaret Wood Farm. The 3rd Division's objective was to push forward to the canal line, to occupy the north end of the tunnel and to establish posts near Bony Point.

Zero hour was set at 6 am on 1 October. Though the night was quiet, with little enemy shelling, it had been dark and wet, and the men were cold and exhausted. When the barrage came down, it was accurate and intense and, as the men left their trenches, Germans were seen moving back from the three strong-points designated as objectives for the 5th Division's attack. The 58th Battalion war diary recalls:

> A German soldier of the 2nd Guards Division walked in and gave himself up to one of the company commanders of the 58th Battalion. He stated he was glad to surrender as he had not eaten in three days and his understrength regiment had taken heavy casualties from the artillery barrage. He said all but thirteen of the fifty Germans in Cabaret Wood Farm were wounded and would also be willing to surrender as they all believed they were fighting inexperienced American troops and had nothing to fear.[1]

As a result, the wood was quickly taken.

The advancing lines moved past the shell-shattered battlefield and out into the rolling grassland, and crops that were relatively undamaged. Even the villages were near complete; undamaged, their grounds and fences remaining, their gardens in flower and fruit trees untouched.

As patrols moved forward, no enemy troops were encountered in the area south-west of Bony, but Germans were still seen in the village. By 1 pm, however, Bony was cleared by men of the 9th Brigade who went on to clear the nearby Knob and Bony Point objectives.

One man who epitomised the determination and courage of the infantry at this time was Lieutenant Norman Dalgleish of the 58th Battalion. After being wounded on the opening day of the attack, 29 September, he continued to lead his men. He was again wounded on 30 September, this time in the arm, but again continued. On 1 October, after assisting in the taking of Cabaret Wood Farm, he was wounded again, this time severely with a shell shard in the face, and was carried out. Covered in blood and unable to speak, Dalgleish first used sign language, then struggled to write and sketch what he knew of the area, the paper splattered with his blood. Later, when taken further back, he asked for his pocketbook and a pencil and wrote a report, with the aid of a nurse, to his superior, noting the advances made that day and including the recommendation of awards for two of his NCOs. He then collapsed, and died a week later on 9 October. An account of this was written up by Pompey Elliott and later read to Dalgleish's father, who 'broke down completely and cried like a child'.[2]

To the north, the 10th Brigade was advancing towards Le Catelet and taking some long-range shelling from German batteries beyond the Beaurevoir Line. German troops were seen pulling out of Le Catelet, and the Australians laid fire on them as they fell back. The 10th Brigade war diary reported that German troops 'were not in a fit state to carry out further attack', but concern remained about the left flank which 'was its tender spot' so machine guns were sent to cover this area. The war diary goes on to report that rations were good and plentiful, 'and apart from the difficulty of supplying the numerous unattached Americans for the first night, there was little trouble'.[3]

At the southern end of the Australian line, the 8th Brigade's 30th and 31st Battalions advanced towards Joncourt. The 30th reported, 'When the barrage dropped it was well defined and fairly intense, our men moving well forward and keeping close contact.'[4] Enemy artillery began to retaliate some five minutes later, with .77 and 5.9-inch guns causing casualties during the advance. At 6.15 am, an enemy aircraft flew low over the advancing Australians but was fired at and driven off, with Lewis gunners resting their weapons on their mates' shoulders and firing at the circling aircraft. The report continued, 'The enemy could now be seen in the vicinity of Mill Ridge. He did not wait for the bayonet, but moved out, some 70 or 80 in one body . . . presenting a favourable target for our men.'[5]

Now the battalions linked up and formed one long advancing line, along with the 32nd British Division moving up on their right. As the barrage lifted, the 30th Battalion dug in quickly in a position overlooking Joncourt. A patrol was sent into the village along the line of the railway, where it was found that the enemy had made a very hurried exit, leaving full packs and equipment behind them. The patrol sent back a runner who informed the battalion that the enemy had vacated and moved to the northern section of the village. From here, German machine-gun and rifle fire hastened the digging-in, and the Australians remained in cover for an hour. At 8.30 am, the decision was made to push on and take the village.

A message was sent from a company of the 30th: 'Am moving through village of Joncourt. Prisoners (few) and booty captured.'[6] Fleeing Germans had established a position in a sunken road, however, and fired on the Australians' flank. The 30th Battalion continued to move forward, then turned and directed heavy fire on the Germans, 'inflicting severe casualties'.[7] The battalion war diary goes on, 'One burst from a Lewis gun dropped four of the Boche at short range. Our rifle fire was also brought to bear to good effect. Favourable targets were being engaged up to 400 and 500 yards, and for the time being we gained superiority of fire. This was due to the excellent manoeuvring for position of the Lewis guns from hole to hole.'[8]

At 9.30 am, groups of Germans were seen assembling in preparation for a counterattack. The 30th Battalion immediately set up defensive positions on the northern outskirts of Joncourt and waited. During this time, two stretcher-bearers moved out into the open to collect a mortally wounded sergeant and were not fired on, but when they moved out a second time they were, and one of the bearers was wounded.

As a prelude to their anticipated counterattack, the Germans began a heavy strafe of Joncourt with high explosive and gas. Fortunately, the Australians found shelter in German dugouts and deep bunkers. After two hours, however, the men were uncomfortable in gasmasks and some tried to get out for fresh air, but they quickly returned as the artillery fire was intense. At 3 pm, the men emerged to find the village destroyed, the formerly prominent buildings a heap of rubble, and fires burning in houses. It was hours before the men could return to the underground shelters, given the lingering gas everywhere.

Keen to finish the Australians, the Germans brought up 77-millimetre guns to within 1500 yards of the village and began to fire over open sights. These guns were quickly engaged by Vickers and Lewis guns and within two minutes had been silenced, and were not used again.

★

By the night of 1 October, the line had advanced; Bony was taken, as were the three difficult tank forts and the village of Joncourt.

When Monash looked at the large wall map at headquarters, he realised that the objectives for the day had been achieved. His men had captured some 3000 Germans but the cost was high, with 2600 Australian casualties in the 3rd and 5th Divisions. Exhausted, these men needed to be relieved; over the night of 1–2 October, they were withdrawn to more secure areas west of the canal and replaced by the 2nd Division. It was the 2nd Division's task on the following morning to take the last real line of German defence – the Beaurevoir Line.

At 8.30 am on 2 October, the British 32nd Division attacked towards Ramicourt under a protective barrage. This time it was the British whose flank was left unsupported as the newly arrived Australian 2nd Division had not moved forward to assist the 16th Lancashire Fusiliers. The 2nd had received no order for the attack; perhaps there had been a hurried and misinterpreted order, or poor communication. While this advance stalled, detailed plans were made for an attack the following day by both British and Australian troops on a front of 11,000 yards.

Overnight, details of the attack and the start time were passed to battalion headquarters. The plan was for an attack by the 5th Brigade on a two-battalion front: the 18th Battalion on the right and the 19th on the left, with the 17th and 20th following. The objective was the villages of Genève, Beaurevoir and Ponchaux, with the advance moving in a north-easterly direction. The 7th Brigade would also be attacking on the left, and the 46th British Division on the right. There were three phases to the attack: first, the capture and mopping-up of the Beaurevoir Line; second, the advance across the La Motte Valley and the establishment of a line on the north-east slopes; and third, the further advance to the high ground along a line stretching south-east from Beaurevoir village.

To provide support, five field artillery brigades were to lay down a barrage for six minutes and move forward 100 yards every four minutes until the high ground was reached, and the artillery barrage would cease at 11 am. Eight tanks were also provided to follow the barrage, four per battalion, along with eight Whippets to assist the 17th and 20th Battalions; available tank numbers were low given the losses of the previous two months. The new anti-tank weapons, in particular a large Mauser anti-tank rifle[9] capable of firing a 13.2-millimetre armour-piercing round through the flimsy British tank armour, had seen tanks easily put out of action. Also to assist the attack of the 5th Brigade were 'gallopers' from the 13th Australian Light Horse Regiment, who would run messages and provide help where required. In the hope of a Haig-style breakthrough, a squadron of light horse was also attached to each battalion headquarters, but these were never used.

By 5.30 am, the men were lined out on the start tapes on the southern outskirts of Estrées waiting for zero hour, set for 6.05 am. The barrage started well and on time, and the men rose and advanced. The German barrage that came down between the jumping-off tapes and the Beaurevoir Line was reported as scattered, and 'did not give much trouble'.[10] The advance saw the 18th and 19th Battalions consolidate a position in the support line of the Beaurevoir system by 7.15 am. The centre companies, however, struck thick wire and heavy machine-gun fire. As no tanks were available, and after a failed attempt to clear the German post, the decision was made to withdraw and call for artillery. At 10.30 am, after the men had been withdrawn, an intensive five-minute barrage fell on the forward section of the German line. Immediately after the barrage stopped, two companies of the 19th Battalion attacked and, after joining with the 18th, who mopped up with them, the trench was secured with 200 prisoners taken, including four officers, along with eighteen machine guns and three trench mortars.

Further to the north, the 7th Brigade also began moving forward. The 25th Battalion had an advance across 1200 yards of open farmland on a 1400-yard frontage to attack a particularly strong section of the German line at Mushroom Quarry. When the barrage fell, they hugged the line of falling shells and, for the first 500 yards, they encountered little resistance. Advanced enemy posts 'surrendered fairly freely . . . the advance was checked here for a few minutes, but the dash and initiative displayed by all ranks succeeded in surrounding and overcoming all resistance . . . the Beaurevoir line was rushed and captured.'[11] The Australians captured a large number of prisoners and machine guns before taking their objective by 7.15 am.

At one point, a company of the 25th came upon 100 Germans lining a bank and firing on advancing British troops of the 151st Brigade further north. They quickly turned Lewis guns on the German position, killing forty and capturing sixty prisoners. The 26th Battalion then passed through the 25th and assisted in the capture of L'Ormisset and Mushroom Quarry.

The 7th Brigade war diary makes mention of the work of the snipers:

The Brigade Sniping Section was used with great effect in the advance. They moved off with the infantry on independent sniping missions, working in pairs. The section claimed 146 direct hits, of which 111 were claimed to be killed. Five enemy machine guns were put out of action by it and three German officers – one a captain, was killed. It reluctantly captured five Germans. A 77mm battery firing at 500 yards range was engaged and silenced for prolonged periods.[12]

As the attack continued, German resistance up to the Beaurevoir Line was not serious but, within the line, German machine gunners in particular held out. The 7th Brigade war diary goes on to state, 'The enemy morale was apparently very mixed; a large proportion did not relish the close fighting. On the other hand, our men used their bayonets with very good result.'[13] Australian casualties were two officers and sixty-one men killed, fourteen officers and 271 men wounded and thirty-seven missing. An estimated 500 Germans were killed and a further 705 captured. Bean records a captured German officer complaining, 'You Australians are all bluff. You attack with practically no men and are on top of us before we know where we are.'[14]

The 7th Brigade now held a line just to the east of Beaurevoir village, north-west of nearby Guisancourt Farm. On the night of 3–4 October, the brigade was relieved by the 7th British Infantry Brigade and moved back to the Nauroy area.

Meanwhile, 5th Brigade's 20th Battalion and two companies of the 17th Battalion had moved through Estrées and pushed past the Beaurevoir Line, which ran along the ridge above the village, with few casualties. They were held up here by a field gun firing from White Cottage as well as a number of concrete pillboxes, some with twenty machine guns.

Nearby, 22-year-old Lieutenant Joe Maxwell of the 18th Battalion had taken charge of his company when the company commander was severely wounded. At 7.15 am, he had sent a message saying he had been held up by heavy machine-gun fire and barbed wire. Having no available tanks to assist, Maxwell then led his men through the dense wire, taking German machine-gun positions as he went[15] by capturing the most dangerous gun and killing and capturing the crew, before taking out other machine guns holding up the advance.

At one point, as Maxwell was charging and firing his revolver, he leapt into a German post only to find he was out of ammunition. He is reported as saying, 'When the Germans before us shouted, *Kamerad*, I was the most pleased and relieved man in France.'[16] One of the surrendering Germans fired and killed an Australian, a cowardly act that brought swift and deadly retribution to these prisoners. Further into the advance, an Australian also shot a surrendering German prisoner. Others about to surrender then hesitated and Maxwell, feeling he needed to apologise and sort out the problem, walked into the group of Germans, taking with him a prisoner and two privates. He soon realised his mistake when a German officer in the trench ordered his men not to surrender, and to capture Maxwell instead. Immediately weapons were pointed at Maxwell, forcing his surrender. He suggested the German officer surrender as there was no way out for him, but he refused, asking Maxwell instead to join him in a drink. At that moment an Australian barrage fell on the trench, killing the German officer and allowing Maxwell to make his escape. Maxwell had already been awarded a Distinguished Conduct Medal and a Military Cross, but his actions on this day were to see him awarded the Victoria Cross.

The 17th and 18th Battalions continued their advance, next coming to the crossroads just on the western outskirts of Beaurevoir village, where they came under artillery fire from a

German 77-millimetre gun. This was quickly put out of action by the Lewis gunners and riflemen, and the gun crew was killed. The other two companies of the 17th Battalion passed through the Beaurevoir Line and captured Wiancourt at 9 am, but found they came under heavy fire as they left the village from a battery of field guns and machine guns firing at a range of 1200 yards.

To press the advance, the 6th Brigade was now brought up, with three battalions – the 22nd, 23rd and 24th – pushing forward to an objective line to the south-west of Beaurevoir village. To assist them, an artillery barrage was arranged for 4.15 pm with eight brigades of Australian artillery. This came down on Beaurevoir and other targets as the three battalions advanced. The right and left battalions met very little resistance, 'but in the centre sector there was several instances where determined resistance was offered by small groups of machine gunners, and an examination of the ground after the attack evinced the fact that bayonets had been used by the men to a greater extent than usual'.[17] Nearby, four 77-millimetre guns were captured 'though the enemy made determined efforts to prevent them falling into our hands'.[18] By 8.30 pm, the battalions were on their objectives and had made contact with their flanking battalions.

By the end of 4 October, the Australians held a 6000-yard front from north of Joncourt to Prospect Hill. On the Australian right flank, the British IX Corps held a further 5000-yard front from Joncourt south to Sequehart. During the attack, the Australians had captured 634 unwounded prisoners, including eleven officers, eight 77-millimetre guns, seven *minenwerfers*, six anti-tank rifles and about sixty-eight machine guns. Enemy dead were estimated to be well over 500. The 5th Brigade had fifty-eight men killed, 391 wounded, 159 gassed and thirty-five missing.

Attention now turned to completing the attack on the surviving sections of the Hindenburg and Beaurevoir lines, and past the remaining undeveloped German defensive lines. Haig still harboured his desire to push his cavalry through the yawning gaps along this new line, but Rawlinson, realising the exhausted state of the Australians, sought to relieve them and secure the lines before further advances could be made. This relief relied on American II Corps, who could not be brought up quickly enough, so the 22nd and 23rd Battalions would remain in place until the Americans' arrival the following night. Monash decided this was a good opportunity to use these battalions, along with the 2nd Pioneer Battalion, to take the fortified Montbrehain, after which they too would withdraw and return to the rear for rest.

The plan was for the two attacking battalions, the 21st and 24th, with the 22nd and 23rd following to mop up, to assemble on the jumping-off tapes at 5.25 am ready to start at zero hour, 6.05 am. Four tanks would be allocated to the two mopping-up battalions plus four tanks, if available, for the 2nd Pioneer Battalion. The attack would be supported by an artillery barrage falling 300 yards to the east, which would then creep forward 100 yards every four minutes. A heavy artillery barrage would also be laid on the village and then, as the battalions closed in, fall on selected targets in the Montbrehain vicinity. The barrage would also include smoke, as this had proved effective over the advance of the previous two months.

Going into this battle were two great mates, Captains Harry Fletcher and Austin Mahony. They had enlisted together from rural Victoria, joined the 24th Battalion as privates and had served at Gallipoli. Fletcher was a Bendigo schoolteacher, while Mahony was a clerk. They had suffered through the fighting at Pozières in July and August 1916, where Mahony was awarded the Military Cross, and each had risen through the ranks. By late 1918, they were both company commanders in the 24th Battalion and, though their company strength was well below that of a usual platoon, they were still together for the attack on Montbrehain.

At 3 am on 5 October, the men of the 24th were turned out of their shelters and ordered to prepare for the attack. As their battalion history states, 'The morning was frosty with the moon shining from a clear sky, and once they were astir the lads were eager for some activity to get their blood circulating with a little more warmth. A few hours later, when they were charging up the slope in the face of heavy fire, their blood was at boiling point.'[19]

The three companies formed up on the tapes one hour before zero hour, shivering and waiting for the barrage to come down. On the right, 'A' Company under Captain Mahony, MC; in the centre, 'B' Company under Captain G. D. Pollington, MM; and on the left, 'D' Company under Captain Fletcher. The men were still feeling the effects of the gas the Germans had laid down at 5.15 am, but by zero hour were keen to move.

At 6.05 am, as planned, the barrage fell ahead of the waiting Australian battalions, but it was thin and inaccurately placed. As telephone lines were quickly laid down and maintained, the first reports came back at 6.20 am from the Pioneers, which stated 'everything seems to be going well',[20] and the CO of the 21st sent a similar message. The Allied barrage provoked a light German retaliatory barrage and an enfilading heavier barrage on the right of the line, which followed the Australian advance. The two attacking battalions continued without the promised tank support, which was late in coming up. As the battalions entered Montbrehain, heavy machine-gun fire raked the 21st Battalion, with one gun firing 'from a window in the first house in the village; two Lewis gunners sliced out the windows with their bullets'.[21] From that point, however, resistance weakened on the 21st's front.

The 24th Battalion came under fire after they left their start line, and they emerged from the railway cutting with heavy fire coming from the north-east of Montbrehain. An enemy strong-point in this area contained 'numerous MG's and 42 Germans. This post put up a desperate resistance. The enemy fought fiercely until our troops were within three yards of their guns. They were eventually overcome and the garrison killed to the man.'[22] Fire then came from a nearby quarry, where more than 100 Germans with forty machine guns were shooting into the advancing lines of the 24th Battalion. After brutal fighting, this strongpoint was taken, along with sixty prisoners plus others in the immediate area. Nearby, a tank firing canister shots helped eliminate four German posts that were holding up Captain Mahony's advance.

Lieutenant George Ingram was awarded the Victoria Cross for his gallantry. His citation mentioned his actions during the attack on Montbrehain; for example, when his platoon was held up by a German strongpoint early in the advance and a heavy fight ensued, he eliminated nine machine guns, killing forty-two Germans.

The Germans began fighting back. The centre company of the 24th became isolated by intense machine-gun fire and a concentrated barrage which inflicted heavy casualties. The Australians established a line of posts and tried to connect them with the companies on their flanks, building a line around the southern side of the village. During this advance, Lieutenant Horrie Clough, while pushing through a hedge, struck his helmet on the barrel of a German machine gun, whereupon his batman, Private John Blankenberg, 'shot the crew as "cowards"'.[23] He had been wounded in action earlier that year, and was to be killed in the fighting that day.

A tank, attempting to relieve the situation, was quickly put out of action. After all the officers of the 24th were either killed or wounded, the senior NCO, Sergeant Major Adrian Burke, decided to dig in on the line they were holding.

A gap now existed between the companies of the 24th Battalion. The Germans counterattacked, pushing the Australians back. Lieutenant Willie McConnochie was fighting for his life, with Germans pushing in from three directions. 'Having a sticky time. Send us a platoon to come up on our right,'[24] he messaged his CO. Two platoons moved forward. 'Am going to hold on till supported,' he sent back. To make matters worse for the Australians, civilians began emerging from cellars; poor, desperate wretches who had been under German occupation for years, and who now crowded around the Australians, elated at their liberation.

Casualties in both battalions were heavy, and two companies of the 19th were brought up; one to support the 21st and one to support the Pioneers. The Pioneers and the 6th Machine Gun Company had followed to the rear of the two battalions as ordered, but as they advanced, they came under heavy fire from the railway line, the quarry and the sunken road, where they dropped into the waist-high crop and out of sight. The Pioneers, though not trained infantry, succeeded in securing the objective, capturing forty Germans and then digging in. They also, with the aid of two tanks, silenced other German posts, but fire from Doon Mill forced them back over the crest of the ridge, where they dug in. An attempt was made to get around the mill, but heavy German fire fell upon any movement by the Australians.

At this point, Lieutenant Norm Wilkinson crawled along the embankment, where he was astonished to see 100 German machine gunners lined along the bank 200 yards ahead. Unseen, he carefully brought up two Vickers guns. They quietly eliminated the two German machine guns protecting the flank, then poured fire into the Germans lining the bank. As Bean says, 'The Germans seemed to melt. Pushing on, Wilkinson and his men found 14 enemy machine guns out of action, 30 Germans killed and 50 wounded. The rest had fled.'[25] A captured German said at the time that if they had they known they were fighting Australians, 'they would not have fought at all'.[26]

The Germans, too, were having a hard day, and they showed great bravery and determination even though no organised counterattacks were mounted. When the Germans observed the Australians were not going to push far past the village, they brought artillery and machine guns forward and fired over open sights into the Australian posts. The 6th Brigade war diary states, 'His MG's were handled very expertly and courageously and pushed far forward while his very heavy losses did not in any way deter him in his efforts to reach and wipe out our posts. It is impossible to accurately estimate the number of enemy killed in this operation, but all ranks say that they have never seen so many enemy dead in such a small area.'[27] Estimates of Germans killed during the day ran well past 500. Over 600 prisoners were also taken, with eight officers and 327 men captured by the Pioneers. The 24th Battalion report on the battle states, 'It is impossible to estimate the number of enemy killed, but never before has it [the battalion] inflicted such heavy casualties.'[28] A German regimental historian wrote, 'only a few survivors came through to bring to regimental headquarters the news of the fearful catastrophe.'[29] The history also noted that the relentless Australian attack saw the

Germans run 'in wild flight before the attack',[30] but also that they did resist at various points including the communal cemetery.

The fighting was so severe and intense that the battalions ran out of ammunition and relied on captured German weapons, especially machine guns, to conserve their own ammunition. The 24th Battalion report noted, 'Vickers Gun, Lewis Gun, Rifle and Revolver ran out of ammunition repeatedly. Extra supplies were sent forward and much was salved from casualties. German guns were freely used on the enemy, and the battlefield was littered with German dead.'[31] Vickers guns played an important part in the fighting, particularly in the 24th Battalion sector. Two Vickers posts each claimed over 100 Germans killed, a claim borne out by the infantry in this area: 'All ranks are unanimous in their praise of the work done by the Vickers M. guns.'[32]

The artillery, after a bad start with a ragged and inaccurate opening barrage, also took credit for a large part of the success of the attack, especially for shelling German artillery, breaking up potential counterattacks and inflicting heavy casualties on the Germans firing from the ridges beyond Montbrehain. At 8 pm, the objectives had been captured and consolidated, and the lines between the battalions linked up and secured.

The outstanding success of the attack on Montbrehain was put down to the aggressive nature of the Australian battalions, in particular the 2nd Pioneer Battalion, which had not been involved in complex infantry operations before. This battalion had no time for any reconnaissance of the forward area, had moved up into position on a dark night and, for the duration of the day, had shown determination in taking German strongpoints and in holding their positions often under heavy artillery and machine-gun fire.

The Australians had captured 150 machine guns plus *minenwerfers*, and vast amounts of artillery pieces and stores. However, the casualties in the three attacking battalions, the 21st, the 24th and the Pioneers, were nine officers and eighty-four other ranks killed, nineteen officers and 271 other ranks wounded, and one officer and sixteen other ranks missing. Among the dead were the great mates Fletcher and Mahony: Fletcher had been killed instantly in the blast of a 77-millimetre shell; Mahony was shot through the temple by a sniper and died two days later.

Montbrehain was a major Australian victory and a severe defeat for the Germans. The enemy was prepared for the attack and had up to 1500 troops in the vicinity, many of them fresh and recently transferred to the area. The smattering of different German regiments – at least ten, it was reported – indicated the confusion that existed in the German army at the time, with men pulled from remnant units under different officers. Such was the defeat at Montbrehain that the Germans were quiet overnight, showed little stomach for a fight, and made no attempt to retake the village the following day. Meanwhile, to the north, the 25th British Division had also captured Beaurevoir to complete the defeat and secure the northern flank.

Unbeknown to the AIF, this was to be the last Australian infantry battle in the war. Although none of them knew it at the time, the war was at last over.

SIXTEEN

The Final Ten Days to Victory

On the night of 5–6 October 1918, the exhausted yet jubilant men of the 6th Australian Brigade were relieved by the 30th American Division. The following day, after a route march from Nauroy to Roisel, the men took the train to the Somme villages of La Chaussée-Tirancourt and Yzeux to the west of Amiens. The war diary of the 24th Battalion records, 'Hard as the fight was and despite the sad memory of departed comrades, all ranks brightened at the thought of the Corps rest. At last we were to spell and its prospect of complete peace and quietness in back areas after seven months' continuous work is very satisfying.'[1]

A similar response was echoed across the wearied and depleted AIF, as the villages and billeting areas swelled with the retiring battalions. Yet, while rest and the rebuilding of battalions were immediate priorities, tight training regimes continued, as did sports competitions, entertainment and local leave to Amiens and nearby villages. Though victory was close, the war continued.

While the five Australian infantry divisions were pulled out of the line and sent for rest, for other Australian units the war went on. The flying squadrons, No.'s 2, 3 and 4, had taken an active part in the offensive from 8 August, operating as far north as Ypres and down to the Somme in support of Australian divisions. During the attack on the Hindenburg Outpost Line, No. 3 Squadron assisted by dropping smoke bombs to provide a continuous line of smoke before the advancing Australians. The squadron also undertook reconnaissance and observation missions, and the men regularly became involved in air-to-air combat with German aircraft, often while protecting photographic flights. The aerial photographs supplied by this squadron played an important role in Monash's planning for the Hindenburg Line assault, in particular the work of the pilots Lawrence Wackett and Max Shelley in photographing the Beaurevoir Line in the face of heavy anti-aircraft fire.

As the Germans fell back, they started to move their troops by trains, which became targets. Stations packed with waiting troops and railway yards, particularly around the main railway hubs near Lille, were also attacked. One raid approached Lille along a shallow line of descent, where 'they were greeted by more bursts of "frightfulness" in the shape of machine gun fire and "flaming onions"[2] in large quantities'.[3] On 18 October, a raid on Lille found the city deserted, with the residents out on the streets waving to the low-flying airmen.

As the German retreat continued, the Australian No. 4 Squadron swapped their Sopwith Camels for the new Sopwith Snipe, a single-seat biplane fighter that came into service just a few weeks before the end of the war. Although it wasn't particularly fast, its manoeuvrability better matched the German fighters. No. 4 Squadron was tasked with high-altitude patrols, while No. 2 Squadron remained in the role of bombing and strafing retreating German troops.

While the flying squadrons continued to bomb and harass the retreating Germans, another group of Australians was fighting a different war. The 1st Australian Tunnelling Company, which had fired the mines at Hill 60 and the Caterpillar at the opening of the Battle of Messines on 7 June 1917, now found themselves with dangerous roles as the enemy fell back towards Germany. The tunnellers had been tasked with clearing booby traps and large delayed mines left behind by the Germans. This was hazardous work as these mines had fuses which were liable to go off at any time.

The tunnellers had an equally difficult task assisting the Royal Engineers. On 1 November, Captain Oliver Woodward was ordered to attach his section of tunnellers to the Royal Engineers of the British 1st Division. They were to bridge a lock on the Canal de la Sambre à l'Oise, fifteen miles north-east of Montbrehain, on 4 November. The prefabricated bridge would allow the passage of the heavy twenty-nine-tonne Mark V tanks. The problem was that Woodward and his men would need to construct it under fire.

On 2 November, Woodward reported to the Royal Engineers and visited the Tank Corps depot at St Benin to measure the width of the tanks and their tracks, and to check on their weight. Late the following day, one of his men, Corporal Albert Davey, a thirty-three-year-old miner from Ballarat West, confided that he'd had a premonition this was his last action. He asked Captain Woodward that, if anything should happen to him, his personal belongings be posted to his wife in Victoria.

The original bridge had been sixty yards from the lock, but this had been blown up by the Germans. The enemy, realising that the only possible crossing point was across the lock gates, had fortified the area, placing two machine guns in the pump house. To allow the engineering work to be done, British troops needed to first secure the area by taking the machine guns and eliminating any

276

resistance, something the Americans had failed to do when they'd captured the area.

On 3 November, Woodward and his tunnellers moved forward, the deep and sticky mud making progress slow, and arrived about half a mile from the lock at 8 pm. The horse-drawn wagons carrying the heavy steel girders were shelled, but the teams made it through, dropping off five tonnes of steelwork and girders. Next, Woodward's men needed to manhandle this material forward to a position 400 yards from the lock and wait there until the lock area was secure.

With the night, a cold drizzle set in. The water trickled down the men's backs and the blackness of the night added to their tension and discomfort. They laid their fingers upon the freezing steel and, with one efficient lift, had the first 800-pound girder balanced on the shoulders of ten men. Slowly and carefully, the line moved forward. The men felt with their feet for rough or broken ground, knowing that if one of them tripped, he would unbalance the rest and the heavy girder could crush them. Even the burst of a shell fifty yards away, its shards whizzing past them, did not halt their progress. Then a machine gun opened fire, its tracer searching out the silent attackers in the darkness.

Slowly the tunnellers edged forward, their shoulders aching under the weight. A slow step, a rebalance, a glance up at the dim horizon and head down as the cold rain beat into their faces. Finally, the men arrived at a sunken road, their assembly point, where they eased the weight off their shoulders and lay down to await the attack. As sunken roads were likely artillery targets, Woodward moved his men out into a nearby field, where they dug shallow shell scrapes and awaited orders to move. When they returned to the sunken road the following day, it was full of English dead who had been caught in the barrage.

Half a mile away, a German 77-millimetre field gun slowly traversed the open ground on the far side of the canal, near the sunken road the tunnellers had so recently vacated. The Germans slid a shell into the breach and pulled the firing cord. The shell arced across the lake, across the canal and crashed to earth among Woodward's men. Earth and mud flew around them, and the rank smell of cordite filled the air. A low moan came from the smoking earth as two wounded men rolled around in agony, while nearby lay the prone and lifeless body of Corporal Davey.

Woodward and his men saw out the night. At 4 am, the German guns fell silent and, as the mist dissipated, Woodward did a quick count of his men and started preparations for zero hour. At 5.45 am, the British artillery barrage crashed upon the Germans on the eastern side of the canal. Then the German artillery opened fire, with shells falling mainly on the sunken road, but some fell among the Australian tunnellers as the British troops advanced and the Royal Engineers edged forward. Leading the attack was Scottish Major George Findlay, MC and Bar, of the British 409th Field Company, who charged across the lock gates in his assault on the pump house. Bullets whistled off the concrete and steel as Findlay charged on, flinging bombs and putting the Germans to flight. For his actions, he was awarded the Victoria Cross.

By 7.30 am, it was considered safe enough for the Australians to begin their bridging of the canal. While the machine guns had been silenced, German artillery, well aware that bridging was underway, heavily shelled the area as the Australians struggled forward with the unwieldy girder sections. Woodward, along with his sergeant, raced across the grassy verge, leapt across the canal gates and began dislodging the coping stones to allow a snug fit for the girders. Quickly the first girder was eased across the gap and lowered into place, but a small calibre shell fell among the men, sending three spinning backwards. By the time the second girder was slid into place, the German bombardment had lifted and their shells were falling one hundred yards forward, where the British infantry was moving out into the open fields.

With the two girders across, the men laid the timber planking. In just two and a half hours, the bridge was ready and the first tanks began their crossing of the lock. This work was undertaken under heavy shellfire, an amazing feat, but five Australians were killed and another five wounded. Here, just a week before the end of the war, they had, in the vernacular of the time, 'gone west', so unfortunate and so desperately unlucky.

Captain Woodward and his men returned to the nearby village of Rejet-de-Beaulieu, where the Australians were buried, the tunnellers with bowed heads saying a last goodbye to five brave mates who had worked so hard, survived so long and had contributed so much, and were now lost to their families back at home. Lying in the weak sun, Woodward notes, 'there was an atmosphere of sadness, more pronounced than usual. I feel that this was entirely due to the fixed belief that we had taken part in the last staged battle of the War, and this thought carried our minds to our comrades who, as it were, had just been given one glimpse of the long expected Armistice, only to lose their lives before it materialised. It was a matter of a few hours, but it was not to be.'[4]

The work of the Australian tunnellers on this occasion was greatly appreciated by General Edward Strickland, the commander of the British 1st Infantry Division, when he wrote, 'The cool gallantry with which they placed the bridges in position under heavy fire after long and arduous hours of labour was magnificent. They have very worthily upheld the very high traditions of the Royal Engineers.'[5]

For this action, Oliver Woodward was awarded a second bar to his Military Cross, one of only four awarded to Australians during the Great War.[6] This action was the last fought by Woodward's tunnellers, and the last action fought by Australians in the Great War.

While Captain Woodward and his men were bridging the canal, the Australian flying squadrons also had a busy day on 4 November. The Australians took to the air in support of the last British attack at Landrecies to the east of Cambrai, engaging in aerial dogfights, low-level attacks on the German airfield at Chapelle-á-Wattines in Belgium and the strafing of troops and transports, and firing on targets of opportunity. However, at the end of the day, the returning Australian aircraft were attacked by an elite German squadron and four Australians were lost. One of these men was Arthur Pallister who had survived four years of war, had five 'kills' and would have been leaving for Australia the following day. These men were likely the last Australians to die in the war, just three days before the Armistice.

By now, German aircraft were finding it hard to respond to Allied air attacks as keeping up operational airfields, fuel, ammunition and servicing was very difficult. On 9 November, they were pursued. They flew low along the road, where for two miles they mercilessly shot up the lines of trucks and horse-drawn wagons, causing great loss of life and the destruction of houses and vehicles. In this attack, Frank Smith, a flight commander with No. 2 Squadron, was shot down and his plane crashed behind German lines. He was pursued by German troops, but hid in a haystack and avoided capture. Soon after, a Belgian farmer, while not prepared to hide him, did provide him with some old clothes which allowed him to pose as a Belgian peasant. Smith even spent a day in an *estaminet* in Enghien, watching German troops retreat eastwards. A few days after the Armistice, he turned up at his squadron mess to the surprise of his mates. Smith was likely the last Australian casualty of the war.

On the eve of the Armistice on 10 November, No. 2 and No. 4 Squadrons were still busy. As the official history states:

> The morning raid between 8.30 and 10.30 found five trains in the blackened Enghien station and the town and roads crowded with troops and transports. The bombs of the S.E.5's damaged a railway bridge, destroyed an anti-aircraft battery, and hit the train and railway station in many places. Leaving the station in a cloud of smoke, the attackers dived upon the road transport, which was still very heavy, and spread panic along the route with their machine guns.[7]

This was the last offensive action by aircraft of the Australian Flying Corps. Their casualties had been proportional to an AIF infantry battalion, with 179 pilots killed, wounded or taken prisoner, a casualty rate of forty-four per cent, compared to the AIF's 1st Division with fifty per cent.[8]

The news from the German home front was grim. The people, destitute and angry, were starving due to the British blockade. The country was torn with civil strife and political upheaval, which led to expressions of grief and antagonism within the army. Nonetheless, many German people had little idea that a surrender was upon them, their nation humiliated and vanquished. They now faced harsh and uncompromising peace conditions, similar to those the Germans had imposed on Russia in 1917.

Germany did not have to look far to see the disintegration of its allies and friends. The Bulgarians had signed an armistice with the Allies in late September. The armies of the Austro–Hungarian Empire were short of supplies, ammunition and transport, confronting desertion on a massive scale. Soldiers, hungry and disenchanted, returned to their towns, villages and farms, desperate to be with their starving families and leave the awful war behind. Such was also the case for the Czech, Croatian and Bosnian armies, who had fought a far-flung war well away from the Western Front and were finished off by the Italians at the Battle of Vittoria Veneto at the end of October. The Austro–Hungarian army sought a separate peace with the Allies, which was signed on 3 November, further reducing Germany's strength.

Similar difficulties faced Germany's other major ally, the Ottoman Empire. The breakthrough by the British in Palestine, helped significantly by the Australian Light Horse, and the taking of Damascus, Beersheba and Gaza throughout October, plus the Turkish retreat into Syria and Macedonia, had left few options for the Ottoman rulers. The remaining Turkish army was seriously short of men, weapons, supplies and, most importantly, a sufficient level of morale to sustain any defence. In early October, the ruling government had resigned and the new government, keen to distance itself from its predecessor, sought a treaty with the United States, even though they had never declared war against America. On 30 October, a four-man Turkish delegation signed the Armistice of Mudros, ending the Turkish Ottoman involvement in the war.

US President Woodrow Wilson had earlier offered Germany a peace plan of Fourteen Points, and on 5 November sent word that the Allied governments were now prepared, on the basis of this plan, to negotiate a lasting peace. Germany quickly realised this was not to be a negotiated peace, but a total and unconditional surrender.

The German army was in full retreat, discarding weapons and equipment and racing to make the German border. On 14 October, the British and French armies had driven the Germans from their strategic railhead at Lille, and on 17 October, Rawlinson's Fourth Army drove them across the River Selle. In this advance, the artillery of the 3rd, 4th and 5th Australian Divisions fought with the British 6th Division (IX Corps), but the Australian infantry, though again called forward by Rawlinson, remained in their rest areas. With Monash on leave, General Hobbs was warned that Australian troops might again be needed, but on the insistence of the Prime Minister Billy Hughes, he told Rawlinson that Australian troops would not be available for three weeks. Meanwhile, the discontent with the reorganisation and disbandment of seven battalions had 'quietly accepted their eclipse'.[9]

The British were unable to keep resupplying the rapidly advancing front, and it was only cavalry units that could maintain contact with the enemy. The British advance was also slowed by delayed-action mines left by the Germans during their retreat, and the dangerous work of clearing these became the task of the Royal Engineers, including the Australian Tunnelling Companies. While the 3rd and 4th Division artillery was withdrawn on 5 November, the 5th Division artillery was delayed in its move to the front by these mines.

Nonetheless, the military situation facing Germany quickly became hopeless, and the Kaiser and chancellor had been informed of the German position in late September. Ludendorff had recommended an immediate ceasefire and the acceptance of Wilson's Fourteen Points, but in late October, completely changed his mind and pressed for the resumption of the war. However, the German army was neither prepared nor equipped to do so, particularly given the troops' low morale and the deep concern for their people at home. Ludendorff was dismissed, and soon after left Germany for neutral Sweden.

On 9 November, Kaiser Wilhelm, unable to retain either his imperial crown or the Prussian crown, and being told the German army would not fight to keep his throne, was forced to abdicate. He had been deeply shocked by the rapid changes in Germany's war situation and the civilian uprisings. The following day, Wilhelm left with his family and a Prussian guard by train for a new home in Holland, which had remained neutral during the war. Here he would remain for the rest of his life, and the Dutch government refused extradition after Article 227 of the Treaty of Versailles directed the Kaiser to be prosecuted for his part in the war. His cousin, King George V, even declared him the greatest criminal in history, while British Prime Minister David Lloyd George strongly supported the widespread view to 'hang the Kaiser'.

Turmoil continued within Germany. The mutiny of soldiers from the German High Seas Fleet in early November led to the executions of seven men, triggering further demonstrations and riots. With the Allies pressing at the gate and driving the last remnants of the German army eastwards, the German Republic was declared and the Social Democrat Friedrich Ebert, a saddle-maker and union activist, became the new chancellor. With the military leaders and the Kaiser gone, nothing to bargain with and an inexperienced leader at the helm, Germany had little hope of a negotiated peace or a softening of the peace terms already on offer. On 8 November, a German delegation led by Matthias Erzberger, a Catholic peace advocate, met with General Ferdinand Foch and French representatives in the Forest of Compiègne. In a railway carriage in the forest, Foch handed the Germans the terms of the surrender and gave them seventy-two hours to consider. Except for an extension of time for the German withdrawal from France, Foch was unwilling to allow any concessions or negotiation. At 5 am on 11 November 1918, it was agreed that the ceasefire and Armistice would take effect at 11 am, Paris time, on that day. The war would be finally over.

The immediate conditions laid upon Germany were severe. The Germans were required to sign an unconditional surrender, and all means of continuing or making war against the Allied powers were to be removed. They were to release all Allied prisoners, but German POWs were not to be released and returned, in order to prevent Germany quickly rebuilding an army. The remnants of the German army were to withdraw within fourteen days from all captured territory and, within a further sixteen days, were to be six miles (ten kilometres) beyond the Rhine into Germany. To eliminate any chance of resuming war, Germany was to hand over 5000 artillery pieces, 25,000 machine guns, 3000 trench mortars, 1700 aircraft, 5000 locomotives and 150,000 rolling stock, while the German High Seas Fleet was stripped of ten battleships, six battlecruisers, eight light cruisers and fifty destroyers. Many of these were scuttled on 21 June 1919 in Scapa Flow.

At 11 am on 11 November, all fighting ceased. The Americans and British continued fighting to the last minute, however, and it is believed that around 10,000 men became casualties, of whom 2700 men died on the last day of the war. According to the Commonwealth War Graves Commission, the last British soldier to die was Private George Edwin Ellison of the 5th Irish Lancers, who was killed at 9.30 am, just ninety minutes before the ceasefire. The last Frenchman to die, killed at 10.50 am, was a runner, Augustin Trébuchon, delivering news of the Armistice to his battalion. The last Canadian was Private George Lawrence Price of the 2nd Canadian Division, who was killed at Mons at 10.58 am. He is recognised as the last Empire soldier to have died. The last American was Private Henry Gunter, killed at 10.59 am, who is recognised officially to be the last Allied man killed in the Great War. His divisional record stated, 'Almost as he fell, the gunfire died away and an appalling silence prevailed.'[10]

The last German killed was a young officer called Tomas. As he approached a group of American soldiers to tell them the war was over, he was shot. It was just after 11 am.

Finally, the war was over.

SEVENTEEN

Armistice at Last

While the men of the AIF had talked about the possibility of a ceasefire or a negotiated peace since August, the reality of it was hard to envision. There seemed no end to the back-and-forth of the war and the mounting casualties.

Men were getting restless. The 30th Battalion history notes, 'time had begun to drag somewhat heavily, the weather was cold, poultry had become scarce and difficult to obtain either by purchase, or more direct means, the few fish remaining in the streams had become detonator shy, and the winter supply of firewood on the farms – particularly that stacked in the open – was fast diminishing, therefore any change, even a return to the front, was not unwelcome.'[1]

Training continued and battalions moved forward into rest areas, while others prepared for a frontline relief. The 46th Battalion was scheduled to move forward on 8 November, but the move was postponed for twenty-four hours. The following day it was postponed again for twenty-four hours. On 10 November, the battalion was about to move forward at 5.30 pm when the move was again postponed for eighteen hours. This was not uncommon, and the men did not expect these postponements had anything to do with a ceasefire. It was a similar case with the 19th Battalion: 'On Monday 11 November the battalion paraded at 0900 in readiness to proceed to the assembly point for enbussing. Again word came through "to dismiss" but to be ready to move on 30 minutes notice. Meanwhile, long tooting of steam railway engines was heard in the distance from the railhead at Peronne and at 1200 unofficial news was received from various sources . . . that an armistice had been signed.'[2]

The 3rd Battalion had also been heading for the front. The battalion history noted, 'On the 10th [November] the battalion was again on the move, busses conveying it to Bazuel, near Le Cateau. The billets in this place were poor and comfortless. Many of the houses had been used as cages for prisoners of war, and on the walls of many of them were scrawled the regimental numbers and names of prisoners, including those of Australians. It was in these cheerless surroundings that we received news of the Armistice.'[3]

News of the ceasefire and Armistice came down to the Australian battalions from divisional headquarters. The official communiqué issued from General Headquarters of the British Army ordering the cessation of fighting was as follows:

Hostilities will cease at 11.00 today, 11th November. Troops
will stand fast on the line reached at that hour which will be
reported by wire to advanced GHQ. Defensive precautions will be
maintained. There will be no intercourse of any description with
the enemy until the receipt of instructions from GHQ. Further
instructions follow. Addressed to all concerned.[4]

The 28th Battalion noted it received the news in this way:

At about 10.50am, a message which nearly stopped the heartbeats
of the pair [sic] was received. Quickly mounting a bicycle,
Lieutenant Vic Pascoe pedalled furiously to the parade ground

and attracted the attention of the Adjutant to hand him the signal. The Brigadier read it to the assembled battalion:

OFFICIAL. GENERAL HEADQUARTERS
REPORTS MESSAGE FROM GENERAL FOCH TO
COMMANDER-IN-CHIEF STOP HOSTILITIES
WILL CEASE ON THE WHOLE FRONT ON
11TH NOVEMBER 1100 HOURS FRENCH TIME
STOP THE ALLIED TROOPS WILL NOT CROSS
UNTIL FURTHER ORDERS THE LINE REACHED ON
THAT DATE AND AT THAT TIME STOP SIGNED
FOCH 6.35am.[5]

While the battalions received the news of the Armistice at different times, and by different means, it is interesting to note that across the AIF, in general the news was taken with no great fanfare by the men. The 3rd Battalion Pioneers noted, 'There was little demonstration among the men of the unit, certainly not much more noise than takes place on pay night, and one found it most difficult to realise that at last the hostilities had ceased, with every probability of their never being resumed.'[6]

The 37th Battalion history noted, 'Men received the news quietly. What seemed an impossibility barely three months before, had become an accomplished fact. Germany was beaten. We had won the war. There was no immediate rejoicing at the victory. The fighting men were rather stunned, and their thoughts flew to the mates they had lost rather than the triumph of the moment. Wasn't it particularly hard luck, they thought, for those killed in the recent fighting.'[7]

Other records of the time mention the great relief felt by the men: 'An immense sigh of relief went around the world. The storm that had threatened to engulf civilisation had ended.'[8]

In the 45th Battalion, 'The troops received the news of the Armistice with feelings of great relief, but with a calmness that was remarkable considering what the cessation of hostilities really meant to them. They felt like one who had awakened from a hideous nightmare, can scarcely believe that it is all over and he is still alive.'[9] Others noted of the men's reaction, 'Men looked into each other's faces, gripped each other by the hand, and felt what they could not speak. And then they set out to celebrate the great day.'[10] The 46th Battalion history records, 'For some it was a great relief, others were dumb and didn't know what to do or what to think. Some men had been away from Australia for four years, and through that time had lived a continuous nightmare of hellish sights and sounds. They had made some friendships that were bonded with hard work and the blood of themselves and others, only to see these friendships torn apart in a split second of blinding light and acrid smoke.'[11]

Some did not actually believe the news to be true:

Everyone was miserable, out of sorts. And thoroughly 'fed up'. Suddenly hooters and sirens could be heard in the distance, followed by the beating of tins and gongs nearer at hand, but no one seemed inclined to interest himself in the matter, and one enthusiast who jumped up and exclaimed, 'The war's over', was told to sit down and not be a blanky fool. So many rumours had been circulating during the last week concerning a fictitious Armistice and cessation of hostilities, that when it did actually eventuate, it was not believed.[12]

Others did not believe the news until they saw it in an English newspaper. The 44th Battalion history notes, 'When the *London Daily Mail* was delivered to us in the late afternoon and we read the news, the men took it all very quietly and calmly. There was no demonstrations at all. In fact there was a certain amount of scepticism.'[13] In the 27th Battery of the 7th Brigade Australian Field Artillery, rumours of peace had been rampant, 'but by most were scarcely credited'. The battalion history takes up the story:

On the dismissal of the stable parade at midday on November 11, Major Doherty gave out that any man who wished to hear an order which had just been received could remain while it was read. Some, however, went to their billets to get their dixies, as dinner was almost ready. The others, when the circular had been read, given the official announcement of the armistice, made the usual dash for the queue at the cook-house, as dinner by then was quite ready. It seemed that dinner was far more important, and any news such as that just received evidently needed days before it was realised.[14]

The surprise of the ceasefire had left battalions confused as orders bearing details of a return to the front were delayed and revised. In the 11th Brigade war diary is a note on 11 November which states, 'General Cannan received an unofficial report that armistice was signed, but this was not confirmed.' Even the following day they were not sure: 'Persistent reports that Armistice has been signed and all French population celebrating the great event. Repeated calls on Division failed to have the report confirmed.'[15]

In *Somme Mud*, Private Edward Lynch writes:

The French people are going clean mad today as they reckon the war is over. Every French man, woman and child is racing around waving flags and wine bottles and telling us, '*Fini la guerre, Monsieur*'. Rumours and furphies are going everywhere . . .

The bugle is blowing 'fall-in' and we line up. Our O.C. gets rid of a few stray frogs from his throat and says, 'A message is just through, men, to say that hostilities ceased at eleven o'clock this morning. That means that the war is over, and –'

'Hooray!' we all yell, very much doubting him. Surely wars don't end like this.

He grins hard, 'I regret to announce that the message is unofficial.[16]

Some battalion war diaries did not even mention the Armistice. The 13th Australian Light Horse Regiment war diary noted for the day, 'Move continued to Le Hergies. Men quartered in bivouacs which were in fair condition. Horses in stables.'[17]

Unlike the sceptical Australians, the French people burst into joyous celebration. Church bells were rung, French flags and bunting were hung in villages and towns and the French national anthem, 'La Marseillaise', was sung. The 22nd Battalion history notes, 'Parades were in progress when the glad news came through, but all work ceased at once. The band, covered with floral tributes, paraded the streets and the Australian flag was hoisted on the church spire amid great manifestations of joy from the assembled villagers.'[18] In Vignacourt, 'the day was given over to revelry, and many a bottle which had been saved by the good folk for this occasion, was produced and shared around. Each little dwelling produced a French flag, which was gallantly displayed in celebration.'[19] The 5th Division history notes that in one village, 'wood and poultry claims against the soldiers were stated to have been suspended for the day.'[20]

In Amiens, the French administration, and the people in particular, showed their gratitude to the Australians. To lead a parade there, Monash chose the band of the 24th Battalion to represent the AIF. By the time the band assembled in the street, the local people had reached a high pitch of excitement, and thousands of Australian troops billeted near Amiens had joined the vast rejoicing throng, marching arm in arm with locals under shopfronts and houses bedecked with the tricolour and decorations. The 24th Battalion history notes, 'The appearance of the Australian band was the signal for a heart-stirring demonstration in honour of the Australian Army. As the band played . . . a wave of intense patriotic fervour swept over the crowd, which made no effort to restrain its feelings, but rejoiced with the utmost abandon and ecstasy.'[21] It goes on to state, 'Australians had pride of place in all the speeches . . . they had the first kisses of the excited women and girls, they had free wine and free meals and everything that a grateful people could bestow upon them.' In the excitement, a member of the 2nd Battalion 'risked his neck to climb to the belfry in the battered church to ring out joy-bells of peace'.[22]

Many war diaries and battalion histories help explain the discrepancy between the French people's celebratory response to the end of war and the Australians' muted one. As noted by the 28th Battalion, 'Perhaps the burden of the war years was so great that it would take some time for the relief to be felt. Rejoicing was more a matter of the individual. In the mass the troops displayed few outward signs of happiness. Truth to tell, many of them repaired to the estaminets and quickly got themselves drunk. For long they had planned what they would do when the good news of the war's end would come; how well and how wildly they would celebrate it, but when the news at last had arrived, their celebrations were mild.'[23]

A note in the 13th Battalion history simply states, 'Australia was near at last; but there was a tinge of sadness and disappointment at the celebrations, sadness at the thought of absent comrades and disappointment at the knowledge that the "old Bat" [battalion] with all its associations would soon be a thing of the past.'[24]

The news of Germany's surrender spread quickly among the Allied armies all along the front. The French soldiers, in particular, enjoyed the news, such was the suffering of their army and their nation. They ignited explosive powder and fired flares, 'the nights weird with its colours' as they 'drank their ration of pinard (red wine) with increased zest'. This celebration would have been joined by the Canadians, the New Zealanders, the Americans and the nations of the British Empire and from the French colonies, filling the cafes and *estaminets* across France and Belgium with song and laughter.

The evening of 11 November, the men began to take in this momentous news: 'Sitting around the braziers in the evenings, all manner of ideas were exchanged. "What did an Armistice mean? Would we go to Berlin? When would we be likely to reach home? What did the future hold for us?" While many other questions came up for discussion, deep down in the hearts of all was an unexpressed feeling of thankfulness that the strife was over.'[25] The men also realised that there was much to do, details to be worked out, terms and conditions implemented and arrangements made for their return to Australia. For many, having been away from home for so long and fighting a war over four years, the announcement of a ceasefire was 'beyond their comprehension'.[26] To others this moment was very strange: 'this sudden eerie silence that had come over the land after years of war; hard to believe that peace had come to take the place of war, and there came over all the feeling not only of victory, but the sense of a job well done. No more was there fear of bombs dropping on camps and billets from the sky, no more the terrifying whine of shells, the aggravating whistle of bullets. All had ceased, and the men could lay aside their gasmasks and put by their guns.'[27]

On 12 November, a Special Order of the Day was received from Marshal Foch which read:

OFFICERS, NON-COMMISSIONED OFFICERS, AND
SOLDIERS OF THE ALLIED ARMIES.
After bringing the enemy's attack to a stand by your stubborn
defence, you attacked him without respite for several months,
with inexhaustible energy and unswerving faith.

You have won the greatest victory in history and have saved
the most sacred of causes, the Liberty of the World.

Well may you be proud.

You have covered your standards with immortal glory, and the
gratitude of prosperity will ever be yours.
(Signed) F. Foch,
Marshal of France
Commander-in-Chief of the Allied Armies

Similarly, General Monash received a message from Australian Prime Minister Billy Hughes:

The government and the people of Australia extend their hardiest
congratulations on the triumphant conclusion of your great effort.
I am specially requested to convey to you their heartfelt thanks
and deep admiration for your brilliant and great leadership, and
for the way in which you and the brave men associated with you
have borne the sufferings and trials of the past four years . . . and
brought the civilized people of the world through adversity to
victorious peace.

The day following the Armistice was bright, clear and cold, as winter was on its way. Training programmes, or more importantly post-ceasefire duty lists, though drawn up, had not been thought about or prepared and, in many cases, both officers and men were unsure what to do. Battalions in the 1st Brigade were sent on a short route march and then directed to work on road and railway repairs in their billeting areas. In the afternoon, sports of various kinds – rugby for the New South Wales and Queensland battalions, and Australian Rules for the Victorians and other state battalions – were organised.

Life for the diggers slipped into an ongoing cycle of route marches, work and cleaning details, inspections, church parades and sports. Men of the 5th Brigade who were then billeted around Vignacourt found themselves filling in trenches and rolling up wire to keep them occupied.

The 7th Brigade war diary notes that on 14 November, 'The CO held a parade of all officers and NCOs . . . he addressed them on the danger of slackness setting-in, now that the hostilities have ceased. He requires a general tightening up of discipline.'[28] In all battalion and brigade war diaries, the focus in the days after the Armistice is recorded as a combination of sport, training programmes and, at night, entertainment to keep the men amused and busy.

The Australian Flying Corps squadrons also awaited new orders and a new role. No. 4 Squadron went to Bickendorf aerodrome in Germany, while No. 2 and No. 3 Squadrons remained in Belgium. The surrendered German planes needed to be checked, guarded and, in some cases, flown to Britain. In many instances, the German pilots had sabotaged their machines, placing sugar in the petrol tanks and loosening the nuts on petrol lines. They were also known to have painted their names and tallies on the aircraft to annoy the Allied pilots sent to secure them.

While No. 4 Squadron enjoyed a leisurely and comfortable time in Germany, the other two squadrons, after completing their work, handed over their aircraft and went back to Britain. Here they were able to lead relatively free lives, with many undertaking educational courses – they did not feel there would be a career in aviation when they returned to Australia – or seeking daytime jobs. Their stay in Britain was also a chance to reunite with their English relatives, to mix in the community and to meet eligible English ladies and marry them.

By the end of the first week of peace, the Australian divisions were preparing to move eastwards, with their destination and their role uncertain. Haig was keen to keep pressure on Germany, and to oversee the extraction and removal of weapons, equipment, transport and supplies that might allow the German forces to be reformed and re-equipped. On the ground, there persisted a mistrust of the Germans' intentions in honouring the ceasefire and Armistice conditions and, above all, a general disbelief that the war was finally over.

EIGHTEEN

The End of the End

In the weeks following the Armistice, two topics dominated the troops' conversation: when they would go to Germany, and when they would go home. Of these, the return to Australia was by far the most important, but the men knew there were other issues to deal with first, not the least being the need to ensure Germany was truly beaten and would not rise again unexpectedly. For this reason, crossing the Rhine and pushing into Germany seemed the immediate challenge and the men felt Australia, through the AIF, needed to be part of this triumphant march forward.

Haig ordered two British armies, the Second and the Fourth, each consisting of four corps of sixteen divisions, to advance on a two-division front. The Australian 1st and 4th Divisions, part of the Fourth Army, were to be the vanguard, with the 4th Division leading on the right and the 1st Division advancing on the left. Their orders were to march towards Germany and halt on the Rhine.

After 20 November, battalions were moving east, often from rest areas around Amiens and nearer the coast, their march taking them through the battlefields of the Somme they knew so well. Back through Corbie and Dernancourt, back through Villers-Bretonneux and Hamel, past Mont St Quentin and through Péronne and Bellenglise and out into the ravaged villages and towns that had seen German occupation for over four years. Here the traumatised villagers cried when they saw their liberators, some falling on their knees with happiness and relief.

As the Australians marched east, they also came across Allied prisoners of war returning westwards, having been released by their German captors. In *Somme Mud*, Private Edward Lynch mentions these unfortunate men:

We see men approaching from along the road towards us. They are in absolute rags and tatters, their clothes a mixture of old, torn uniforms, British, French and Fritz. The fellows are filthy. The poor wretches are staggering as they walk from sheer weakness, for they're just skin and bone, scarecrows on legs.

A tall, gaunt figure sways towards us from the bunch of scarecrows. 'Can you spare us a coupla tins of bully beef? I belonged to the 29th Battalion. Got knocked and taken prisoner at Fleurbaix (Fromelles) in July sixteen. There's two other Aussies in the mob.'

We look at him and his mates. Prisoners of war. Poor, half-starved wretches. All dirty yellow skin, hollow cheeks and sunken, hopeless eyes. Food and cigarettes are being handed out everywhere. Handed out to be clutched at by long, claw-like, grasping fingers that shake. How we pity these poor beggars! How we thank our lucky stars we escaped the ordeal of being prisoners of war. We look upon fellow men reduced to skin-clad skeletons and are sickened . . .

The fellows bite like starved dogs. Animal hunger shows in their every movement. They say they were left behind to fend for themselves when Fritz retreated. Now they're in no one's care, but just have to depend upon getting food from passing battalions until some organised effort is made to collect and care for them.[1]

Believing they would be part of the army of occupation and the triumphant crossing of the Rhine, the Australians formed specialist units for the expected tasks ahead. In one case, a request went to the 3rd Australian Division for a composite company to act as Australian Headquarters Guard Company. The order for men specified, 'A-class men, fit for hard marching under hard conditions. They must be willing if required, to remain on the Western Front for a long time.' These men were to be 'of good physique, good character and should be good "drills" – if in possession of a decoration so much the better'.[2]

However, the AIF's hope of seeing Germany was crushed: 'at Sains, they were sadly disillusioned by the arrival of a number of British troops which were stated to have just come from England and who were reported to be going to Cologne instead . . . There was considerable bitterness at the prospect of being done out of what the men so eagerly looked forward to – a trip into Germany to enable them to treat the Germans in a manner in keeping with their own treatment of the inhabitants of the French and Belgian villages during the years of German occupation.'[3]

In the end, No. 4 Squadron of the Australian Flying Corps were the only Australians who went into Germany. A small group of men from the 1st Australian Tunnelling Company also entered Germany, albeit without authority. With time to waste near the German border, Oliver Woodward and a group of tunnellers had set out for the frontier. They travelled about two miles into a forest near Malmedy, along a dirt road, when they came upon two poles painted black and white to signify the border. As Woodward wrote in his diary, 'I formed the party in line and at slow march with a modified form of goose step we crossed the Border. Thus no member of the party could claim that he was the first man of the 1st Australian Tunnelling Company to set foot in Germany.'[4]

The Australians' exclusion from the army of occupation was seen as typical of the British attitude to colonial troops, who believed they had won the war for Britain. In fact, the exclusion was simply a result of the fact that the men of the AIF, unlike British troops, were far from Australia, had never been granted leave home and needed to be quickly repatriated. As a consequence, the Australians were told they would march into Belgium to await their return first to England, and then Australia. As the 22nd Battalion history states, 'This was a disappointment to some of the men, but the prospect of getting home sooner more than compensated for the loss of the opportunity of seeing the Fritz and his family at home.'[5] The destination for the Australians became the Belgian industrial city of Charleroi, some thirty miles south of Brussels and about seventy-five miles south-east of Ypres.

It must be remembered that the end of the war, at least for the Allies, came quite suddenly and unexpectedly, and planning had been well underway in August 1918 for spring offensives in early 1919. The Allied nations had given little thought to the repatriation of the men. What was quickly realised, however, was that for the AIF this enormous process would be played out in three stages: first, repatriation, the return to Australia by sea of 180,000 men now in Europe; second, once home, the demobilisation of the AIF and the other services; and third, the rehabilitation of these men, not only back into the civilian workforce, but also the repair of the mental and physical wounds of so many damaged men.

While planning for the return began, the AIF were settling into a comfortable routine in the villages and suburbs around Charleroi. As Private Earnest Pitman wrote, 'We are in real good billets here and are having a fairly easy time generally. We have about two route marches per week. When on parade we generally have more games than drill. The people who live up here seem a good bit different from those down on the Somme. They are more friendly and do not fleece us quite so much when we buy bread or milk from them. The kiddies here can talk German a lot and are also fast learning to be able to swear in English.'[6] From here, the men could visit Brussels, the picturesque town of Dinant and the battlefield of Waterloo. There was also leave to Britain, 'yet the universal longing was for none of these so much as for Australia. "When are they going to send us home?" was the question uppermost in every mind.'[7]

Following the Armistice, General Monash and his staff had quickly begun planning for the repatriation of the men to Australia. On 16 November, the Demobilisation and Repatriation Branch was formed, with General Cyril White presiding. On 21 November, Monash was appointed by Prime Minister Hughes to be Director-General of Repatriation and Demobilisation. This scheme was launched with all divisional commanders on 26 November at Brewery Château, Le Cateau, and was introduced to brigade and battalion commanders.

One condition not known to the men was that they had to be 'released' by Field Marshal Haig. For his part, Haig needed men in Europe, and he would only release them when he felt confident of the peace negotiations with Germany, which were unlikely to occur before February 1919.

General Monash was faced with the gigantic task of shipping back to Australia these 180,000 men – plus at least 7000 dependants – but his first problem was the lack of available ships. Prime Minister Hughes had directed that the returning men must come back in comfortable, modern ships, with a band, a non-alcoholic canteen and quality food. But ships of any class and quality were simply not available, as every nation sought ships to bring their troops home.

For Monash, the big question was how to determine the order of the men's return. Consideration was given to returning battalions as a single unit, allowing them to return to their state capitals to victory marches and a rousing welcome. In the end, Monash decided that fairness must prevail and introduced a policy that those who had been the first to leave Australia would be the first to return, meaning that the men who had embarked from Australia in 1914 and 1915, and who had served the longest, were the first to receive their ticket home. Two other criteria were also taken into consideration: whether a man had a family, and whether there was a job for him to return to.

To compound the shipping problem, the Australian authorities had to consider the English wives and children of Australian servicemen. Initially it was proposed that wives and children would be sent to Australia first, but that would mean these new immigrants would have to survive for upwards of a year before their husbands could be provided transport home. Instead, 'family ships' were requisitioned for the men, their English wives and their children to be sent home together. By May 1919, this was quite a logistical problem as an average of 150 Australian soldiers were getting married each week in England. Monash also had to take into account the 40,000 wounded men and those convalescents from hospitals across England who required special transport, medical services and staff, as well as a shipping strike in February 1919.

The health of the men was also a focus of concern, and a reason for Monash to get men onto ships bound for Australia quickly. The repatriation process took place at the height of the influenza pandemic, which began in January 1918 and continued until late

1920. The social and political conditions of the time – the starvation, the overcrowding, the huge numbers of people crammed together in hospitals and medical facilities, the poor hygiene of people caught up in the war and the weakened immune systems of a vast population – intensified the spread of the disease. The US Census Bureau estimated a mortality rate of 50 to 100 million people, three to five per cent of the world's population, the most devastating pandemic in history. Influenza was, therefore, of great concern to the Australian medical authorities, and prompted an urgency about getting the men away from the contagious areas they were in, as soon as possible. Ships were required to have wider spacing between hammocks, with fewer men per ship, and staff were to watch for symptoms in potentially sick men who could transport the virus to Australia.

Another major problem for General Monash was keeping the men occupied while they waited for available ships. Monash realised he needed to redirect the focus of his men and give them a new motive. He explained the process as that of moving from a 'fighting morale' to a 'reconstruction morale', whereby men might become 'a useful member of the nation'.[8]

Many men had joined the AIF directly from school and had no trade or professional training. They would be returning unskilled and ill-prepared, and competing against men who had remained at home for the duration of the war. To address this, three types of training were offered: basic educational training, including literacy, arithmetic and other educational courses for those short of simple skills; technical training in everything from mechanical skills, agriculture and trade training; and professional training that was undertaken by both Sydney and Melbourne University.

Further, as the scheme gathered momentum, education fell into two categories: training and education within the AIF, and training within schools and universities in Britain and on the Continent. Courses were offered in the trades: bricklaying, tiling, bookkeeping, shorthand, carpentry, forestry, motor mechanics and telegraphy. Men went to art school to learn painting, while others worked to get their school matriculation or diplomas that might give them access to jobs on their return. To provide on-the-job training, men were sent to work in factories, railways and mines. Rural courses were very popular, including mixed farming, wool classing, animal husbandry, fruit growing and dairying, as many men were reluctant to return to the cities, seeking instead a quieter life in the bush.[9]

Another issue on the home front was the shortage of teachers, books and pencils. Textbooks in particular could not be found, even for the staff, and some, like *Beef, Mutton, and Wool* by Lieutenant William Kelly of the 48th Battalion, were especially written for popular courses.

As effective as these schemes sounded in theory, not everyone was happy. One battalion history noted, 'The education scheme with the unit was handicapped in various ways. There was no suitable accommodation. Most classes had to be held under very miserable conditions in rough sheds generally with an earth floor and often with no windows. Tables and seats were rare and the cold at most times through the Somme winter made study almost impossible . . . The total effect educationally of the Battalion's efforts was no doubt negligible, but the main result was attained of keeping a good proportion of all ranks fairly busy during the mornings.'[10] For all the criticism, Bean notes, 'Yet no part of the AIF's war effort more richly repaid the nation . . . turning men's thoughts to their own and the nation's future, and to the problems of peace.'[11]

Nevertheless, there was also an increase in serious crime and acts of insubordination, which came on the back of the earlier battalion mutinies, particularly the 1st Battalion mutiny on 21 September, when 119 men had refused to go back into the line. These men were charged with desertion rather than mutiny (which carried the death penalty), and all but one were found guilty. Some were subsequently sent to prison at Broadmoor, England, but in most cases their sentences were not enforced after the cessation of hostilities. Privates Rigby Catorall, Vere Stanley Scott and Alexander Hutchinson were all found guilty of desertion; they were each given ten years' penal servitude. In other cases, individuals found not guilty of desertion were charged instead with being absent without leave. One was Private Glennan, who went missing for nearly six weeks and received ninety days' field punishment. Private Arthur Anderson received sixty days. Private Charles John Moore was charged with 'neglect to the prejudice of good order and military discipline',[12] referring to a self-inflicted wound. Although he pleaded not guilty, he was found guilty and sentenced to sixty days' forfeiture of pay.

Other restless and angry soldiers sitting around in camps, waiting for ships and demobilisation, took the law into their own hands. Not only Australian, but also British and Canadian troops, were expressing their frustration. Strikes had stopped coal and food supplies, and men were on half-rations and freezing. Between November 1918 and June 1919, Canadian troops were involved in thirteen riots and serious disturbances, the most notorious in Kinmel Park in North Wales, where five men were killed and twenty-three injured. Of the seventy-eight men arrested, twenty-five were convicted of mutiny, with sentences of ten years' penal servitude.

In the 8 December issue of *The Two Blues*, a battalion newspaper, an editorial discussed the matter of demobilisation: 'Is it going to be [as] hard to demobilise as it was to beat Fritz? We all recognise the difficulties and will cheerfully wait our turn, but nevertheless the Southern Cross is calling us, we feel, more strongly than ever. We want to see it shining brightly above us as we smoke our pipes in our gardens on our great wide plains or our mountains or near our surf.'[13]

Preparations began for a final Christmas in Europe. The battalions were now celebrating their fourth Christmas on active service, and everyone attempted to make this a joyous and memorable occasion. On Christmas Day, men went to church services and sang carols. The 39th Battalion history records:

On Christmas day, each company dined as a unit. At 12.30 pm the men sat down to a dinner which would have done credit to any chef in the prosperous times of peace. When dinner was over, every man received a Christmas box from the Brigade Comforts Fund. The battalion officers donated a sum of money to provide a Christmas treat for the children of the village of Bouillancourt and a Christmas tree was placed in a large marque. Numbers of happy kiddies in high glee and full of excitement were present. Lieutenant Charles Mason made an excellent 'Father Christmas' and distributed toys from the tree. After the children received their toys they were given cocoa, cake and chocolates.[14]

Christmas 1918 was probably the first time that a serious effort was made to involve the local people in unit celebrations. In the 7th Battalion, the inhabitants of Couillet, a suburb of Charleroi, 'lent us table linen, ornaments, flowers, flags, cutlery and crockery. The battalion cooks supplied the dinner. The waiting was done by the officers and sergeants. A three course meal was served, washed down by bottles of good beer and a rum issue,'[15] with others noting, 'with the assistance of the hospitable Belgian people, the soldiers were able to make the celebration worthy of the glad season'.[16] However, not all Christmas dinners went well. The 17th Battalion 'spent its fourth Christmas in surroundings as cheerless as the preceding three'.[17] In spite of this, as the 24th Battalion history notes, 'At all the festive gatherings the memory of the gallant dead was affectionately honoured.'[18]

One Christmas dinner had a surprising outcome. As the No. 4 Squadron AFC celebrated their Christmas dinner at the aerodrome at Birkendorf near Cologne, a young French orphan by the name of Henri Heremene wandered into the mess. In rags and starving, he was immediately fed and looked after by the men, and quickly became the squadron's mascot. Young Henri had lost both parents in the war and had bestowed himself on a number of British regiments from the age of six. Now about eleven, he was given the nickname 'Digger', and attached himself to an aircraft mechanic, Private Tim Tovell. When the squadron moved back to England in February 1919, Henri was hidden in an oat sack and carried on Tovell's back.

On 6 May 1919, about 800 AFC men travelled by train to Southampton. At the wharf, under heavy skies and drizzling rain, they received a tremendous send-off by the Southampton mayor, along with his council, citizens and a brass band. But unbeknown to the mayor, another little drama was playing out that day: the smuggling on board of young Henri, this time in a large sports bag. Some days out, Henri was discovered by the captain, but was allowed to remain on the ship. He was given permission to land and, after disembarking in Sydney, travelled with Private Tovell to Queensland, where he was welcomed into the family. In 1926, Henri went to Melbourne to work as a civilian for the RAAF, but was killed on 24 May 1928 after a motorcycle accident.

Into the new year of 1919, men were steadily leaving in drafts from France and Belgium for the embarkation ports in the south of England. Many transferred to the divisional camps on the Salisbury Plain, where they went back into the barracks and billets they had known earlier in the war. By this time, both local leave and leave into London or for trips around the United Kingdom was readily available, but 'lack of money was the only difficulty which faced many would be tourists. The Commonwealth Bank in London had never been so busy in its existence, and the cable lines to Australia were almost monopolised by urgent messages for bank drafts.'[19]

In European billets and in camps around Salisbury in England, Australian troops, impatient to get back home, were proving a nuisance for both the Military Police and the constabulary. Well understanding the irritation and the lack of discipline within Australian units in Europe, British authorities made every effort to get them first to England and then load them onto ships to get them out of the way. As a result, by the end of March 1919, all but 50,000 Australians had been sent home, and this number was down to just 5000 by the end of May.

As groups of 1000 men assembled and moved out, there were emotional farewells. In the 31st Battalion, the first draft left on 27 December 1918, 'and the remainder of the original men and nine officers left on the 13th January'.[20] For the men of the 40th Battalion, the first draft left on 17 February 1919, 'and it was only then that we realised that the brotherhood of men existed no longer as a battalion of infantry. We drank in fellowship together, pledged ourselves to meet again in Tasmania, and from a sentiment born of the sadness of farewell, for once felt sorry that the war was over.'[21]

From around Salisbury, from the villages of Codford, Sutton Veny and Larkhill, trains took the men to various ports along the south coast of England. The train trip was often met by cheering crowds offering flowers, cups of tea and buns, while others stood by the railway line and waved and wished the men 'bon voyage'. Similar crowds met the men at Plymouth and Davenport and, as the ships of excited diggers moved away from the quays, ships of the Royal Navy lined their passage seaward, salutes were fired and cheer after cheer came from the Jack Tars lining the ships' rails.

The sea voyage took them south and into the Atlantic. In *Somme Mud*, Private Lynch writes:

We've had a week at sea now. Times are good as is the food and we have very little drill to worry us. There are plenty of books to read and we have two bands and a concert party on board. The sea has been calm and we've only had two inoculations so far . . .

The days are very hot, but the sea is becoming unsettled and the old *Beltana* is doing over 300 miles a day.

. . . We enjoy Cape Town, but in a calmer, mature manner than when we bubbled over on our wild days there three years ago on our way to the war.

Then it was across the wind-blown, freezing stretch of the South Indian Ocean to Fremantle, Adelaide or Melbourne. Often troops from New South Wales and Queensland disembarked in Melbourne and then had to endure the slow train north. Private Lynch relates the last run into Central Station in Sydney:

We're running through the outer suburbs now. Every suburban train we pass is screeching a welcome. Front gardens and backyards are filled with happy, waving people . . . Flags are fluttering ahead. We're running into a flag-bedecked platform at Central and the train glides to a standstill . . . An officer calls our names and each man is handed a leave pass. On towards the barrier we move and we're through and into a motor car and being whisked away along streets lined with thousands of cheering people. The car stops near the Domain. We get out. A laneway is open before us, a laneway fenced with friendly faces. [22]

Lynch, like 180,000 other diggers, was home at last. What lay ahead for these men, the pain and sorrow, the physical and mental wounds they carried, would be with them until death, but for now they were at home and among family, and the realisation was sinking in that they had survived and returned.

Acknowledgements

First my thanks to my publisher Meredith Curnow. I have now worked with Meredith on four books, and have always been grateful for her patience, support and help through the anguish of the edit. I would also like to thank my editors, Tom Langshaw and Deonie Fiford.

My thanks to Dr Roger Lee, Brad Manera and Dr Peter Stanley for historical back-up and suggestions. Thank you, too, to Elise Edmonds, Senior Curator at the State Library of New South Wales, for her suggestions with soldiers' diaries.

Thanks to the staff at the Australian War Memorial and its Research Centre, especially for the online resources available to historians and writers. I must thank Dr Peter Pedersen and his co-author Chris Roberts for the wonderful *ANZACS on the Western Front: The Australian War Memorial Battlefield Guide*, an indispensable publication for anyone researching or wandering the battlefields.

Similarly, thanks to the National Archives of Australia for the personal files of men enlisted in the Great War, again an indispensable resource.

My thanks to my wife, Heather, for giving me the time to write, and to my grandchildren for the spontaneous visits and disruptions. I am very lucky.

Finally, to my friends and colleagues who seemed to continually ask, 'When will the book be out?' – you have kept me going and kept me focused. Thank you.

Structure of the
AIF Infantry

1st Division	1st Brigade	(1st–4th Battalions) – NSW
	2nd Brigade	(5th–8th Battalions) – Victoria
	3rd Brigade	9th Battalion – Queensland
		10th Battalion – SA
		11th Battalion – SA
		12th Battalion – Tasmania, WA, SA
4th Division	4th Brigade	13th Battalion – NSW
		14th Battalion – Victoria
		15th Battalion – Queensland, Tasmania
		16th Battalion – WA, SA
2nd Division	5th Brigade	(17th–20th Battalions) – NSW
	6th Brigade	(21st–24th Battalions) – Victoria
	7th Brigade	25th Battalion – Queensland
		26th Battalion – Queensland
		27th Battalion – SA
		28th Battalion – WA
5th Division	8th Brigade	29th Battalion – Victoria
		30th Battalion – NSW
		31st Battalion – Queensland, Victoria
		32nd Battalion – SA, WA
3rd Division	9th Brigade	(33rd–36th Battalions) – NSW
	10th Brigade	(37th–39th Battalions) – Victoria
		40th Battalion – Tasmania
	11th Brigade	41st Battalion – Queensland
		42nd Battalion – Queensland
		43rd Battalion – SA
		44th Battalion – WA
4th Division	12th Brigade	45th Battalion – NSW
		46th Battalion – Victoria
		47th Battalion – Queensland, Tasmania
		48th Battalion – SA, WA
	13th Brigade	49th Battalion – Queensland
		50th Battalion – SA
		51st Battalion – WA
		52nd Battalion – SA, WA, Tasmania
5th Division	14th Brigade	(53rd–56th Battalions) – NSW
	15th Brigade	(57th–60th Battalions) – Victoria

Notes

1: Back on the Somme

1   Bean, C. E. W., (ed.), *Official History of Australia in the War of 1914–18* [hereafter *Official History*], Angus & Robertson, Sydney, Vol. V, p.5
2   Bean, *Official History*, Vol. V, p.11
3   Bean, *Official History*, Vol. V, p.17
4   11th Australian Infantry Brigade War Diary, 25 December 1917
5   14th Australian Infantry Brigade War Diary, January summary
6   6th Australian Infantry Brigade War Diary, 18 January 1918
7   Bean, *Official History*, Vol. V, pp.28–29
8   Bean, *Official History*, Vol. V, pp.30–31
9   Stanley, P., *Bad Characters: Sex, Crime, Mutiny, Murder and the Australian Imperial Force*, Pier 9, Murdoch Books, Sydney, 2010, p.158
10 Gammage, B., *The Broken Years: Australian Soldiers in the Great War*, Penguin Books Australia, Melbourne, 1975, p.243

2: The German March Offensive: All or Nothing

1   3rd Australian Infantry Brigade War Diary, 21 March 1918
2   8th Australian Infantry Brigade War Diary, 21 March 1918
3   14th Australian Infantry Brigade, War Diary, Appendix 12, 'Report on enemy raid 21st March'
4   14th Australian Infantry Brigade War Diary, 22 March 1918, p.28
5   14th Australian Infantry Brigade War Diary, 21 March 1918, p.27
6   15th Australian Infantry Brigade War Diary, 30 March 1918
7   14th Australian Infantry Brigade War Diary, 23 March 1918, p.29
8   8th Australian Infantry Brigade War Diary, 23 March 1918
9   8th Australian Infantry Brigade War Diary, 31 March 1918
10 Gorman, Captain E., MC, *With the Twenty-Second: A History of the Twenty-Second Battalion AIF*, H. H. Champion, Australian Authors Agency, Melbourne, 1919, p.75
11 14th Australian Infantry Brigade War Diary, 28 March 1918, p.36
12 Lynch, E., *Somme Mud*, Random House, Sydney, 2006, p.146
13 14th Australian Infantry Brigade War Diary, 28 March 1918, p.37
14 White, T. A., *The Fighting Thirteenth: A History of the Thirteenth Battalion AIF*, 13th Battalion A.I.F. Committee, Sydney, 1924, p.122
15 Ibid.
16 White, *The Fighting Thirteenth*, p.123
17 Bean, *Official History*, Vol. V, p.128
18 13th Battalion War Diary, 'Extract from Daily Intelligence Summaries', 27–28 March 1918
19 13th Battalion War Diary, pp.129–30
20 Bean, *Official History*, Vol. V, p.141

21 Bann, S., *The Inventions of History: Essays on the Representation of the Past*, p.45
22 General Haig's Special Order of the Day, 11 April 1918
23 Bean, *Official History*, Vol. V, p.156
24 Ibid.
25 12th Australian Infantry Brigade War Diary, 28 March 1918
26 Bean, *Official History*, Vol. V, p.360
27 Bean, *Official History*, Vol. V, p.416

3: Saving Amiens

1 Bean, *Official History*, Vol. V, p.175, quoted in Williams, H. R., *The Gallant Company: An Australian Soldier's Story of 1915–18*, Angus & Robertson, Sydney, 1933, pp.183–85
2 Ibid.
3 33rd Battalion AIF War Diary, 30 March 1918
4 Lieutenant Colonel Morshead Intelligence Report of 33rd Battalion AIF, 31 March 1918, Appendix 22
5 Ibid.
6 Ibid.
7 Bean, *Official History*, Vol. V, p.307
8 Lieutenant Colonel Morshead Intelligence Report of 33rd Battalion AIF, 31 March 1918
9 35th Battalion War Diary, 4 April 1918
10 Quoted in Pedersen, P., *Anzacs on the Western Front: The Australian War Memorial Battlefield Guide*, Wiley & Sons, Milton, 2012, p.327
11 Ibid.
12 33rd Battalion War Diary, Appendix
13 Bean, *Official History*, Vol. V, p.355
14 Bean, *Official History*, Vol. V, p.452
15 Bean, *Official History*, Vol. V, p.499
16 Bean, *Official History*, Vol. V, p.500
17 Bean, *Official History*, Vol. V, p.507
18 Bean, *Official History*, Vol. V, p.540
19 Ibid.
20 Bean, *Official History*, Vol. V, p.553
21 Bean, *Official History*, Vol. V, p.569
22 Bean, *Official History*, Vol. V, p.573
23 Bean, *Official History*, Vol. V, p.575
24 Bean, *Official History*, Vol. V, p.580
25 Bean, *Official History*, Vol. V, p.603
26 Ibid.
27 Ibid.
28 Ibid.
29 Bean, *Official History*, Vol. V, pp.609–10
30 Bean, *Official History*, Vol. V, p.625
31 Bean, *Official History*, Vol. V, p.626
32 Bean, *Official History*, Vol. V, p.638
33 13th Australian Infantry Brigade War Diary, Appendix 31, p.24. Telegram from General Staff, Fourth Army, 26 April 1918
34 Edgar, P., *To Villers Bretonneux*, Australian Military History Publications, Loftus, 2006, p.251

35 Ibid.
36 Bean, *Official History*, Vol. V, pp.672–73
37 Bean, *Official History*, Vol. V, p.638
38 Bean, *Official History*, Vol. V, p.646
39 White, *The Fighting Thirteenth*, p.132

4: Hamel: A Test of New Tactics

1 Bean, *Official History*, Vol. VI, p.249
2 Bean, *Official History*, Vol. VI, p.246
3 Bean, *Official History*, Vol. VI, p.262
4 Bean, *Official History*, Vol. VI, p.273
5 Bean, *Official History*, Vol. VI, p.283
6 White, *The Fighting Thirteenth*, p.144
7 Browning, N., *The Westralian Battalion: A History of the 44th Battalion*, Advance Press, Bassendean, 2004, p.315
8 Browning, *The Westralian Battalion*, p.315
9 Bean, *Official History*, Vol. VI, p.284
10 Marks, D. G., *Sundry Jottings*, Sydney, 1919, p.91
11 Bean, *Official History*, Vol. VI, p.293
12 Bean, *Official History*, Vol. VI, p.290
13 Bean, *Official History*, Vol. VI, p.293
14 White, *The Fighting Thirteenth*, p.144
15 Bean, *Official History*, Vol. VI, p.306
16 Rule, E. J., *Jacka's Mob*, Military Melbourne, Melbourne, 1999, p.305
17 Bean, *Official History*, Vol. VI, p.305
18 Ellis, A. D., *The Story of the Fifth Australian Division*, Hodder & Stoughton, London, 1920, p.326
19 Bean, *Official History*, Vol. VI, p.301
20 Bean, *Official History*, Vol. VI, pp.316–17
21 Bean, *Official History*, Vol. VI, p.327
22 Monash, General Sir John, *The Australian Victories in France in 1918*, Hutchinson, London, 1920, p.62
23 Steel, R. J. and McWilliams, J., *Amiens: Dawn of Victory*, Dundurn Press, Toronto, 2001, p.16
24 Bean, *Official History*, Vol. VI, p.335

5: Nibbling East

1 Keatinge, M. B. B., *The War Book of History of the Third Pioneer Battalion*, John Burridge Military Antiques, Swanbourne, 1989, p.108
2 Dollman, W. and Skinner, H. M., *The Blue and Brown Diamond: A History of the 27th Bn AIF 1915–1919*, Lonnen & Cope, Adelaide, 1921, p.145
3 Cutlack, F. M., *Official History of Australia in the War of 1914–1918*, Vol. VIII, The Australian Flying Corps, p.308
4 Cutlack, *Official History*, Vol. VIII, p.309
5 Green, F. C., *The Fortieth: A Record of the 40th Battalion, AIF*, Naval Military Press Ltd, Sandhurst (UK), 2007, p.146
6 Ibid.
7 Gorman, E., *With the Twenty-Second*, p.88
8 Harvey, W. J., *The Red and White Diamond: The Authorised History of the 24th Battalion AIF*, p.246

Notes

9 Harvey, *The Red and White Diamond*, p.259
10 19th Battalion War Diary, Intelligence Report Appendix s
11 Lynch, *Somme Mud*, p.221
12 Lynch, *Somme Mud*, p.259
13 13th Battalion War Diary, August 1918 Part 1, Summary of Operations 31.7.1918 to 4.8.1918, Appendix 9
14 Marks, D., *Diary*, Entry 1 August 1918, p.94
15 Dean, A. and Gutteridge, E. W., *The Seventh Battalion AIF: Resume of the Activities of the Seventh Battalion in the Great War 1914–1918*, p.145
16 Keatinge, *The War Book of History of the 3rd Pioneers*, p.109
17 Browning, *The Westralian Battalion*, p.340
18 Gorman, E., *With the Twenty-Second*, p.80
19 Harvey, *The Red and White Diamond*, pp.257–58

6: The Days Before the Allied Offensive

1 Bean, *Official History*, Vol. VI, p.505
2 Ibid.
3 Browning, N., *Fix Bayonets: The History of the 51st Battalion AIF*, p.186
4 8th Australian Infantry Brigade War Diary, July 1918, Appendix 29, image 81
5 8th Australian Infantry Brigade War Diary, July 1918, Appendix 29, image 82
6 From his citation for the Distinguished Conduct Medal, which he received in this action.
7 Ellis, A. D., *The Story of the Fifth Australian Division*, p.319
8 Bean, *Official History*, Vol. VI, p.522
9 Ibid.
10 Bean, *Official History*, Vol. VI, p.523
11 Polanski, I. L., *We Were the 46th: History of the 46th Battalion in the Great War 1914–18*, p.79
12 Lynch, *Somme Mud*, p.177
13 Ellis, *The Story of the Fifth Australian Division*, p.327
14 Ibid.
15 Bean, *Official History*, Vol. VI, p.504
16 Bean, *Official History*, Vol. VI, p.525
17 Serle, G., *John Monash: A Biography*, Melbourne University Press, Melbourne, 1982, p.343; and Bean, *Official History*, Vol. VI, p.525
18 Bean, *Official History*, Vol VI, p.525. See also 15th Australian Infantry Brigade War Diary, Appendix 7
19 Green, F. C., *The Fortieth*, p.149
20 Carne, W. A., *In Good Company: History of the 6th Machine Gun Company AIF*, p.328
21 Browning, *The Westralian Battalion*, p.346
22 Paterson, A. T., *The Thirty-Ninth: The History of the Thirty-Ninth Battalion AIF*, p.214
23 Bean, *Official History*, Vol. VI, p.529
24 Browning, *The Westralian Battalion*, p.345

7: *Der Schwarze Tag*: The Black Day

1 Browning, *The Westralian Battalion*, p.348
2 Doneley, B., *Black over Blue: The 25th Battalion, AIF at War 1915–1918*, p.145
3 Bean, *Official History*, Vol. VI, p.531
4 Browning, *The Westralian Battalion*, p.348

5 Dollman, V. D. and Skinner, H. M., *The Blue and Brown Diamond: History of the 27th Battalion AIF 1915–1919*, p.151
6 Bean, *Official History*, Vol. VI, p.543
7 Keatinge, *War Book of the Third Pioneer Battalion*, p.113
8 Longmore, C., *Eggs-a-Cook: The Story of the Forty Fourth*, p.155
9 Bean, *Official History*, Vol. VI, p.533
10 MacKenzie, K. W., *The Story of the Seventeenth Battalion AIF*, p.260
11 Doneley, *Black over Blue*, p.145
12 Doneley, *Black over Blue*, p.262
13 Dollman and Skinner, *The Blue and Brown Diamond*, p.153
14 Longmore, *Eggs-a-Cook*, p.156
15 Green, F. C., *The Fortieth*, p.150
16 Lynch, *Somme Mud*, pp.258–59
17 Longmore, *Eggs-a-Cook*, p.156
18 Longmore, *Eggs-a-Cook*, p.157
19 Browning, *The Westralian Battalion*, p.355
20 Ibid.
21 Browning, N., *Leane's Battalion: The History of the 48th Battalion AIF 1916–1919*, p.280
22 Bean, *Official History*, Vol. VI, p.572
23 Ibid.
24 Bean, *Official History*, Vol. VI, pp.570–71
25 White, *The Fighting Thirteenth*, p.150
26 White, *The Fighting Thirteenth*, p.151
27 Bean, *Official History*, Vol. VI, p.569
28 Browning, *Leane's Battalion*, p.277
29 While the train's complete undercarriage, bogies and gun were returned to Australia after the war and displayed, everything but the barrel was dismantled and disposed of in the early 1960s. Today, the barrel can be seen at the Australian War Memorial in Canberra.
30 Bean, *Official History*, Vol. VI, p.562
31 Ellis, *The Story of the Fifth Australian Division*, p.336
32 Bean, *Official History*, Vol. VI, p.606

8: Pushing on from the Blue Line

1 Bean, *Official History*, Vol. VI, p.614
2 Bean, *Official History*, Vol. VI, p.606
3 McNicol, N. G., *The Thirty-Seventh: History of the Thirty-Seventh Battalion AIF*, Modern Printing Co., Melbourne, 1936, p.218
4 Bean, *Official History*, Vol. VI, p.614
5 Ibid.
6 Bean, *Official History*, Vol. VI, p.615
7 8th Australian Infantry Brigade War Diary, 8 August 1918
8 15th Australian Infantry Brigade War Diary, #3, report on operations, 11 August 1918, Appendix 8
9 15th Australian Infantry Brigade War Diary, Image 5
10 4th Australian Infantry Brigade War Diary, Image 6
11 15th Australian Infantry Brigade War Diary, 9 August 1918
12 Dollman and Skinner, *The Blue and Brown Diamond*, p.157

13 Downing, W. H., *To the Last Ridge*, p.148
14 Bean, *Official History*, Vol. VI, p.440
15 1st Battalion War Diary, Appendix 8, 'Report on Operations on the 9/8/18'
16 Bean, *Official History*, Vol. VI, p.651
17 Jordan, L., *Stealth Raiders*, Penguin Random House, Sydney, 2017, p.191
18 Bean, *Official History*, Vol. VI, p.682

9: Green Slopes Above the River

1 Bean, *Official History*, Vol. VI, p.687
2 McNicol, N. G., *The Thirty-Seventh*, p.219
3 Bean, *Official History*, Vol. VI, p.687
4 Ibid.
5 Browning, *The Westralian Battalion*, p.363
6 Bean, *Official History*, Vol. VI, p.691
7 Ibid.
8 McNicol, *The Thirty-Seventh*, p.223
9 Bean, *Official History*, Vol. VI, p.699
10 51st Battalion War Diary, August 1918, Appendix 12
11 Bean, *Official History*, Vol. VI, p.711
12 Harvey, N. K., *From Anzac to the Hindenburg Line: The History of the 9th Battalion*, p.233
13 Harvey, *From Anzac to the Hindenburg Line*, p.237
14 White, *The Fighting Thirteenth*, p.153
15 Wanliss, N., *The History of the Fourteenth Battalion AIF*, p.331
16 Ibid.
17 34th Battalion War Diary, 20 August 1918
18 Beaver, E., *Short History of the 34th Battalion AIF*, p.41
19 9th Australian Infantry Brigade War Diary, 22 August 1918
20 *Short History of the 34th Battalion AIF*, 34th Bn Association, p.41
21 Ibid.
22 Bean, *Official History*, Vol. VI, p.768
23 9th Australian Infantry Brigade War Diary, 28 August 1918
24 Ibid.
25 Ibid.
26 Bean, Vol VI, p.776

10: Eastwards on the Roman Road

1 Green, *The Fortieth*, p.154
2 Bean, *Official History*, Vol. VI, p.710
3 Brahms, V., *The Spirit of the Forty-Second*, p.92
4 6th Australian Infantry Brigade War Diary, Appendix 36 (Image 78), titled 'Report on Operations, 8th–19th August 1918'
5 MacNeil, A. R., *The Story of the Twenty-First: Being the Official History of the 21st Battalion AIF*, p.21
6 Ibid.
7 White, *The Fighting Thirteenth*, p.153
8 Ibid.
9 White, *The Fighting Thirteenth*, p.154

10 Monash, *Australian Victories*, p.163
11 Ibid.
12 Bean, *Official History*, Vol. VI, p.733
13 Bean, *Official History*, Vol. VI, p.736
14 Wren, E., *Randwick to Hargicourt: History of the 3rd Battalion AIF*, p.319
15 Bean, *Official History*, Vol. VI, p.740
16 1st Australian Infantry Brigade War Diary, August 1918, Appendix 11, 'Report on Operations in Proyart Sector 22nd–27th August 1918'
17 Ibid.
18 Bean, *Official History*, Vol. VI, p.753
19 Bean, *Official History*, Vol. VI, p.754
20 Bean, *Official History*, Vol. VI, p.759
21 Bean, *Official History*, Vol. VI, p.761
22 Bean, *Official History*, Vol. VI, p.769
23 Lock, C. B. L., *The Fighting 10th: Souvenir of the 10th Battalion AIF 1914–1919*, p.100

11: Mont St Quentin: What Presumption

1 Monash, *Australian Victories*, p.168
2 Monash, *Australian Victories*, p.217
3 Quoted in Serle, *John Monash*, p.353
4 Quoted in Serle, *John Monash*, p.352
5 Quoted in Serle, *John Monash*, p.355
6 Bean, *Official History*, Vol. VI, p.822
7 Monash, *Australian Victories*, p.181
8 Bean, *Official History*, Vol. VI, p.805
9 Bean, *Official History*, Vol. VI, p.806
10 17th Battalion War Diary entry for 31 August 1918
11 Bean, *Official History*, Vol. VI, p.809
12 Mackenzie, *The Story of the Seventeenth Battalion*, pp.281–82
13 17th Battalion War Diary, 31 August 1918, 'Report on Operations 27–31 August 1918', Appendix 15
14 Bean, *Official History*, Vol. VI, p.809n
15 Ibid.
16 Bean, *Official History*, Vol. VI, p.811
17 Mackenzie, *The Story of the Seventeenth Battalion*, p.283
18 Quoted in the 20th Battalion War Diary, 31 August 1918
19 Ibid.
20 Mackenzie, *The Story of the Seventeenth Battalion*, p.283
21 18th Battalion War Diary, 31 August 1918
22 *Newcastle Morning Herald and Miners Advocate*, 5 September 1918, p.5
23 Mackenzie, *The Story of the Seventeenth Battalion*, p.286
24 Casualties in the 40th Battalion were one officer and 29 other ranks killed, and six officers and 123 other ranks wounded. Green, *The Fortieth*, p.184
25 Green, *The Fortieth*, p.181
26 Bean, *Official History*, Vol. VI, p.829
27 Bean, *Official History*, Vol. VI, p.813
28 Bean, *Official History*, Vol. VI, p.815
29 Bean, *Official History*, Vol. VI, p.873n

30 Telegram from General Rawlinson to the 2nd Division, 5th Australian Infantry Brigade War Diary, September 1918, Appendix 4, p.26
31 Serle, *John Monash*, p.355
32 Bean, *Official History*, Vol. VI, p.817
33 Ibid.
34 *Warwick Examiner and Times*, 4 September 1918, p.5

12: Taking Péronne

1 Ross St Claire, *Our Gift to the Empire: 54th Australian Infantry Battalion 1916–1919*, p.210
2 St Claire, *Our Gift to the Empire*, p.211
3 St Claire, *Our Gift to the Empire*, p.212
4 From his citation for the Distinguished Conduct Medal.
5 Quoted in St Claire, *Our Gift to the Empire*, p.214
6 Harvey, *The Red and White Diamond*, p.282
7 The battalion history notes that the 'more than usual proportion of killed to wounded was due to the fact that there was little or no shelter for a man when once hit'. Ibid.
8 15th Australian Infantry Brigade War Diary, Report of Operations 1–5 September 1918, Appendix 1, p.3
9 History of the 59th Battalion, p.19
10 Bean, *Official History*, Vol. VI, p.857
11 Bean, *Official History*, Vol. VI, p.861
12 15th Australian Infantry Brigade War Diary, Report of Operations 1–5 September 1918, Appendix 1, p.8
13 Bean, *Official History*, Vol. VI, p.854
14 Quoted in St Claire, *Our Gift to the Empire*, p.227

13: The Hindenburg Outpost Line

1 *The Forty First*, compiled by members of the Intelligence Staff, p.127
2 Ibid.
3 Browning, *The Westralian Battalion*, p.383
4 Browning, *The Westralian Battalion*, p.379
5 Bean referred to this as 'the first recorded mutiny in the AIF' in *Official History*, Vol. VI, p.875
6 59th Battalion War Diary, 5 September 1918, p.10
7 Bean, *Official History*, Vol. VI, p.875. Bean in fact quoted the wrong date. It was not 14 September but 5 September.
8 Longmore, *Eggs-a-Cook*, p.166
9 Bean, *Official History*, Vol. VI, p.886
10 Lynch, *Somme Mud*, pp.297–98
11 Longmore, *Eggs-a-Cook*, p.170
12 Wallace, N. V., quoted in Browning, *Leane's Battalion*, p.302
13 Ibid.
14 White, *The Fighting Thirteenth*, p.156
15 Ibid.
16 Browning, *Leane's Battalion*, p.305
17 Bean, *Official History*, Vol. VI, p.898
18 Bean, *Official History*, Vol. VI, p.911

19 Browning, *Leane's Battalion*, p.306
20 Browning, *Leane's Battalion*, p.309
21 White, *The Fighting Thirteenth*, p.157
22 Ibid.
23 White, *The Fighting Thirteenth*, p.158
24 The German 58th I.R. (119th Division) had twenty-seven men killed or wounded, and twelve officers and 294 other ranks captured.
25 Chataway, T. P., *History of the 15th Battalion 1914–1918*, p.313
26 Lynch, *Somme Mud*, p.293
27 Lynch, *Somme Mud*, p.294
28 Bean, *Official History*, Vol. VI, p.909
29 Chataway, *History of the 15th Battalion*, p.232
30 Bean, *Official History*, Vol. VI, p.914
31 Harvey, *From Anzac to the Hindenburg Line*, p.245
32 Ibid.
33 Wren, *Randwick to Hargicourt*, p.326
34 The 46th Battalion history states they captured seventeen officers and 496 other ranks. Polowski, *We Were the 46th*, p.92
35 Polowski, *We Were the 46th*, p.91
36 Bean, *Official History*, Vol. VI, p.926
37 Rule, *Jacka's Mob*, p.327
38 Wanliss, *The History of the Fourteenth Battalion AIF*, p.341
39 Browning, *Leane's Battalion*, p.316
40 Ibid.
41 Ibid.
42 Bean, *Official History*, Vol. VI, p.906
43 Gill, I., *Fremantle to France: 11th Battalion AIF 1914–1919*, p.68
44 Bean, *Official History*, Vol. VI, p.931
45 Bean, *Official History*, Vol. VI, pp.931–32
46 Bean, *Official History*, Vol. VI, p.933
47 Ibid.

14: Taking the Hindenburg Line

1 Bean, *Official History*, Vol. VI, p.942
2 Bean, *Official History*, Vol. VI, p.943
3 Green, *The Fortieth*, p.191
4 *The History of the 39th Battalion AIF*, p.233
5 30th Battalion War Diary, 26 September 1918
6 30th Battalion War Diary, 28 September 1918
7 Ibid.
8 Green, *The Fortieth: A Record of the 40th Battalion AIF*, p.193
9 Fairey, E., *The Story and Official History of the 38th Battalion AIF*, p.78
10 'Narrative of Operations carried out by 38th Battalion from 1900 on 27/9/18 to 2/10/18', Appendix 5, p.1
11 Fairey, *The Story and Official History of the 38th Battalion AIF*, p.78
12 Fairey, *The Story and Official History of the 38th Battalion AIF*, p.79
13 Fairey, *The Story and Official History of the 38th Battalion AIF*, p.81
14 Fairey, *The Story and Official History of the 38th Battalion AIF*, p.235

15 Green, *The Fortieth*, p.194
16 29th Battalion War Diary, 29 September 1918
17 Ibid.
18 Ibid.
19 30th Battalion War Diary, 29 September 1918
20 Ellis, *The Story of the Fifth Australian Division*, p.370
21 Ibid.
22 Yockelson, M., *Borrowed Soldiers: Americans Under British Command, 1918*, p.189
23 Yockelson, *Borrowed Soldiers*, p.184

15: Montbrehain: The Last Attack

1 58th Battalion War Diary, Appendix 1, Narrative of Operations carried out.
2 McMullin, R., *Pompey Elliott*, Scribe, Melbourne, 2002, p.494
3 10th Australian Infantry Brigade War Diary, Narrative Report on Operations, Appendix 12
4 Appendix 2; Narrative of Operations of 'D' Coy 30th Battalion AIF attached to 32nd Battalion during the attack and capture of Joncourt, 1st October 1918, p.2
5 Ibid.
6 Ibid.
7 Ibid.
8 Ibid.
9 These were introduced in early 1918 and, by the end of the war, 15,800 had gone into service.
10 5th Australian Infantry Brigade War Diary, Appendix 6, p.4
11 7th Australian Infantry Brigade War Diary, 'Report on Operations on October 3rd 1918', Appendix 4a, October 1918
12 Ibid.
13 Ibid.
14 Bean, *Official History*, Vol. VI, p.1021
15 Maxwell had already been awarded a Distinguished Conduct Medal and a Military Cross, but his actions on this day were to see him awarded the Victoria Cross.
16 Carlyon, L., *The Great War*, Macmillan, Sydney, 2006, p.721
17 5th Australian Infantry Brigade War Diary, Appendix 6, Report on Operations 27 Sept/3 October 1918, p.6
18 Ibid.
19 Harvey, *Red and White Diamond*, p.295
20 6th Australian Infantry Brigade War Diary, Appendix 22, Report on Operations 5th October 1918, p.7
21 Bean, *Official History*, Vol. VI, p.1034
22 6th Australian Infantry Brigade War Diary, Appendix 22, Report on Operations 5th October 1918, p.7
23 Bean, *Official History*, Vol. VI, p.1037
24 Bean, *Official History*, Vol. VI, p.1040
25 Bean, *Official History*, Vol. VI, p.1037
26 Bean, *Official History*,Vol. VI, p.1036
27 Ibid.
28 24th Battalion Report on the attack on Montbrehain by the 24th Battalion 5th Operations, Appendix 2, p.3

29 Bean, *Official History*, Vol. VI, p.1042
30 Ibid.
31 24th Battalion Report on the attack on Montbrehain by the 24th Battalion 5th Operations, Appendix 2, p.3
32 24th Battalion Report on the attack on Montbrehain by the 24th Battalion 5th Operations, Appendix 2, p.10

16: The Final Ten Days to Victory

1 24th Battalion War Diary, 6 October 1918
2 A German 37-millimetre revolving barrelled anti-aircraft gun which discharged five flares in rapid succession.
3 Molkentin, M., *Fire in the Sky: The Australian Flying Corps in the First World War*, Allen & Unwin, Sydney, 2010, p.319
4 Woodward, O. H., *Personal Diary*, Vol. II, p.111
5 Woodward, O. H., *Personal Diary*, Vol. II, p.112
6 Australian War Memorial Encyclopedia Statistics – Military
7 Cutlack, *Official History*, Vol. VIII, The Australian Flying Corps, p.384
8 Molkentin, *Fire in the Sky*, pp.336–37
9 Bean, *Official History*, Vol. VI, p.1048
10 Trueman, C. N., 'November 11th 1918'

17: Armistice at Last

1 Sloan, H., *The Purple and Gold: A History of the 30th Battalion*, p.222
2 McGuinness, P., *Boldly and Faithfully: History of the 19th Battalion AIF*, p.308
3 Wren, *Randwick to Hargicourt*, p.329
4 McNicol, *The Thirty-Seventh*, p.257
5 Kahan, H. K., *The 28th Battalion AIF: A Record of War Service*, p.103
6 Keating, *War Book of the Third Pioneer Battalion*, p.142
7 McNicol, *The Thirty-Seventh*, pp.259–60
8 McNicol, *The Thirty-Seventh*, p.260
9 Lee, J. E., *The Chronicle of the 45th Battalion AIF*, p.75
10 Harvey, *The Red and White Diamond*, p.308
11 Polanski, *We Were The 46th*, p.96
12 Newton, L. M., *The Story of the Twelfth: A Record of the 12th Battalion during the Great War*, p.200
13 Browning, *The Westralian Battalion*, p.403
14 *With the 27th Battery in France*, p.167
15 11th Australian Infantry Brigade War Diary, 11–12 November 1918
16 Lynch, *Somme Mud*, pp.311–12
17 Hunter, D. J. *My Corps Cavalry*, p.94
18 Gorman, *With the Twenty-Second*, p.103
19 MacKenzie, *The Story of the Seventeenth Battalion*, p.297
20 Ellis, *The Story of the Fifth Division*, p.394
21 Harvey, *The Red and White Diamond*, p.309
22 Taylor, F. W. and Cusack, T.A., *Nulli Secundus: A History of the Second Battalion AIF 1914–1919*, p.337
23 Kahan, *The 28th Battalion AIF*, p.103
24 White, *The Fighting Thirteenth*, p.163
25 Sloan, *The Purple and Gold*, p.222

26 St Claire, *Our Gift to the Empire*, p.244
27 Taylor and Cusack, *Nulli Secundus*, p.337
28 Corfield, R., *Hold Hard, Cobbers*, Vol. 1, p.188

18: The End of the End

1 Lynch, *Somme Mud*, pp.314–15
2 9th Australian Infantry Brigade War Diary, Appendix 10
3 Chataway, *History of the 15th Battalion*, p.235
4 Woodward, O. H., *The War Story of Oliver Holmes Woodward, Captain 1st Australian Tunnelling Company, AIF*, p.125
5 Harvey, *The Red and White Diamond*, p.314
6 Browning, *Leane's Battalion*, p.332
7 Gorman, *With the Twenty-Second*, p.105
8 Bean, *Official History*, Vol. VI, p.1057
9 St Claire, *Our Gift to the Empire*, p.244
10 Ibid.
11 Bean, *Official History*, Vol. VI, p.1072
12 13th Battalion War Diary, May 1918
13 Davies, W., *The Boy Colonel*, Random House, Sydney, 2013, p.394
14 *The Thirty-Ninth: The History of the 39th Battalion AIF*, p.245
15 Dean and Gutteridge, *The Seventh Battalion AIF*, pp.132–33
16 Harvey, *The Red and White Diamond*, p.316
17 MacKenzie, *The Story of the Seventeenth Battalion*, p.298
18 Harvey, *The Red and White Diamond*, p.317
19 Harvey, *The Red and White Diamond*, p.315
20 MacNeil, *The Story of the Twenty-First*, p.25
21 Green, *The Fortieth*, p.203
22 Lynch, *Somme Mud*, pp.330–34

Recommended Reading List

1st–15th Australian Infantry Brigade war diaries 1915–1919; Australian War Memorial, Canberra, www.awm.gov.au/collection/records/awm4/subclass.asp?levelID=1776
Various battalion war diaries; Australian War Memorial, Canberra, www.awm.gov.au/collection/records/awm4/subclass.asp?levelID=1742

Bean, C. E. W., *Anzac to Amiens*, Penguin Books Australia, Melbourne, 1993
—— (ed.), *Official History of Australia in the War of 1914–18*, Angus & Robertson, Sydney: Vol. I, The Story of Anzac, 1921; Vol. II, The Story of Anzac, 1937; Vol. III, The AIF in France, 1937; Vol. IV, The AIF in France, 1933; Vol. V, The AIF in France During the Main German Offensive, 1918, 1933; Vol. VI, The AIF in France During the Main German Offensive, 1918
Carlyon, Les, *The Great War*, Macmillan, Sydney, 2006
Davies, W., *The Boy Colonel*, Random House, Sydney, 2013
Downing, W. H., *To the Last Ridge: The World War I Experiences of W. H. Downing*, Duffy & Snellgrove, Sydney, 1998
Edgar, P., *To Villers-Bretonneux*, Australian Military History Publications, Loftus, 2006
Gammage, W., *The Broken Years: Australian Soldiers in the Great War*, Penguin Books Australia, Melbourne, 1975
Jordan, L., *Stealth Raiders*, Penguin Random House, Sydney, 2017
Lynch, Private E., *Somme Mud*, Random House, Sydney, 2006
Marks, D. G., *Sundry Jottings*, Sydney, 1919, catalogued as Marks War Diary, 7 August 1914–21 December 1918, MLMSS 2879, Mitchell Library, Sydney
Maxwell, J., VC, *Hell's Bells and Mademoiselles*, Angus & Robertson, Sydney, 1939
McMullin, R., *Pompey Elliott*, Scribe, Melbourne, 2002
Mitchell, G. D., *Backs to the Wall: A Larrikin on the Western Front*, Allen & Unwin, Sydney, 2007
Molkentin, M., *Fire in the Sky: The Australian Flying Corps in the First World War*, Allen & Unwin, Sydney, 2010
Monash, General Sir John, *The Australian Victories in France in 1918*, Hutchinson, London, 1920
Pedersen, P., *ANZACS on the Western Front: The Australian War Memorial Battlefield Guide*, John Wiley & Sons, Milton, 2012
Rule, E. J., *Jacka's Mob*, Military Melbourne, Melbourne, 1999
Serle, G., *John Monash: A Biography*, Melbourne University Press, Melbourne 1982
Stanley, P., *Bad Characters: Sex, Crime, Mutiny, Murder and the Australian Imperial Force*, Pier 9, Murdoch Books, Sydney, 2010
State Library of New South Wales, Records of the European War Collecting Project, established by the Trustees of the Mitchell Library in 1918

Wanliss, N., *The History of the 14th Battalion AIF: Being the Vicissitudes of an Australian Unit During the Great War*, Melbourne, 1929
White, T. A., *Diggers Abroad: Jottings by a Digger Officer*, Angus & Robertson, Sydney, 1920
Yockelson, M., *Borrowed Soldiers: Americans Under British Command, 1918*, University of Oklahoma Press, Norman, 2008

Battalion histories (in numerical order)

Taylor, F. W. and Cusack, T. A., *Nulli Secundus: A History of the Second Battalion AIF 1914–1919*
Wren, E., *Randwick to Hargicourt: History of the 3rd Battalion AIF*
Dean, A. and Gutteridge, E. W., *The Seventh Battalion AIF: Resume of the Activities of the Seventh Battalion in the Great War 1914–1918*
Harvey, N. K., *From Anzac to the Hindenburg Line: The History of the 9th Battalion*
Lock, C. B. L., *The Fighting 10th: Souvenir of the 10th Battalion AIF 1914–1919*
Gill, I., *Fremantle to France: 11th Battalion AIF 1914–1919*
Newton, L. M., *The Story of the Twelfth: A Record of the 12th Battalion During the Great War*
White, T. A., *The Fighting Thirteenth: A History of the Thirteenth Battalion AIF*, 13th Battalion A.I.F. Committee, Sydney, 1924
Wanliss, N., *The History of the Fourteenth Battalion AIF*
Chataway, T. P., *A History of the 15th Battalion 1914–1918*
MacKenzie, K. W., *The Story of the Seventeenth Battalion AIF*
McGuinness, P., *Boldly and Faithfully: History of the 19th Battalion AIF*
MacNeil, A. R., *The Story of the Twenty-First: Being the Official History of the 21st Battalion AIF*
Gorman, E., *A History of the 22nd Battalion AIF*
Harvey, W. J., *The Red and White Diamond: The Authorised History of the 24th Battalion AIF*
Doneley, B., *Black over Blue: The 25th Battalion, AIF at War 1915–1918*
Dollman, W. and Skinner, H. M., *The Blue and Brown Diamond: History of the 27th Battalion AIF 1915–1919*
Kahan, H. K., *The 28th Battalion AIF: A Record of War Service*
Sloan, H., *The Purple and Gold: A History of the 30th Battalion*
Edwards, John, *Never a Backward Step: History of the 33rd Battalion AIF*
Beaver, E., *Short History of the 34th Battalion AIF*
McNicol, N. G., *The Thirty-Seventh: A History of the Thirty-Seventh Battalion, AIF*
Fairey, E., *The Story and Official History of the 38th Battalion AIF*
Paterson, A. T., *The Thirty-Ninth: The History of the Thirty Ninth Battalion AIF*
Green, F. C., *The Fortieth: A Record of the 40th Battalion, AIF*
The Forty First – compiled by members of the Intelligence Staff
Browning, N., *The Westralian Battalion: A History of the 44th Battalion*
Longmore, C., *Eggs-a-Cook: The Story of the Forty-Fourth*
Lee, J. E., *The Chronicle of the 45th Battalion AIF*
Polanski, I. L., *We Were the 46th: History of the 46th Battalion in the Great War 1914–18*
Browning, N., *Leane's Battalion: The History of the 48th Battalion AIF 1916–1919*
Browning, N., *For King and Cobbers: The History of the 51st Battalion AIF 1916–1919*
Browning, N., *Fix Bayonets: The History of the 51st Battalion AIF*
St Claire, R., *Our Gift to the Empire: 54th Australian Infantry Battalion 1916–1919*
Corfield, R., *Hold Hard, Cobbers: 57th and 60th Battalions AIF*

Histories of other units

Keatinge, M. B. B., *The War Book of the Third Pioneer Battalion*

Cutlack, F. M., *Official History of Australia in the War of 1914–1918*, Vol. VIII, The Australian Flying Corps

Carne, W. A., *In Good Company: History of the 6th Machine Gun Company AIF*

Ellis, A. D., *The Story of the Fifth Australian Division*

Hunter, D. J., *My Corps Cavalry*

Woodward, O. H., *The War Story of Oliver Holmes Woodward Captain 1st Australian Tunnelling Company, AIF*

Index of Names and Places

Discover a
new favourite

Visit **penguin.com.au/readmore**